W9-CNM-822

GEORGE J. ANNAS is the Director of the Center for Law and Health Sciences, Boston University School of Law, Assistant Professor, Boston University School of Medicine, and Lecturer in Legal Medicine, Boston College Law School. He has taught courses in health law; law, medicine and public policy; patients' rights; human experimentation; health planning and regulation; and genetics and law. He is a member of the Massachusetts Board of Registration and Discipline in Medicine, and former Chairman of the Massachusetts Health Facilities Appeals Board. Professor Annas has written extensively in both the legal and health care literature, is editor-in-chief of *Medicolegal News*, and coeditor of the text, *Genetics and the Law*. He has degrees in economics, law, and public health from Harvard University, where he was a Joseph P. Kennedy, Jr. Fellow in Medical Ethics while studying for his M.P.H. degree. He is a member of the bar of the Commonwealth of Massachusetts and of the State of Minnesota.

Also in this Series

AN AMERICAN
CIVIL LIBERTIES
UNION HANDBOOK

THE RIGHTS OF HOSPITAL PATIENTS

THE BASIC ACLU GUIDE TO A HOSPITAL PATIENT'S RIGHTS

George J. Annas

General Editors of this series:
Norman Dorsen, *Chairperson*
Aryeh Neier, *Executive Director*

A DISCUS BOOK/PUBLISHED BY AVON BOOKS

To the Sick, and the Healers
who treat them as Persons

AVON BOOKS
A division of
The Hearst Corporation
959 Eighth Avenue
New York, New York 10019

ISBN: 0-380-00286-8

First Discus Printing, March, 1975.
Third Printing

DISCUS TRADEMARK REG. U.S. PAT. OFF. AND
FOREIGN COUNTRIES, REGISTERED TRADEMARK—
MARCA REGISTRADA, HECHO EN CHICAGO, U.S.A.

Printed in the U.S.A.

Acknowledgments

The author wishes to acknowledge the great help provided in all phases of this book by health lawyers Leonard H. Glantz and Joseph M. Healey. Thanks are also due to Professors Sylvia Law of New York University School of Law, Frances Miller of Boston University School of Law, and John Robertson of the University of Wisconsin Law School for reading and commenting on the manuscript. Special thanks are due to Norma Swenson for her critical comments, not all of which were heeded, on the chapter on women, to health lawyer Kenneth Wing for his ideas on informed consent and confidentiality, and to Barbara Popper for reviewing the chapter on children. Elizabeth Keel, Mary F. Annas, George J. Annas, Sr. and Ann Campbell helped enormously in making the text intelligible. Finally, I wish to thank Professor William J. Curran of Harvard University for introducing me to the field of patients' rights and teaching me much of what I know about the subject.

Table of Contents

Preface

This guide sets forth your rights under present law and offers suggestions on how you can protect your rights. It is one of a continuing series of handbooks published in co-operation with the American Civil Liberties Union.

The hope surrounding these publications is that Americans informed of their rights will be encouraged to exercise them. Through their exercise, rights are given life. If they are rarely used, they may be forgotten and violations may become routine.

This guide offers no assurances that your rights will be respected. The laws may change and, in some of the subjects covered in these pages, they change quite rapidly. An effort has been made to note those parts of the law where movement is taking place but it is not always possible to predict accurately when the law *will* change.

Even if the laws remain the same, interpretations of them by courts and administrative officials often vary. In a federal system such as ours, there is a built-in problem of the differences between state and federal law, not to speak of the confusion of the differences from state to state. In addition, there are wide variations in the ways in which particular courts and administrative officials will interpret the same law at any given moment.

If you encounter what you consider to be a specific abuse of your rights you should seek legal assistance. There are a number of agencies that may help you, among them ACLU affiliate offices, but bear in mind that the ACLU is a limited-purpose organization. In many communities, there are federally funded legal service offices which provide assistance to poor persons who cannot afford the costs of legal representation. In general, the rights that the ACLU defends are freedom of inquiry and expression; due process of law; equal protection of the laws; and privacy. The authors in this series have discussed other rights in these books (even though they sometimes fall outside the ACLU's usual concern) in order to provide as much guidance as possible.

These books have been planned as guides for the people directly affected: therefore the question and answer format. In some of these areas there are more detailed works available for "experts." These guides seek to raise the largest issues and inform the non-specialist of the basic law on the subject. The authors of the books are themselves specialists who understand the need for information at "street level."

No attorney can be an expert in every part of the law. If you encounter a specific legal problem in an area discussed in one of these handbooks, show the book to your attorney. Of course, he will not be able to rely *exclusively* on the handbook to provide you with adequate representation. But if he hasn't had a great deal of experience in the specific area, the handbook can provide helpful suggestions on how to proceed.

Norman Dorsen, General Counsel
American Civil Liberties Union

Aryeh Neier, Executive Director
American Civil Liberties Union

The principal purpose of these handbooks is to inform individuals of their rights. The authors from time to time suggest what the law should be. When this is done, the views expressed are not necessarily those of the American Civil Liberties Union.

Introduction

Each year 34 million Americans are admitted to hospitals, and each of us will be hospitalized an average of eleven times before we die. While we spend almost $40 billion annually on hospital care, few patients are completely satisfied with the way they are treated in hospitals. Patients rightfully resent the all-too-common impersonalized and patronizing manner in which they are dealt with. Such actions on the part of health care providers both undermine the human rights of patients and perpetuate patient-consumer ignorance of medical treatment and health care. If hospitals are not to become human rights wastelands, vigorous action must be taken by patients, consumers, nurses, health care workers, and physicians to promote and protect patient rights.

This book is built on two fundamental premises: (1) the American medical consumer possesses certain interests, many of which may properly be described as rights, that he does not automatically forfeit by entering a hospital; (2) most hospitals fail to recognize the existence of these interests and rights, fail to provide for their protection and assertion, and frequently limit their exercise without recourse for the patient. Patients should not be required to relinquish basic human rights upon entering a health care institution. Human rights can be protected without decreasing either the efficacy or the efficiency of medical treatment.

Many of the legal rights of hospital patients have been enunciated by the courts in the context of malpractice suits brought against physicians by former patients. Most malpractice cases involve physicians who have not only injured their patients but have done so either negligently or intentionally. Cataloguing these cases, as is necessary to outline the legal rights of hospital patients, often presents physicians and hospitals in a less than favorable light. Such

descriptive materials are nonetheless essential to an understanding of basic patient rights. It is not the intention of
this book, however, to castigate medical professionals for
occasional past misdeeds. The intention is to inform both
consumers and health care providers of the legal rights of
hospital patients. It is hoped that this information will
encourage patients to assert their rights and reinforce
hospital personnel in their efforts to enhance patient rights.

Most of the chapters in this book deal with the specific
right expressed in the chapter title. There are some exceptions. Chapter I sets forth the theoretical framework of
the book, and Chapter II describes how the hospital is organized. Chapter III gives an overview of the types and
sources of laws that govern hospitals. The final chapter describes a new professional, a "patient rights advocate,"
and suggests how the introduction of such a person into
the hospital setting might further enhance individual patient rights. While all hospital patients are protected by essentially the same rights, some groups have special problems. Therefore, separate chapters have been included on
women, children, and the terminally ill.

Most of the material cited in the footnotes is available
in legal and medical libraries. Appendix C contains a
guide to this literature and informs those interested how to
obtain specific information in these libraries. Appendix E
lists a number of organizations involved in the legal rights
of hospital patients. Common medical terms and abbreviations are defined in Appendices A and B, and Appendix D
sets forth a "model" Patient Bill of Rights.

I

The Patient's Rights Movement

The patient's rights movement is difficult to define. That it is not as well organized and identifiable as other consumer movements can be explained by a number of factors. When individuals are sick, their first priority is to regain their health. Under these circumstances hospitalized patients often give up rights that they would otherwise vigorously assert. In the words of Dr. Oliver Wendell Holmes[1]:

> The persons who seek the aid of the physicians are very honest and sincere in their wish to get rid of their complaints ... There is nothing men will not do, there is nothing they have not done, to recover their health and save their lives. They have submitted to be half-drowned in water, and half-cooked with gases, to be buried up to their chins in earth, to be seared with hot irons like slaves, to be crimped with knives, like codfish, to have needles thrust into their flesh, and bonfires kindled on their skin, to swallow all sorts of abominations, and to pay for all this, as if to be singed and scaled were a costly privilege, as if blisters were a blessing, and leeches were a luxury.

There are three reasons why there are few organized groups of hospital patient-consumers in the patient's rights movement. First, the average person in a hospital is by definition sick and therefore not in a very good position to exercise his own rights, let alone to organize to help protect and assert the rights of others. Second, the average length of stay in most American acute-care hospitals is about 8 days, hardly long enough to build any type of an inpatient organization. Third, outside the hospital most Americans prefer not to think about hospitalization, just as they prefer not to think about death, to continue to smoke, to drive after drinking, and to engage in other activities that may seriously affect their health.

Local patient's rights movements have been built around neighborhood health centers, outpatient clinics of some large hospitals, comprehensive health-planning agencies, and an occasional free clinic. On the whole, however, it can be said that there is no unified consumer movement in health care in this country.

The attention of the American people, however, is beginning to center on the hospital for other reasons. First among these is the rising cost of hospital care and the movement, now endorsed by both major political parties, toward some form of comprehensive national health insurance. Others include the series of well-publicized medical-care events in which the protection of the rights of individual patients has been questionable. These include the disclosure of a study of syphilis by the U.S. Public Health Service in which treatment was withheld from 400 black males with the disease; revelations concerning experimentation with aborted fetuses; reports of failure to treat severely impaired infants; the unconsented sterilization of young black women by HEW-financed family-planning clinics; and the rise in the incidence of malpractice litigation and the amounts of the awards. Medical advances in the areas of increased technology to prolong life, amniocentesis to detect genetic defects prior to birth, organ transplantation and artificial implants, behavior modification through drug therapy and surgery, and increased specialization in medicine all tend to increase the technological and decrease the human aspects of medical care. To maintain a balance in which the patient retains the power to make the ultimate decisions regarding his care and medical treatment, explicit recognition and protection of the legal rights of patients are essential.

What is meant when a patient says "I have a legal right to 'X'?"

Many a scholar's life has been spent trying to define the term "right." The history of that concept is as old as the institutions of Western civilization.[2] The purpose here, however, is simply to clarify the terms used in this volume. The statement "I have a right" performs several functions and has several different meanings. Which function and which meaning are generally not made clear to the listener and may not even be clear to the person making the statement. Possible meanings include[3]:

1. Because I am a citizen of this country, I possess "X" as a legal right created by the Constitution, by legislative action or by prior court determination.
2. Because of my relationship with another party, there is a strong possibility that a court of law would recognize "X" as my legal right.
3. I believe that "X" should be recognized as a right even though a court of law would probably not recognize it as such.

As these examples demonstrate, there is no single or absolute definition. To understand any definition, it is necessary to understand the purpose for which the definition is sought, the audience for which it is intended, and the identity of the definer. In regard to the concept of a right, it is most helpful to consider that a continuum exists.

At one end would be all of those rights that are recognized as legal rights. These include the *rights of citizenship* arising under the Constitution and its Amendments, the laws of the fifty states, and court decisions. Holland, in his treatise on jurisprudence, refers to such a right as "a capacity residing in one man of controlling, with the assent and assistance of the state, the actions of others."[4] This is the type of right described in Statement I, and is a *legal right*.

Somewhere near the middle of the continuum are those rights that, with a high degree of probability, would be recognized as legal rights by a court of law. In most situations, all that is needed is the appropriate justiciable controversy to present the court with the opportunity to recognize a new legal right. This type of right involves a reasonable expectation of what a court of law would do if called on to deal with the issue. Such a right is described by Statement II and is a *probable legal right*.

At the other end of the continuum are statements of what the law ought to be, based on a political or philosophical conception of the nature and needs of man. In making a declaration of what we believe should be, we are making a political statement. Such rights may be considered of fundamental importance and pre-exist recognition by positive law. The early civil rights movement provides numerous examples, as does the United Nations' Universal Declaration of Human Rights. This is the kind of right described in Statement III and may be termed a *human right*.

This volume is primarily concerned with legal rights and probable legal rights. However, at times certain human rights, although not currently recognized by law, will be advocated when their existence is important to patients.

Is there a legal right to health care in the United States?

No. While specifically set out in documents of both the United Nations and the World Health Organization, the right to health care appears neither in the U.S. Constitution nor in our Declaration of Independence, although "life, liberty and the pursuit of happiness" are all made rather difficult without proper health care. The strongest Congressional expression on the subject is found in the preamble to the 1966 Comprehensive Health Planning Act, which states that "the fulfillment of our national purpose depends on promoting and assuring the highest level of health attainable for every person." While people who qualify for Medicare and Medicaid enjoy a right to have some of their medical bills paid, there is no legal right to demand that services be rendered (except in emergency situations discussed in Chapter IV). The adoption of a program of national health insurance would, by itself, serve only to expand the payment right without addressing itself to the problem of access to services.[5]

What characteristics of the present doctor-patient relationship in the hospital context make it difficult for patients to assert their rights?

There are five characteristics of the doctor-patient relationship in decision-making that make it difficult for patients to retain the power to make the final decisions concerning their care while they are in the hospital. These characteristics can be outlined as follows[6]:

1. Ambiguous identification of the decision-maker.
2. Ambiguous identification of the person or entity that commands the decision-maker's loyalty.
3. Control of pertinent medical information by the attending physician.
4. Lack of reporting or review of the ultimate treatment decision.
5. Justification of the decision, on occasion, on the basis of some public policy rather than on the needs of the individual patient.

While this list is not meant to be either all inclusive or universal, a patient can, by using it as a checklist, determine just how likely it is that he or she will be able to make the final decision concerning what treatment, if any, will be given. For example, the real decision-maker may be a dying patient's family (Characteristic 1); the physician's loyalty may lie with the parents or with a colleague engaged in a research protocol rather than the child-patient (Characteristic 2); the physician may refuse to share information regarding diagnosis or prognosis with a patient (Characteristic 3); or a physician may make a decision to discontinue all treatment on the basis that it is too expensive given society's other needs (Characterstic 5). Characteristic 4 now pervades all medical decision-making since, as will be discussed later, often the only way a patient can get a decision or procedure reviewed is to bring a malpractice action.[7]

Is there any reason to believe that patients will ever regain the decision-making power from the medical profession?

Frequently one hears the objection that the legal system has no legitimate interest in interfering with the current doctor-patient relationship. Even a cursory glance at the history of the past century demonstrates the inherent weakness of such a position.

There are an extraordinary number of precedents suggesting that the law is willing to encourage the shifting of

power in relationships that have been protected by the
law, in some cases, for centuries. Examples include buyer-
seller, landlord-tenant, debtor-creditor, employer-employee,
warden-prisoner, police-suspect, teacher-student, parent-
child, and those involving minorities, such as blacks,
children, and the elderly.

Several things are evident from this listing. First, prior
status of a relationship established, by force of law or by
force of habit, is not itself sufficient justification for con-
tinuation of that status. Second, when there is sufficient
justification, in terms of basic constitutional rights or fundamental human fairness, the legislature, the judiciary,
and the executive can and will act to redefine the relationship. Third, the process of redefinition may take many
paths. It may involve federal or state legislation or regulations enforced by an administrative agency. It may involve
injunctive relief or an executive order. No matter the
form, however, the effect is qualitatively the same.

The conclusion is, therefore, that a legal re-definition of
the doctor-patient relationship is neither a radical nor un-
precedented suggestion.[8]

NOTES

1. O. W. Holmes, The Young Practitioner, in W. H. Daven-
   port, ed., THE GOOD PHYSICIAN, (MacMillan, New
   York 1962) at 176.
2. Those interested in pursuing the concept of a "right" in
   the legal literature are referred to E. Pollack, HUMAN
   RIGHTS (1971); J. Austin, THE PROVINCE OF
   JURISPRUDENCE (1954); Hoffeld, FUNDAMENTAL
   LEGAL CONCEPTIONS (1919); C. Hill, RIGHTS
   AND WRONGS (1969).
3. These three distinctions, or others like them, have been
   suggested by a number of commentators, among them
   Professor Charles H. Baron of Boston College Law
   School. See Annas, *A.H.A. Bill of Rights,* 9 TRIAL 59
   (Nov., 1973).
4. Holland, ELEMENTS OF JURISPRUDENCE (1893).
5. See Chapter XVI for a discussion of the payment
   mechanism under the Medicare and Medicaid programs.
6. These characteristics are discussed in considerably more
   detail in Annas, *Medical Remedies and Human Rights:
   Why Civil Rights Lawyers Must Become Involved in*

Medical Decision-Making, 2 HUMAN RTS. 151, 156-64 (1972).

7. Details concerning such suits are set out in Chapter XVII.

8. The ideas in this section, as well as some of those in other parts of this chapter, are discussed in more detail and with extensive footnotes in Annas & Healey, *The Patient Rights Advocate: Redefining The Doctor-Patient Relationship in the Hospital Context*, 27 VAND. L. REV. 243 (1974).

II
How the Hospital Is Organized

Describing how hospitals are organized and administered is somewhat like describing the secondary schools. The differences in student bodies (patient populations) and teachers (medical staff) may be more important than the similarities in organizational structure. Nevertheless, it may be useful for patients to have a general introduction to the hospital scene, so long as it is remembered that the generalities that are set forth in this chapter must be modified by the particular circumstances that exist in each hospital.

What kinds of hospitals are there?

There are approximately 7,000 hospitals in the United States. They can be classified either by type of ownership or service. About 2,000 of these hospitals are owned by local, state, or federal government. Of the remainder, about 1,000 are for profit, private hospitals, also termed proprietary hospitals, most of which are small, having fewer than 100 beds. The majority of other hospitals are private, nonprofit institutions, also called charitable or voluntary hospitals.

Hospitals may specialize in their services, such as pediatrics or obstetrics, or in diseases such as cancer or TB, but the trend is for hospitals to be "general," capable of handling most medical problems. If a hospital is affiliated with a medical school and has a training program including medical students, interns, and residents, it can also be termed a "teaching hospital." There are only about 620 teaching hospitals in the United States, but they have almost one-half of the nation's hospital beds.[1]

10

Most patients are, therefore, seen in non-profit (government or private) general teaching hospitals.

Who runs the hospital?

In theory the hospital's board of trustees or the board of directors has the supreme authority. Its responsibility is to see that the hospital renders adequate service to its patients at an efficient cost. Most boards, however, are composed of leading members of the business community and others who seldom have either the time or inclination to get deeply involved in the management of the institution.

The *executive director* (sometimes called the *administrator* or *superintendent*) of the hospital is appointed by the board to manage the hospital, in terms of housekeeping and business functions, on a day-to-day basis. The job of directing the medical aspects of patient care is usually in the hands of a separate group, with a separate hierarchy—the medical staff. A joint committee with representatives of both management and the medical staff often functions to provide a liaison between the two groups.[2]

How are the hospital's goals determined?

For decades economists assumed that major corporations were guided exclusively by the profit motive and that their goal was only to maximize profits. Galbraith has made a rather persuasive argument that once enough profits have been generated to assure survival, large firms have other goals, usually to maximize growth "consistent with the provision of revenues for the requisite investment."[3] Moreover, since industry is growing increasingly more complex, the nature of these goals and how they will be implemented are no longer in management's hands but in the hands of production and design experts whom Galbraith terms the "technostructure." It is this group that actually runs the corporation.

An analogous movement can be seen in larger hospitals. Once they have reached the point at which they can deliver a wide range of competent health care services and have been accepted by the community as quality hospitals, their goals are likely to shift. The goal becomes to develop increasing expertise in specialized areas, often backed by increasingly sophisticated and expensive medical equipment. Like Galbraith's technostructure, the senior physicians on the medical staff are able to dictate to the hospital management the types of equipment and staffing that are necessary to develop these specialized capabilities, like open-heart surgery and cobalt therapy. This, in turn, adds to the prestige of the institution and therefore to the prestige of the members of its medical staff.

This institutional quest for glory and the demands of specialization and subspecialization may make some sense on a regional or multistate level. When every hospital in a community constructs the same array of expensive and redundant equipment to keep their staffs happy, however, gross waste in medical resources follows. But the progression is logical as soon as the hospital decides to replace the goal of maximizing the health of the community with the goal of internal growth in specialized expertise.

To summarize, the health industry's experts in production and design are its medical staff; their goal is to maximize their capabilities of providing specialty care and to advance their reputations "consistent" with the provision of ordinary medical services for the requisite patient population. Some 23 states, and more recently the federal government, are attempting to halt this unregulated growth of hospitals by requiring that applications for expansion of services be approved by a state agency, which must certify that there is a public "need" for the proposed services.[4] The resources presently available to such programs, however, almost certainly doom them to limited successes at best.

Even if one rejects the above-outlined view of how hospitals operate, the traditional view does not necessarily give the health of the community primacy. A leading hospital text[5] defines the goals of the hospital as:

> caring for the sick and injured;

> providing an educational facility for doctors, nurses, and other health care personnel;

> promoting public health in the community by preventing disease and accidents; and

encouraging active research in the field of human medicine.

As will become apparent in later chapters, these goals are not always completely compatible, and patient care may be compromised by those who rank either education or research ahead of the rights of individual patients.

Who is in charge of an individual patient's care?
If the *referring physician*, the one who sent the patient to the hospital, is a member of the hospital staff or has staff privileges, he or she will continue in charge and is termed the *attending physician*.[6]

If the referring doctor doesn't have staff privileges, another physician, usually a *resident*, will be put in charge. Problems arise when patients admitted through a clinic or an emergency ward do not know who is in charge of their care. The hospital has a duty to put someone in charge of your care, and you have a right to know who that person is.

Who are the other doctors in a teaching hospital?
A *resident* usually is a house officer who has completed medical school and a one-year internship. He is still in training, although it could be his fourth or fifth year of residency, and he or she may be as capable as anyone on the hospital staff to treat patients.

Interns are in their first year after medical school.[7] They are also in training and accompany residents on rounds.[8] They are available for questions or complaints when the "attending" and the resident are not on the floor. Approximately 35 percent of all interns and residents are graduates of foreign medical schools. While many speak English, some do not. If the doctor who wants to treat you does not speak your language, you can refuse to let him touch you without an interpreter.

You may also be seen by *medical students*. They are usually in their third or fourth year of school but may have just started. They will often accompany the "team" on rounds, and one is usually assigned to each patient. They may be introduced to you as "doctor" or "student doctor." Unless "M.D." follows their name on an identifying tag, they are not *licensed to practice medicine,* even within the hospital. You cannot be examined by anyone, M.D. or not, without your permission.[9]

In most hospitals interns and residents begin their training on or about July 1. Therefore, during the summer months you are more likely to be seen by someone who has just started on the job training than during the rest of the year.[10]

While you are in the hospital, you may also be seen by *consultants,* who are generally specialists. Specialization is regulated by the medical profession through American Specialty Boards. There are currently 22 such boards, each of which requires an applicant to complete an internship and three to seven years of approved training and practice before issuing a certificate, which makes the doctor a "board-certified specialist." While no law requires specialists to be certified, those that have certification are generally the best since they have both specialized training and have agreed to devote at least 90 percent of their practice time to their specialty. The 22 specialties are: allergy and immunology, anesthesiology, colon and rectal surgery, dermatology, family practice, internal medicine, neurological surgery, nuclear medicine, obstetrics and gynecology, ophthalmology, orthopedic surgery, otolaryngology, pathology, pediatrics, physical medicine and rehabilitation, plastic surgery, preventive medicine, psychiatry and neurology, radiology, surgery, thoracic surgery, and urology.[11] It is your right to know whether the consultant is board certified and exactly why the consultant has been called before he or she examines you.[12]

A medical staff may be divided into a number of classifications, including the following: *active staff,* the regular membership; *associate,* junior membership; *consulting,* a doctor who can consult but not admit; *courtesy,* a doctor who only occasionally uses the hospital; *emeritus,* for retired doctors; *house staff,* interns and residents; *honorary,* for noted doctors not heavily involved in the hospital.

Staff appointments are usually renewable annually. In exchange for this privilege staff doctors are usually required to give some of their time in service to the hospital. This may take the form of committee membership, teaching, research, or covering the emergency ward, and it varies considerably from one hospital to another.[13]

Biographical information on all physicians licensed to practice medicine can be obtained by consulting the *American Medical Directory,* published biennially by the American Medical Association (AMA). *The Directory of Medical Specialists,* published by A. M. Marquis, Who's Who, Inc.,[14] gives a more comprehensive biography, lists all diplomates of the American Specialty Boards, and gives the requirements for board certification in each specialty. Both of these publications should be available in the hospital library. Information regarding licensure requirements can be found in the state medical practices act for the state in which the hospital is located.

Once a patient is in a hospital room, which staff members is the patient most likely to see?

Doctors will generally spend between 5 and 10 minutes a day with the average patient. This means that about 99 percent of the time patients will be cared for by the nursing staff of the hospital. Nurses are responsible for *nursing,* which can be defined as delivering basic medical and health care to the patient. Their duties may include such things as administration of medication (prescribed by a doctor), changing bandages and dressings, drawing blood, regulating and recording dietary intake and output, monitoring blood pressure, observing the patient's overall condition, and seeking immediate help in the event of a change in the patient's status. It is not uncommon for the nursing staff on a floor to be organized as follows:

> the nursing *supervisor* will supervise all nursing care in a particular building or area. If your questions are not adequately answered by the head nurse on the floor, ask for the nursing supervisor. The supervisor reports to the *director of nursing.*

> a *head nurse,* who supervises the nursing personnel on the floor

> a staff of *registered nurses* or "R.N.s," which means they have graduated from a 2 to 4 year

nursing program and passed a registration examination

a staff of "L.P.N."s or *licensed practical nurses* (these are nurses with 1 to 1½ years of practical experience who have passed a licensing examination)

nurse's aides and orderlies, who will assist the nursing staff in more routine matters such as bathing patients, moving patients, making beds, collecting bed pans, giving back rubs, etc. They have had about two weeks of formal training.

nursing students—students either in a hospital-based nursing program or from a university-based degree program.

Larger hospitals will also have other specialized personnel in such fields as respiratory therapy and physical therapy, transportation and dietary, who may also see the patient often, depending on the problem. Some hospitals have more than 85 separate job descriptions for various medical personnel. *Social workers* and *chaplains* are available for patients who wish to see them. You may, of course, refuse to see them.

Generally aides and nurses will be assigned to specific rooms on a floor, so that a patient can expect to see the same faces when ringing for aid. Most hospital personnel work 8-hour shifts. A typical hospital's shifts will be from 7 A.M. to 3 or 3:30 P.M. (day), 3 P.M. to 11 P.M. (evening) and 11 P.M. to 7 A.M. (night). A patient can anticipate some delay in responding to rings for aid during the first half-hour period of each shift because during this time the staff coming in is reviewing progress reports on the patients they will be caring for during their shift.

How is the hospital's medical staff oganized?

The organization of the hospital's medical staff is determined by the medical staff's bylaws, written rules that govern the conduct of the physicians who practice medicine in the hospital. While these bylaws vary from hospital to hospital, they will usually include a statement of purpose, a list of required qualifications of staff members, a descriptive outline of the staff's organization, a statement concerning staff functions (which will usually be assigned to particular committees), a statement on the range of patients each class of doctor may care for, and the types of treatments the doctor may use. Finally there will be a list of staff rules and regulations concerning such things as record keeping, tissue removal and examination, tests that must be performed on all patients admitted to the hospital, consent procedures, and the signing of physician orders.[15]

Who is in charge of the hospital staff?

The staff usually has an overall president or *chief of staff*. The staff is often further subdivided into specific departments (such as medicine, surgery, pediatrics, obstetrics, etc.), each with its own *chief of service*. If a patient cannot get satisfaction concerning a medical complaint from his attending physician, one person who can take appropriate action is the chief of service. The patient should not hesitate to contact the chief of service if he believes he is being mistreated, or if the attending physician refuses to answer his questions.

What committees in the hospital structure are most likely to directly affect patient care?

Hospitals may have as many as 30 to 35 committees, each responsible for various aspects of patient care and the management of the hospital. Some of the more important ones are described below. If a patient has a complaint directly involving an area over which one of these committees has jurisdiction, direct communication with the chairman or a member of the committee may bring action on it.

Executive Committee: This committee consists of the chiefs of service, elected members of the staff, and other officers. It is the main decision-making body of the medical staff.

Tissue Committee: This committee is charged with reviewing tissues, removed from patients, and patient records to help ensure that only necessary surgery is performed in the hospital.

Cancer Committee: This committee is usually charged with the development of an overall plan for the treatment, care, and follow-up of cancer patients. It reviews the medical care of all patients with this diagnosis.

Research and Human Trials Committee: This committee should review all proposed medical research in the hospital before it commences to ensure that the scientific design is sound, the potential benefits outweigh the risks, and the informed consent of each patient involved is obtained.

Utilization Review Committee: This committee is designed to review all admissions to the hospital (or a sample thereof) to determine if the number of days that the patient stayed in the hospital was medically necessary. Its purpose is to help decrease the average patient's length of stay. The average length of stay is about 4.5 days for patients aged 1 to 14, 6.5 days for patients aged 15 to 44, 10 days for patients aged 45 to 64, and about 14 days for those patients 65 or older.

What are some common abbreviations used in hospitals?
Like the space program, modern medicine has a tendency to say everything in terms of the first letters of the words that make up the full description of the place or test. The operating room, for example, is commonly referred to as the "OR," the emergency room or ward as the "ER" or "EW," the outpatient department as the "OPD," and intensive care unit as the "ICU" and the coronary care unit as the "CCU." A listing of the most common such abbreviations appears in Appendix B of this volume.

NOTES

1. J. Knowles, The Hospital, 9 *Scientific American*, Sept. 1973, 128, 135.
2. See W. J. Curran & E. D. Shapiro, LAW, MEDICINE & FORENSIC SCIENCE (2nd ed.), Little, Brown, Boston, 1970 at 602. One survey found that 70 percent of the seats on the boards of large Manhattan hospitals were held by businessmen, bankers, lawyers and accountants. *New York Times*, March 18, 1974, at 23, col. 1.

3. J. K. Galbraith, THE NEW INDUSTRIAL STATE, Houghton Mifflin, Boston, 1967 at 176. As Galbraith notes, the goal of expansion "in the output of many goods is not easily accorded a social purpose. More cigarettes cause more cancer. More alcohol causes more cirrhosis. More automobiles cause more accidents, maiming and death; also more preemption of space for highways and parking; also more pollution of the air and the country-side." Id., at 164.

4. See W. Curran, *National Survey and Analysis of Certifica-tion-of-Need Laws: Health Planning and Regulation in State Legislatures, 1972*, Chicago, American Hospital Association, 1973; Havighurst, *Regulation of Health Facili-ties and Services by "Certificate of Need,"* 59 VA. L. REV. 1143 (1973); C. Havighurst, ed., *REGULATING HEALTH FACILITIES CONSTRUCTION*, American Enterprise Institute For Public Policy Research, Washington, D.C., 1974.

5. M. MacEachern, HOSPITAL ORGANIZATION AND MANAGEMENT (3rd ed.), Physicians Record Co., Berwyn, Ill., 1962 at 29.

6. Medical staff may be either "open" or "closed." If the staff is open, any licensed physician may admit a private patient and care for him there. On a closed staff, only those physicians whose applications for staff membership have been reviewed and approved by the hospital's governing board may admit and care for patients (this is the usual arrangement).

7. In 39 states a graduate of a medical school is required to complete a one-year internship before he is eligible for licensure. That year he may legally practice medicine only in the facility in which he is training.

8. "Rounds" are usually made in the early morning, between 7 and 10 A.M. (when the doctors arrive) or in the late afternoon between 4 and 6 P.M. (before the doctors leave). During this time each patient is checked for a varying period of time (usually short) to see how he or she is progressing.

9. See Chapter VI, Informed Consent to Treatment.

10. As one writer has described it:

Each summer more than eight thousand graduates of American medical schools enter the first year of house-staff training. The first of July, the medical world's famous beginning date for the house-staff year, is a time of dispersion, upheaval, and

loss.... More than 1,500 hospitals lose a large
part of the house-staff they have trained. Yester-
day's interns join the ranks of more than 22,000
American-trained residents. In many hospitals a
large number of foreign graduates arrive for their
first experience in an American hospital, and more
move along in residency.

E. Mumford, INTERNS: FROM STUDENTS TO
PHYSICIANS, Harvard U. Press, Cambridge, 1970 at
33.

11. *See* Appendix A, Common Medical Terms, for the defi-
nitions of these specialities.
12. *See* Chapter VI, Informed Consent to Treatment.
13. *See* generally C. Eisele, ed., THE MEDICAL STAFF
IN THE MODERN HOSPITAL, McGraw-Hill, New
York, 1967, and M. Roemer & J. Friedman, DOCTORS
IN HOSPITALS, John Hopkins Press, Baltimore, 1971.
14. The latest edition is the 15th, 1972-73.
15. Much of this material is taken from an unpublished
teaching handout of Professor Duncan Neuhauser of the
Harvard School of Public Health.

III

Rules the Hospital Must Follow

Hospitals are not sovereign islands. Their affairs must be conducted within the framework of the law. In particular, hospitals supported to any substantial degree by the state or federal government must ensure that those human rights guaranteed by the United States Constitution are afforded to all patients.[1] Other hospitals to which this standard has yet to be applied are bound by the regulations of the state that apply directly to hospitals, by the standards of the Joint Commission on Accreditation of Hospitals (JCAH) if they are so accredited, and by their own internal bylaws and policies.

Until the mid-1960's, the medical profession and its trade organization, the AMA, had almost complete authority in setting and regulating medical practice in the hospital. In the past decade, however, courts have found the *hospital* liable in a number of instances for the conduct of physicians practicing therein. This has led to a movement by hospital administrators and their organization, the American Hospital Association (AHA), to achieve a measure of control over medical decision-making.[2] If the hospital is going to be held liable for the actions of doctors, the administrators properly reasoned, they have the right to exercise some control over the doctors. The major step in this direction of interest to patients was the promulgation of the AHA's Patient Bill of Rights.

In this chapter we will examine some of these external and internal rules that the hospital must follow under the law. A review of these materials reveals that the combination of public policing and self-enforced rules is insufficient to protect the rights of hospital patients.

21

What state laws must a hospital follow?

Most of the state laws that directly relate to hospitals are found in the public health laws and hospital licensing laws of the state and in the regulations promulgated under the authority of these laws by the state agency that has the duty to enforce them. While all states now license hospitals, prior to World War II fewer than a dozen states had any laws regulating hospitals. It was the passage by Congress of the Hill-Burton Hospital Construction and Survey Act of 1946 that led most of the states to adopt a licensing statute since such a statute was a prerequisite to obtaining federal construction funds. Since this was a construction bill, it should not be surprising that most of the standards set forth in these statutes pertained to construction design and adequacy of the physical plant rather than the quality of care delivered in the hospitals. Moreover, even on these limited criteria, enforcement has been generally lax and "regulations are often worded as recommendations rather than requirements; words like sufficient, adequate, and reasonable are common, especially in standards dealing with patient care."[3]

Recently about half of the states have passed so-called "certificate of need" legislation, which requires that before any hospital expands or substantially changes its services, it must obtain from the state a formal declaration that there is a public "need" for such a change or expansion. Like Hill-Burton, this remains a "brick and mortar" approach to hospital care, with almost no attention being paid to the quality of care provided in the institutions.

While states have the power to affect directly the quality of care in hospitals, they have been loath to exercise it and have in general been content to limit their activities to buildings and construction.[4]

What is the Joint Commission on Accreditation of Hospitals (JCAH)?

The JCAH is the only private accrediting agency of national significance. It was founded in 1952 by the AMA, the AHA, the American College of Physicians, the American College of Surgeons, and the Canadian Medical Association (which has since dropped out and formed its own group in Canada). Representatives of the American Association of Homes for the Aging and the American Nursing Home Association were added later. The organization inspects hospitals on a voluntary basis and designates them "accredited" if they measure up to a set of published criteria. While submission to such an examination is optional, since 1965 a JCAH-accredited hospital has been automatically eligible to be certified as a reimbursable provider under Medicare, provided it also complies with federal utilization review requirements. Until 1970 JCAH standards dealt mainly with the medical staff organization and record keeping. New standards been added in areas such as the emergency ward, anesthesia, nursing, environmental services, and dietary services. Not covered are such critical areas as outpatient department and experimentation.

The basis of the standards is the JCAH's view that "hospital governing bodies have the overall responsibility for the conduct of the hospital in a manner consonant with the hospital's objective of delivering a high quality of patient care."[5] About 4,800 hospitals are JCAH accredited, about 2,000 being inspected each year.[6] Hospitals get six weeks prior notice of all inspections. While since 1973 consumers with specific complaints have had the right to be heard by the inspection team, most visits continue to be conducted as friendly consultations.[7]

Which standards of the JCAH are most relevant to patient rights?

In the broad view, they all are since their general purpose is to promote quality patient care. In a more narrow sense, however, patient rights are dealt with most explicitly in the preamble of the standards of the JCAH which provides in relevant part:

> *Equitable and humane treatment at all times and under all circumstances is a right.* This principle entails an obligation on the part of all those involved in the care of the patient to recognize and to respect his individuality and his dignity. This means creating and fostering relationships founded on mutual acceptance and trust. In practical terms, it means that *no person should be denied impartial access to treatment or accommodations which are available and medically in-*

dicated, on the basis of such consideration as race, color, creed, national origin or the nature of the source of payment for his care.

Every individual who enters a hospital or other health facility for treatment retains certain rights to privacy, which should be protected by the hospital without respect to the patient's economic status or the source of payment for his care. Thus, representatives of agencies not connected with the hospital, and who are not directly or indirectly involved in the patient's care, should not be permitted access to the patient for the purpose of interviewing, interrogating or observing him, without his express consent given on each occasion when such access is sought.

The individual's dignity is reflected in the respect accorded by others to his need to maintain the privacy of his body. To the extent possible, given the inescapable exposure entailed in the provision of needed care, the patient should be aided in maintaining this privacy. The design and furnishings of examination and treatment areas, in the emergency department and outpatient facilities as well as in other parts of the hospital, should be so planned as to facilitate the maintenance of the patient's privacy, and, as far as possible, to shield him from the view of others.

Another important aspect of the patient's right to privacy relates to the *preservation of the confidentiality of his disclosures.* The setting in which the patient's history is taken, for example, should be such that he can communicate with the physician in confidence. This is true of the emergency department as well as of other parts of the hospital. In many teaching hospitals, and particularly in those which are closely affiliated with medical schools, all patients, regardless of their economic status, may be expected to *participate to some extent in clinical training programs* or in the gathering of data for research purposes. For all patients, regardless of the source of payment for their care, this *should be a voluntary matter.* The level of the patient's participation in such activities should in no way be related to the nature of the source of payment for his care.

In many large hospitals, the patient may be seen by several physicians during the course of his treatment. He has the *right to know the identity of the physician who is primarily responsible for his care.* In addition, the patient has the *right to be informed as to the nature and purpose of any technical procedures which are to be performed upon him,* as well as to know by whom such procedures are to be carried out. The *patient has the right to communicate with those responsible for his care, and to receive from them adequate information concerning the nature and extent of his medical problem, the planned course of treatment and the prognosis.* In addition, he has a right to expect adequate instruction in self care in the interim between visits to the hospital or to the physician. In the matter of communication, ethnic and cultural considerations are highly significant, and should be taken into account by *providing interpreters* where language barriers are a continuing problem. (italics mine)

Is the Preamble an integral part of the JCAH Standards?
Yes. This is the only reasonable way to read the final paragraph of the Preamble, which provides:

> The spirit and intent expressed in this preamble relative to the hospital patient's rights and needs and the observance of these in practice will be considered as a persuasive factor in the determination of a hospital's accreditation, *in the same manner as are any of the standards of this volume.* (italics mine)

What is the AHA Bill of Rights?
The AHA Bill of Rights was approved as a national policy statement after a three-year study by the AHA's board of trustees and four consumer representatives. When it was released to the press in January 1973, the AHA said that while none of its 7,000 member hospitals would lose accreditation if it failed to adopt the statement and make copies available to all patients, it expected its members to endorse the statement.[8] While response has been mixed, it is probably fair to say that most hospitals have adopted or are in the process of considering a statement similar to that promulgated by the A.H.A.

What does the AHA Bill of Rights provide?
The exact text of the AHA Bill of Rights is:

1. The patient has the right to considerate and respectful care.

2. The patient has the right to obtain from his physician complete current information concerning his diagnosis, treatment, and prognosis in terms the patient can be reasonably expected to understand. When it is not medically advisable to give such information to the patient, the information should be made available to an appropriate person in his behalf. He has the right to know, by name, the physician responsible for his care.

3. The patient has the right to receive from his physician information necessary to give informed consent prior to the start of any procedure and/or treatment. Except in emergencies, such information for informed consent should include but not necessarily be limited to the specific procedure and/or treatment, the medically significant risks involved, and the probable duration of incapacitation. Where medically significant alternatives for care or treatment exist, or when the patient requests information concerning medical alternatives, the patient has the right to such information. The patient also has the right to know the name of the person responsible for the procedures and/or treatment.

4. The patient has the right to refuse treatment to the extent permitted by law and to be informed of the medical consequences of his action.

5. The patient has the right to every consideration of his privacy concerning his own medical care program. Case discussion, consultation, examination, and treatment are confidential and should be conducted discreetly. Those not directly involved in his care must have the permission of the patient to be present.

6. The patient has the right to expect that all communications and records pertaining to his care should be treated as confidential.

7. The patient has the right to expect that within its capacity a hospital must make reasonable response to the request of a patient for services. The hospital must provide evaluation, service, and/or referral as indicated by the urgency of the case. When medically permissible, a patient may be transferred to another facility only after he has received complete information and explanation concerning the needs for and al-

ternatives to such a transfer. The institution to which the patient is to be transferred must first have accepted the patient for transfer.

8. The patient has the right to obtain information as to any relationship of his hospital to other health care and educational institutions insofar as his care is concerned. The patient has the right to obtain information as to the existence of any professional relationships among individuals, by name, who are treating him.

9. The patient has the right to be advised if the hospital proposes to engage in or perform human experimentation affecting his care or treatment. The patient has the right to refuse to participate in such research projects.

10. The patient has the right to expect reasonable continuity of care. He has the right to know in advance what appointment times and physicians are available and where. The patient has the right to expect that the hospital will provide a mechanism whereby he is informed by his physician of the patient's continuing health care requirements following discharge.

11. The patient has the right to examine and receive an explanation of his bill regardless of source of payment.

12. The patient has the right to know what hospital rules and regulations apply to his conduct as a patient.

A much more complete and detailed bill of rights is set forth in Appendix D of this volume.

What is the legal significance of the JCAH Preamble, the AHA Bill of Rights, and other similar documents on patient rights?

Comedian Johnny Carson caught some of the spirit of the AHA Bill of Rights on his January 9, 1973, show. He noted that some rights, like the right of a comatose patient not to be used as a doorstop, the right of a patient who has had an autopsy to seek further medical consultation, and the right of a patient, no matter what the extenuating circumstances, to refuse to be given a sponge bath with "Janitor In A Drum," had somehow been overlooked by the AHA.

It is no secret to the members of the medical and legal professions that their traditional "codes of ethics" are more properly labeled codes of professional etiquette. The codes generally are concerned with interprofessional relationships on such topics as referrals, fees, and advertising rather than with the ethics involved in physician-patient or attorney-client relationships. Perhaps this is all one should expect of any group charged with regulating its own conduct. The JCAH Preamble and the AHA Bill of Rights follow the pattern. Their thrust is toward encouraging etiquette and courtesy in the doctor-patient relationship in the hospital context, not toward informing the patient of his rights.

The "rights" to "considerate and respectful care," to "every consideration of privacy," to "reasonable response to requests of a patient for services," to "obtain information as to any relationships with educational institutions," to "expect reasonable continuity of care," to "examine and receive an explanation of a bill regardless of source of payment," and "to know what hospital rules and regulations apply to his conduct as a patient" are essentially matters of staff courtesy. For example, no law forces a doctor to be respectful to a patient.

As for the remainder of the listed "rights," the rights of "complete current information concerning diagnosis, treatment and prognosis," to "receive from his physician information necessary to give informed consent, to refuse treatment to the extent permitted by the law," and "to be advised if the hospital proposes to engage in or perform human experimentation affecting his care or treatment" are all fairly simple concepts relating to informed consent.[9] The list is, therefore, essentially a combination of rudimentary statements of courtesy and basic concepts concerning informed consent. This has led one commentator to term the title "not only pretentious, but deceptive" and to describe the entire AHA effort as akin to "the thief lecturing his victim on self-protection."[10] While one must agree that hospitals have a long way to go to equal strides taken in the areas of employer-employee, landlord-tenant, and debtor-creditor relationships, the document deserves legal analysis before facile criticisms are hurled its way.

If adopted as official hospital policy, for example, a Patient Bill of Rights could be used in court as evidence against a hospital. Specifically, patients could sue hospitals to require that they provide for the rights enumerated. The mechanics of suing a doctor or a hospital are discussed in Chapter XVII.

While some courts have argued that to permit the introduction into evidence of self-imposed standards would only discourage the use of such standards,[11] the trend is certainly toward allowing their admission. The JCAH standards and hospital bylaws, for example, were admitted in one case to serve as "evidence of custom" to aid the jury in determining the standard of care to which the hospital should be held.[12] It is possible that a court would allow the admission of a document like the AHA Bill of Rights, even if the defendant hospital had not officially adopted it, on the grounds that it would give the jury an indication of the practices of other hospitals.

Does adoption of a bill of rights increase the patient's ability to sue the hospital if his rights are violated?

It is difficult to envision an action for "inconsiderate or disrespectful care." It might be that someone would sue to see his bill, even though a third party was paying it, but this is also unlikely. Defining "reasonable continuity of care" is not likely to come to court unless the hospital does such a poor job that a consumer group brings a class action. The five provisions dealing with informed consent probably do not increase the hospital's present responsibilities.[13] While imaginative lawyers could probably come up with some type of action based on each of the twelve AHA rights, the only two that delineate a hospital policy more clearly than current JCAH standards are:

5. . . . privacy . . . Case discussion, consultation, examination, and treatment are confidential and should be conducted discreetly. Those *not directly involved in this case must have the permission of the patient to be present.*

7. . . . When medically permissible, a patient *may be transferred* to another facility *only after* he has received *complete information and explanation* con-

cerning the needs for and alternatives to such a transfer. (italics mine)

The first of these considerably strengthens the standard set out in the Preamble of the JCAH standards:

> Every individual who enters a hospital ... retains certain rights of privacy ... Thus, representatives of *agencies not connected with the hospital*, and who are not directly or indirectly involved in the patient's care *should not* be permitted access to the patient for the purpose of interviewing, interrogating or observing him *in any way detrimental to his condition* or obstructive to the care being provided. (italics mine)

In this case the vagueness of the Preamble is replaced by a rule that requires specific patient permission (although a written requirement would be preferable) for him to be viewed by medical students or house staff not "directly involved" in his care. Such permission would, of course, also be necessary for him or his case to be presented at any type of class or at grand rounds. Without his permission the patient would have a potential action for invasion of privacy that he might not otherwise have under the state's common law.

As to transfer, the JCAH standard is set out in the "Emergency Services" section:

> ... no patient should *arbitrarily* be transferred if the hospital where he was initially seen has means for adequate care of his problem. (italics mine)

Here the term "arbitrarily" is expanded to require articulation of the precise reason transfer is deemed necessary. Transfer of an invalid for an improper reason might thus be more easily proved.

The conclusion that the AHA Bill adds only marginally to any potential hospital liability is inescapable. No hospital should therefore be deterred by any considerations of liability from adopting it as hospital policy. Another conclusion is that these documents add to patient rights mainly by making patients and hospital personnel *aware* of some of the rights of hospital patients.

Have any states mandated Patient Bills of Rights by law?

As of the publication of this volume only one state, Minnesota, had required by law that a particular version of a Patient Bill of Rights be posted in all hospitals and distributed to all patients.[14] The bill enacted in May 1973 was, however, only a watered-down version of the AHA Bill of Rights and probably has done little to enhance patient rights in the state.[15] Indeed, since it has the official stamp of approval from the Minnesota legislature, some doctors might feel that the *only* rights they must afford hospital patients are those set forth in the statute. If this is the case, the bill in Minnesota may do patients more harm than good. The lesson is that if you want to make a patient Bill of Rights law, make sure that it includes all of the elements you think are important for the protection of Patient rights. The bill does, nonetheless, have one strong section that makes anyone who intentionally abuses or culpably neglects a patient liable to a fine of up to $1,000 and up to a year in prison.

What is the general rule concerning the ability of a patient to sue a hospital for violation of a hospital rule or regulation?

In general, violation of a rule or regulation that is designed primarily for the safety of hospital patients will constitute negligence if this violation results in injury to the patient.[16] This rule was applied in one case in which a consultation was sought by the patient but refused.[17] The court cited the JCAH standards (since the hospital was accredited and had agreed to be bound by these standards) on consultation, which provided in part that "The patient's physician is responsible for requesting consultation when indicated. It is the duty of the hospital staff through its chief of service and executive committee to make certain that members of the staff do not fail in the matter of calling consultants as needed." A malpractice award was upheld as a result. In reaction, the JCAH revised this standard by lowering it to state only that "the use of consultations, and the qualifications of the consultant, should be reviewed as part of medical care evaluation."[18]

Can a hospital be held liable for permitting a doctor whom it knows or should know is practicing bad medicine to continue to practice medicine in the hospital?

This question was answered in the affirmative by a lower court judge in the fall of 1972 in California. In that case a doctor, John G. Nork, was found to have performed at least 13 unnecessary laminectomies, some that crippled the patient for life. The patient who was suing Dr. Nork had suffered multiple injuries due to the unnecessary surgery performed on him. The court awarded $2 million in punitive damages as well as $1,700,000 in compensatory damages to the patient. The hospital settled with the patient and the amount assessed against Dr. Nork was affirmed on appeal. While this lower court case is not precedent in any jurisdiction, it has received extensive publicity in the medical and hospital literature, and is probably the beginning of a trend to hold hospitals accountable for failure to monitor the performance of the physicians it permits to practice within its walls. In discussing the liability of the hospital the court notes[19]:

> The hospital has a duty to protect its patients from malpractice by members of its medical staff when it knows or should have known that malpractice was likely to be committed upon them. Mercy Hospital had no actual knowledge of Dr. Nork's propensity to commit malpractice, but it was negligent in not knowing ... because it did not have a system for acquiring the knowledge; it did not use the knowledge available to it properly; it failed to investigate the Freer case [a previous malpractice charge against Dr. Nork] ... Every hospital governing board is responsible for the conduct of their medical staff.

In an analogous Arizona case the court found that when a hospital had undertaken to monitor and review the performance of staff doctors and to restrict or suspend their privileges if they had demonstrated an inability to perform a certain procedure, it would be held liable for failure to take action against a physician who had demonstrated such inability.[20]

For what other acts might a hospital be held liable?

The following examples are illustrative of areas in which the hospital may be liable for action or inaction. The listing is not meant to be inclusive.

A hospital may be held liable for failure to require that instruments be counted after surgery, even if not counting them is common practice.[21] Likewise, failure of a hospital radiology department to obtain and check the medical history of a patient referred for x-ray may be negligent, even though it was common practice not to check.[22] A hospital violates good standards if it allows, because of lack of sterile technique, a patient or employee with a known infectious condition to infect a previously noninfected patient.[23]

Good standards require a nurse or other hospital employee to immediately report defective or inadequate hospital equipment.[24] A nurse is also required to read the "signals of danger" and bring these to the immediate attention of a doctor,[25] and if the doctor persists in a course of action that may be to the detriment of the patient, the nurse has an obligation to report this in such a way as to insure the patient's safety.[26] A hospital should not transfer a patient if it may worsen the patient's condition,[27] must not injure a bedridden patient while turning the patient over,[28] nor may it permit a patient to be burned by a heating lamp, hot-water bottle, or similar device.[29]

NOTES

1. For the implications of receipt of Hill-Burton funds, for example, see Chapter V, on Admission and Discharge. For Medicare-related requirements, see Chapter XVI, Payment of Hospital Bills.

2. Eg. *Darling v. Charleston Community Memorial Hospital*, 33 Ill. 2d 326, 211 N.E. 2d 253 (1965), *cert. denied*, 383 U.S. 946 (1966); *Steeves v. U.S.*, 294 F. Supp. 446 (1968).

3. Worthington & Silver, *Regulation of Quality of Care in Hospitals: The Need for Change*, 35 LAW & CONT. PROB. 305, 309 (1970).

4. E.g., Mass. Gen. Laws ch. 111, §25C–G. See generally, Havighurst, *Regulation of Health Facilities and Services by "Certificate of Need,"* 59 VA. L. REV. 1143, 1144

(1973) for a list of the state statutes in 23 states. In 1972 the federal government adopted a "mini" certificate of need program that provided that new construction not approved by a properly designated state agency might not receive Medicare and Medicaid reimbursement for the capitalization portion of the hospital bill related to the new construction. Pub. L. No. 92–603, §221 (H.R. 1, §1122, 1972). Comprehensive Health Planning, which started with the promise of being truly "comprehensive," has also slipped back into a brick and mortar approach in its "review and comment" functions. (42 U.S.C. §246) *And see* Comment, *Comprehensive Health Planning— Federal, State, Local: Concepts and Realities,* 3 WISC. L. REV. 839 (1970).

5. JCAH *Manual, supra.,* note 5 at 3.

6. See generally, Worthington & Silver, *supra.,* note 3; and JCAH, ACCREDITATION MANUAL FOR HOSPITALS: 1970, Chicago, 1970 at 1–2. The *Manual* is available for $2.25 from the JCAH, 875 North Michigan Avenue, Chicago Ill. 60611 (pub. No. H-101); A loose-leaf edition, which includes an updating service, is also available for $8 (Pub. No. H-100).

7. *Medical World News,* Jan. 25, 1974 at 4–5. The public is still barred, however, from being present with the inspection team during their tours of the hospital without the permission of the hospital. The secretary of HEW may also, if he receives a substantial number of consumer complaints about a hospital, institute a separate accreditation survey for the purposes of Medicare reimbursements, regardless of JCAH findings. See also Lablin, Outfit That Accredits Hospitals Helps Set Quality of Patient Care, *Wall St. J.,* Jan. 13, 1975 at 17, col. 1.

8. *New York Times,* Jan. 9, 1973 at 1.

9. See generally Chapter VI, Informed Consent to Treatment.

10. Gaylin, The Patient's Bill of Rights, *Saturday Review of Science,* March 1973 at 22.

11. E.g., *Fonda v. St. Paul City Ry.,* 71 Minn. 438, 74 N.W. 166 (1898).

12. E.g., note 2; *supra.,* Stone v. Proctor, 259 N.C. 633, 131 S.E. 2d 297 (1963); Pederson v. Dumouchel, 72 Wash. 2d 73, 431 P. 2d 973 (1967).

13. At least one commentator, Don Harper Mills, has argued, however, that hospitals should move slowly in this direction since they might be setting themselves up as guaran-

tors to the patient that the doctor will perform at a certain standard of disclosure and candor, a guarantee that they may not be able to enforce.

14. The complete text of the bill of rights mandated by Ch. 688, St. 1973 is:

(1) Every patient and resident shall have the right to considerate and respectful care;

(2) Every patient can reasonably expect to obtain from his physician or the resident physician of the facility complete and current information concerning his diagnosis, treatment and prognosis in terms and language the patient can reasonably be expected to understand. In such cases that it is not medically advisable to give such information to the patient the information may be made available to the appropriate person in his behalf;

(3) Every patient and resident shall have the right to know by name and specialty, if any, the physician responsible for coordination of his care;

(4) Every patient and resident shall have the right to every consideration of his privacy and individuality as it relates to his social, religious, and psychological well being;

(5) Every patient and resident shall have the right to respectfulness and privacy as it relates to his medical care program. Case discussion, consultation, examination, and treatment are confidential and should be conducted discreetly;

(6) Every patient and resident shall have the right to expect the facility to make a reasonable response to the requests of the patient;

(7) Every patient and resident shall have the right to obtain information as to any relationship of the facility to other health care and related institutions insofar as his care is concerned and:

(8) The patient and resident have the right to expect reasonable continuity of care which shall include but not be limited to what appointment times and physicians are available.

290 NEW ENG. J. MED. 32 (1974), and Minnesota: A Patient-Rights Law, *Medical World News*, Oct. 26, 1973 at 27. HEW has also adopted a Patient Bill of Rights for Skilled Nursing Facilities participating in Medicare

and Medicaid programs. 39 *Fed. Reg.* 35774-5 (Oct. 3, 1974).

16. *Kapuschinsky v. United States,* 248 F. Supp. 732 (D.S.C., 1966).

17. *Steeves v. United States,* 294 F. Supp. 446 (1968). This case is discussed in some detail in Chapter VIII, Consultation, Referral, and Abandonment.

18. JCAH *Manual,* supra. note 5 at 40. Cf. Worthington & Silver, supra., note 3 at 311, n. 28.

19. *Gonzales v. Nork,* Sup. Ct. Cal., Co. Sacramento, Nov. 19, 1973 (slip opinion, at 194) (Judge B. Abbott Goldberg).

20. *Purcell v. Zimbelman,* 500 P. 2d 335, 341, 18 Ariz. App. 75 (1972); see also, *Joiner v. Mitchell Co. Hospital Authority,* 125 Ga. App. 1, 186 S.E. 2d 307 (1971).

21. *Leonard v. Watsonville Community Hospital,* 305 P. 2d 36 (Cal., 1957).

22. *Favalora v. Aetna Casualty & Surety Co.,* 144 So. 2d 544 (La., 1962).

23. *Helman v. Sacred Heart Hospital,* 62 Wash. 2d 136, 381 P. 2d 605 (1963).

24. *Rose v. Hakin,* 335 F. Supp. 1221 (D.C.D.C., 1971); Annot., 14 A.L.R. 3d 1254 (1967).

25. *Valentin v. La Société Francaise de Bienfaisance Mutuelle de Los Angeles,* 76 Cal. App. 2d 1, 172 P. 2d 359 (1946); *Duling v. Bluefield Sanitarium, Inc.,* 149 W. Va. 567, 142 S.E. 2d 754 (1965). A hospital may also be liable for negligence in connection with the preparation, storage, or dispensing of medications to patients. See *Ball Memorial Hospital v. Freeman,* 245 Ind. 71, 196 N.E. 2d 274 (1964 ; Annot., 9 A.L.R. 3d 579 (1966).

26. *Goff v. Doctor's General Hospital of San José,* 333 P. 2d 29 (Cal. App., 1958).

27. *Alden v. Providence Hospital,* 127 App. D.C. 214, 382 F. 2d 163 (1963).

28. *St. John's Hospital & School of Nursing, Inc. v. Chapman,* 434 P. 2d 160 (Okla., 1967). A hospital may also be liable for permitting patients to use toilet facilities when they are unable to, or for having slippery floors. See, e.g., Annot., 36 A.L.R. 3d 1235 (1971) Annot., 16 A.L.R. 3d 1237 (1967).

29. Annot., Hospital's Liability for Injury to Patient from Heat Lamp or Pad or Hot Water Bottle, 72 A.L.R. 2d 408 (1960).

IV
The Emergency Ward

The typical emergency ward plays at least three roles: trauma (sudden injury) center, outpatient center, and backup center.[1] The first is its traditional one. The U.S. Public Health Service estimates that each day trauma kills 310 Americans, injures 137,000, confines 32,000 to bed, and leaves 1,100 with some degree of permanent impairment.[2] Second, emergency wards are increasingly being called on to act as the primary source of medical care for the surrounding community, especially for the poor.[3] Visits to hospital ambulatory clinics and emergency wards increased from 65 million in 1954 to more than 200 million in 1974, and more than twice as many patients are seen in emergency rooms annually than are admitted to hospitals.[4] Finally, persons who have their own private physicians but cannot reach them (e.g., at night or on weekends) use emergency rooms for primary health services. What evidence there is indicates that because emergency wards do not view the provision of primary care as their major function, they are not particularly well-equipped to handle the non-emergency problems of these last two groups.[5]

Must a hospital render service to someone who comes to an emergency room for treatment?

The general rule is that if an emergency is found to exist, a hospital with emergency facilities is required to render service. No completely satisfactory definition of an emergency has been formulated. In general, an emergency is an injury or acute medical condition liable to cause death, disability, or serious illness.

37

Examples of emergency conditions that require the *immediate* attention of a physician *to prevent loss of life* include[6]:

> massive hemorrhage from major vessels (heavy bleeding);
>
> cardiac arrest (heart attack);
>
> cessation or acute embarrassment of respiration (breathing stopped);
>
> profound shock from any cause (collapse with increased heart rate and white skin tone);
>
> rapidly acting poison;
>
> anaphylactic reactions (allergic response);
>
> acute epidural hemorrhage (collection of blood within brain following head injury);
>
> acute overwhelming bacteremia and toxemia (release of bacteria into blood stream; decrease in blood pressure, increase in temperature);
>
> severe head injuries;
>
> penetrating wound of the pleura ōr pericardium (heart or lung wound);
>
> rupture of an abdominal viscus (any internal organ of abdomen);
>
> acute psychotic states (sudden and complete change in personality).

An emergency condition need not be this serious, however, and could include cuts that require stitches, broken bones, and high fever. The principal case dealing explicitly with the right to receive emergency treatment, for example, involved a 4-month-old baby with diarrhea and fever.[7] The family physician prescribed medication by phone on the second day of the illness and saw the child during office hours the third day.

The child did not sleep at all the third night, and on the morning of the fourth day the parents, knowing their doctor was not in that day, took him to an emergency room. The nurse on duty refused to examine the child, saying hospital policy forbade treating anyone already under a doctor's care without first contacting the doctor, which she was unable to do. The parents took their child home and made an appointment to see their family doctor that night. The child died of bronchial pneumonia during the afternoon.

The court ruled that the parents could recover from the hospital for refusal to treat in an "unmistakable emergency." Their reasoning was that people should be able to rely on an "established custom" of the hospital to render aid in such cases in its emergency room. One who requires emergency aid but is refused treatment is worse off for having been delayed in obtaining treatment. The court applied the principle that if one voluntarily undertakes to render services to another, that service cannot be negligently terminated to the detriment of one who has relied on it.[8]

At least two other cases have presented the same issue. In the first, the plaintiff, who was suffering from frostbite, was being treated by a doctor who attempted to gain admission for his patient. The hospital refused, and not until a week later did the patient gain admission to another hospital.[9] In the second case the plaintiff attempted to receive treatment for an obviously broken arm, which the hospital refused.[10] Both courts adhered to the rule establishing a right to emergency treatment when such treatment is customarily given. Almost every court faced with the question of emergency has repudiated the old doctrine that a hospital need only accept those whom it chooses.[11]

It is also possible for a state to impose a duty on hospitals to administer emergency care. Illinois, New York, and California are among states that have already done so.[12] In none of these cases is a distinction made between the duty of private and public hospitals. The only case making such a distinction indicates that a public hospital may be held to a higher standard.[13] In neither case may a hospital refuse treatment on the basis of the prospective patient's race.[14]

How long must a patient wait to be seen?

The patient should be seen within a reasonable time, and in case of an emergency this means very quickly. In *New Biloxi Hospital v. Frazier*[15] the patient entered the emergency room bleeding from a shotgun wound in his arm. He was observed but not treated for two hours, at which time he was transferred to another hospital. He died shortly after arrival. The court found the hospital responsible for the results of the delay in rendering aid.

The American College of Surgeons has recommended that "Medical staff coverage should be adequate to insure that an applicant for treatment will be seen by a physician within fifteen (15) minutes after arrival."[16] An argument can be made that this recommendation has such standing in the medical community that hospitals may be legally accountable if they fail to live up to it.[17]

Does a patient have a right to be seen by a physician?

The patient with an emergency condition should be seen and examined by a physician.

Both the federal government in the *Medicare Conditions of Participation* and the American College of Surgeons in their *Standards for Emergency Departments in Hospitals* specify that "every applicant for treatment should be seen by a physician."[18] One legal commentator, William Regan, has speculated that a physician who fails to respond to an emergency call might even be charged with abandonment of a patient even though he has never seen him because of the agreement he made to see emergency patients when he agreed to be "on call."[19] Attorney Charles Letourneav, after reviewing the literature, concluded that "only a physician should be permitted to make a diagnosis of an emergency."[20]

A hospital that operates an emergency room or ward must, to be accredited, "have some procedure whereby the ill or injured person can be assessed, and either treated or referred to an appropriate facility, as indicated."[21] While this standard does not specify that any more than a nurse or clerk need make the assessment, what case law there is indicates that if there is reasonable basis for suspecting an emergency exists, a patient has a right to be examined and treated by a physician. In *Citizen's Hospital Association v. Schoulin*,[22] for example, an automobile accident victim was brought in with back pain. A nurse examined him and found no injury. She refused to either call a doctor or admit the patient. The following day, in another hospital, he was found to have a broken back. The first hospital was held liable.

Similarly, in *O'Neill v. Montefiore Hospital*,[23] the patient was taken to an emergency ward with chest pain and shortness of breath. He told the nurse on duty he thought he was having a heart attack. Because he did not have the proper type of health insurance, however, she refused to admit him or call his physician to the hospital. The patient returned home and died, and the court decided that the hospital could be found liable for the death.

After an emergency patient begins receiving treatment, is a hospital required to continue treatment?

Generally, a hospital must continue to provide service until a patient can be transferred or discharged without harm.

In one case,[24] a woman with a stab wound was examined and had her wound cleansed and dressed by an intern. She was then transferred to another hospital where she died a short while later during exploratory surgery. The court found that the hospital had not supplied adequate emergency treatment prior to ordering a transfer, and this contributed to the patient's death.

Another case involved a victim of an auto accident.[25] After pulse and bloodpressure checks and a brief abdominal exam, the intern in charge left the person unattended. After about 45 minutes the patient was transferred to another hospital where he died 30 minutes later from internal injuries. The court found that the hospital had failed to provide adequate emergency treatment.

In implementing its provisions for payments to hospitals that do not participate in Medicare, HEW has also promulgated standards for establishing when an emergency ends. The regulation provides: "An emergency no longer exists when it becomes safe from a medical standpoint to move the individual to a participating hospital or other institution, or to discharge him."[26]

Under the standard, one court ordered Medicare benefits to a woman for her entire 86-day hospitalization.[27] The court was persuaded by her doctor's statement that he would not have taken responsibility for her discharge if it had occurred any earlier. Under this rationale it would seem that as long as an emergency condition dictated the original hospital treatment, the hospital remains obligated throughout the entire period of required hospitalization.[28]

The JCAH has stressed that patients are not merely to be shored up sufficiently to facilitate their enduring a trip to some other facility. Its standard for emergency service provides that "no patient should be arbitrarily transferred if the hospital where he was initially seen has means for adequate care of his problem."[29] As previously discussed, the AHA Patient Bill of Rights goes even further.[30]

May a hospital condition emergency care on prepayment or demonstration of an ability to pay?

All indications from the case law are that it may not.

In one case,[31] an 11-year-old boy was taken to a hospital for an emergency appendectomy. Two hours later, after having been placed in bed and given medication, the hospital discharged him because his mother could not immediately pay $200. Although the court properly treated the case as an issue of negligent discharge rather than as one of refusal to administer emergency aid, the case is an example of a court finding that essential hospital treatment must be administered without regard to cost or ability to pay.

Several states have addressed the issue of cost in their statutes obligating hospitals to extend emergency aid. In one state the law requires: "The person [to be treated], if able, or the person responsible for accompanying such person, shall execute an agreement to pay the charges for such services or care."[32] Another statute requires that the hospital must "not before admission question the patient or any member of his or her family concerning insurance, credit or payment of charges, provided however, that the patient or a member of his or her family shall agree to supply such information promptly after the patient's admission."[33]

In the process of adopting a broad obligation on the part of hospitals to render emergency aid, the Wisconsin Supreme Court has said: "It would shock the public conscience if a person in need of medical emergency aid would be turned down at the door of a hospital having emergency service because that person could not at that moment assure payment for the service."[34] In this case the court was not directly concerned with a refusal to aid for lack of the patient's ability to pay but was construing a state law requiring counties to pay hospital costs for the medically indigent. Nonetheless, the implication is that the duty to render emergency aid when the hospital has the facilities cannot be obviated by the patient's poverty.

The same rationale would seem to apply to patients with emergency conditions who had outstanding unpaid bills at the hospital. The hospital could not refuse to treat their emergency conditions simply because their past bills were not paid up.[35]

What if a hospital has no emergency room?

Over 90 percent of all general hospitals have emergency rooms. However, in the absence of a statutory obligation, a person seeking emergency aid at a hospital without an emergency room might lawfully be turned away.

New York has enacted a statute requiring every general hospital to "admit any person who is in need of hospitalization."[36] But even this provision would not reach those situations in which emergency assistance short of full hospitalization was required. A dilemma is also presented by a hospital that lacks emergency facilities and admits only patients of doctors who are on the hospital staff. One court has, however, implied that if "elements of a critical emergency were present," a duty might be created even when the hospital had no emergency room and only admitted patients of staff doctors.[37]

A hospital may also be obligated to provide some minimum amount of emergency service if it has chosen to participate in the Medicare program.[38] A hospital may qualify for participation in the program either by satisfying federal regulations or by being accredited by the JCAH. The federal regulations require every participating hospital to have "at least a procedure for taking care of the occasional emergency case it might be called upon to handle."[39] JCAH requires "a well-defined plan for emergency care, based on community need and on the capability of the hospital."[40]

Must the physician in the emergency room notify your doctor before treating you?

Some hospitals have an "unwritten rule" that if a patient of another staff physician comes to the emergency room, the emergency-room physician must call the other physician to get his permission to treat the patient. There seems little doubt that this is bad medical practice. A leading medicolegal commentator has reacted as follows[41]:

> This is ridiculous. It is absolutely imperative that all physicians involved realize that the patient who comes to the emergency department is the sole responsibility of the emergency department physician and remains such until another physician *arrives* to take over the patient ... it is improper to have to await any permission before commencing treatment.

Can a consumer group sue a hospital to compel them to improve their emergency services?

In 1971 a consumer group sued the District of Columbia General Hospital to bring its emergency-room standards up to "acceptable medical" levels. The court agreed that when the emergency room was understaffed, there were likely to be substantial delays before a patient was seen and that such delays could cause aggravation of injuries and even death. Indeed, while the case was pending, a patient died in the emergency room after waiting for more than 6 hours without being seen. Following this incident, the hospital agreed to hire additional personnel. The court, on the hospital's promise of improving the standard of medical care delivered in the emergency room, said it would continue to watch the situation to make sure the promises were kept. The case stands for the proposition that a court may, under appropriate circumstances, order a hospital to bring its practice of medical care up to its own rules "and the standards of accepted medical practice in the community."[42]

NOTES

1. Torrens & Yedbab, *Variations Among Emergency Room Populations: A Comparison of Four Hospitals in New York*, 7 MED. CARE 60 (1970).
2. Freese, Trauma: The Neglected Epidemic, *Saturday Review*, May 13, 1972, at 58.
3. Shortliffe, Hamilton & Naroian, *The Emergency Room and the Changing Pattern of Medical Care*, 258 NEW ENG. J. MED. 20 (1958); Weinerman, Ratner, Robbins

& Lavenhar, *Yale Studies in Ambulatory Medical Care,* 56 AM. J. PUB. HEALTH 1037.

4. J. Knowles, The Hospital, *Scientific American,* Sept., 1973,) 128, 130; Shaffer, More Americans Turn to Emergency Rooms and Receive Poor Care, *Wall St. J.,* Oct. 5, 1971 at 1, col. 6. Lublin, More Community Hospitals Employ Physicians to Treat Emergencies During the Small Hours, *Wall St. J.,* Dec. 9, 1974 at 36, col. 1.

5. Brook & Stevenson, *Effectiveness of Patient Care in An Emergency Room,* 283 NEW ENG. J. MED, 904, 907 (1970).

6. Flint, EMERGENCY TREATMENT AND MANAGEMENT (3rd ed.), 1965 at 88.

7. *Wilmington General Hospital v. Manlove,* 54 Del. 15, 174 A. 2d 135 (1961).

8. *Restatement of Torts 2d,* §323

9. *Stanturf v. Sipes,* 447 S.W. 2d 558 (Mo. 1969).

10. *Williams v. Hospital Authority of Hall County,* 119 Ga. App. 626, 168 S.E. 2d 336 (1969).

11. See Powers, *Hospital Emergency Service and the Open Door,* 66 MICH. L. REV. 1455 (1968).

12. Ill. Rev. Stat. Ch 111 ½, §86 (Smith-Hurd Supp. 1972); N.Y. Public Health Law S2805-b (McKinney 1973); Cal. Health and Safety Code §1407.5 (West 1970).

13. *Williams v. Hospital Authority of Hall County,* 119 Ga. App. 626, 168 S.E. 2d 336 (1969).

14. *Cypress v. Newport News Gen. & Nonsectarian Hospital Ass'n.,* 375 F 2d 648 (4th Cir. 1967).

15. 245 Miss. 185, 146 So. 2d 882 (1962).

16. BULLETIN OF THE AMERICAN COLLEGE OF SURGEONS, at 112 (May-June, 1963).

17. Cf. Annas, A.H.A. *Bill of Rights,* 9 TRIAL 59 (Nov., 1973).

18. Letourneav, *Legal Aspects of the Hospital Emergency Room,* 16 CLEV.-MAR. L. REV. 50, 60. This concept is important since few of the nation's approximately 6,000 non-teaching hospitals have any doctor on duty in the emergency ward at night. Lublin, supra. note 4.

19. *Id.* at 60.

20. *Id.* at 65.

21. Joint Commission on Accreditation of Hospitals, ACCREDITATION MANUAL FOR HOSPITALS, (1970) at 71.

22. 48 Ala. 101, 262 So. 2d 303 (Ala. App. 1972). See also, *Thomas v. Corso,* 265 Md. 84, 288 A. 2d 379 (1972).

23. 11 App. Civ. 2d 132, 202 N.Y.S. 2d 436 (1960).

24. *Jones v. City of New York*, 134 N.Y.S. 2d 779 (Sup. Ct. 1954), *mod*, 143 N.Y.S. 2d 628 (App. Div. 1955).
25. *Methodist Hospital v. Ball*, 50 Tenn. App. 460, 362 S.W. 2d 475 (1961). See also Mulligan v. Wetchler, 332 N.Y.S. 2d 68 (Sup. Ct. 1972).
26. 20 C.F.R. §405.191(b)(2) (1973).
27. *Brewerton v. Finch*, 320 F. Supp. 68 (N.D. Miss. 1970).
28. 213 J.A.M.A. 674 (1970).
29. JCAH *Manual, supra* note 21.
30. See *supra.*, Chapter III, Rules the Hospital Must Follow.
31. *LeJeune Road Hospital v. Watson*, 171 So.2d 202 (Dist. Ct. App. Fla. 1965).
32. Cal. Health and Safety Code, §1407.5 (West 1970).
33. New York Public Health Law, §2805-b (1) (1973).
34. *Mercy Medical Center of Oshkosh v. Winnebago County*, 206 N.W. 2d 198, 201 (Wis. 1973).
35. See *infra.* Chapter XVI, Payment of Hospital Bills.
36. N.Y. Public Health Law 2805-b (1) (McKinney 1973).
37. *Hill v. Ohio County, Kentucky*, 468 S.W. 2d 306 (Ky. 1971).
38. See generally, 42 U.S.C. §1395 *et seq.*
39. 20 C.F.R. §405.1033 (1973).
40. JCAH *Manual, supra* note 21.
41. N. Chayet, Merry-Go-Round Dizzies Emergency Room, *Medical Tribune*, Jan. 9, 1974, at 28, col. 4.
42. *Greater Washington, D.C. Area Council of Senior Citizens v. District of Columbia*, D.D.C., Civil Action No. 275–71, Sept. 27, 1971 (Judge Barrington Parker) (unpublished opinion).

V

Admission and Discharge

Most of this book is concerned with what happens to the patient during his stay in the hospital. This chapter concentrates on the legal problems at the beginning and end of the patient's stay: admission to the hospital and discharge from the hospital. Problems seldom arise when the patient's physician has made formal arrangements in advance for the admission or discharge of the patient. However, in the absence of a specific agreement between the patient's physician and the hospital (e.g., a patient who presents himself for admission or who wishes to leave before his doctor wants him to), many legal issues can arise. This chapter deals with the most frequently occurring problem areas. For problems involved with the admission of an emergency patient, see Chapter IV.

What conditions may a hospital place on the admission of a non-emergency patient?

The general rule is that the non-emergency patient has no absolute right to be admitted to a hospital.[1] This is another way of saying that there is no universal legally enforceable right to hospital care in the United States.[2]

Teaching hospitals may encourage the admission of cases that would be "interesting" for their staffs to work on and discourage the admission of more routine cases. Even this criterion may vary from hospital to hospital. In one study comparing the admission policies of a community teaching hospital with those of a university-based teaching hospital, for example, an intern at the community hospital said proudly, "not a single patient needing hospitalization has been refused admission during the previous year." A resident at the university-based hospital, on the other hand, argued that it was important that the admitting physician screen patients for teaching purposes.[3]

This does not mean, however, that a hospital may place any condition it pleases on patient admission. While private hospitals may "screen" admissions based on a number of criteria, *they may not refuse admission on the basis of race, color, or national origin.*[4] As discussed in Note 15, *duration residency requirements* can ordinarily not be used as a basis to deny admission, either.

May a hospital demand a down payment or deposit before agreeing to admit a non-emergency patient?

In a case that made the newspapers, New York's Mount Sinai Hospital initially refused to admit one of Israel's former top generals following a stroke because he could not produce $3,080.00 in advance (the projected cost of a two-week stay). Even though his physician had made arrangements for his admission, he was kept over an hour in the waiting room until a local Israeli official delivered a check for the full amount. The director of the hospital defended the action by saying that he did not consider the general's condition "critical," and that "if we [had] been given $1,000.00 we would have settled."[5]

As a result of this incident the *New York Times* polled a number of area hospitals. Most responded that they followed New York law, which required them to admit emergency patients without inquiring into their financial status.[6] University Hospital, for example, said it "never turned anyone away." Montefiore Medical Center said, "We admit the patient and then try to collect." And Beth Israel Hospital said that its "policy was to treat anyone who presented himself as an emergency."[7]

The foregoing illustrates at least two facts: (1) Hospital admission policies vary (even in a state with a law forbidding the examination of a patient's financial status in emergency circumstances); *and* (2) Hospitals can and do require nonemergency patients to make deposits before admission in some cases. When the patient involved is insured under Medicare, Medicaid, or some form of public assistance, hospitals often have special offices to process both admissions and collections. Generally, of course, deposits are required only of those who have no private or public health insurance. Indeed, it is illegal for a hospital to require a deposit from a Medicare or Medicaid patient.[8]

Poverty lawyers have argued that admissions discrimination on the basis of economic status is unconstitutional as a denial of equal protection under the 14th Amendment.[9] To date, however, this argument has not been successful in the courts. Even when it does succeed, however, it will not mean that a poor person can demand admission to hospitals, but only that hospitals cannot decide whether or not to admit patients on the basis of ability to pay.[10]

What steps must a hospital take before a patient is considered admitted?

The question is important because while a hospital may not be duty-bound to care for a non-emergency patient, once the hospital has initiated treatment, it has a duty to continue to provide it until the patient can be safely discharged.

The old rule was that such a duty did not arise until the patient was *formally* admitted, which involved the actual completion of admission forms; an initial evaluation of the patient's condition was not sufficient action to constitute admission.[11] Recently, however, courts have begun to expand the concept of admission to include many acts by hospital employees. One commentator has warned[12]: "Hospitals should be aware that virtually any act on behalf of the patient will constitute admission and assumption of the duty to treat."

Two cases in which no forms were signed illustrate this point. In one, the dressing of the patient in a hospital gown for examination was found sufficient to constitute admission.[13] In another, the actions of a nurse in attempting to contact a doctor to care for the patient was sufficient to constitute assumption on the part of the hospital of a responsibility for the patient's health.[14]

When may a person legally be refused admission to a government hospital?

Government hospitals are generally established by statute or ordinance, and this law (or regulations promulgated under its authority) generally spells out the conditions under which admission to the hospital may be refused. Most of these requirements are concerned with residency and financial status. In order for a patient to demonstrate a "right" to be admitted, he must be able to show that he meets the requirements of the statute or regulation.[15] Any hospital can properly refuse admission to the "professional patient" who travels from state to state seeking shelter rather than medical care.

Must hospitals receiving funds under the federal Hill-Burton Program make special efforts to provide free or below-cost services for the poor?

While one of the requirements for hospitals receiving monies (for construction and modernization) under the Hill-Burton Act of 1946 was to provide a "reasonable volume of services to persons unable to pay therefore,"[16] no attempts were made to define or enforce this requirement until the 1970s. As a direct result of a number of lawsuits giving both the indigent and the medically indigent (those not indigent but unable to pay their medical bills) the right to sue hospitals receiving Hill-Burton funds but not offering services to the poor,[17] HEW has recently promulgated new regulations designed to require such hospitals to provide some free or low-cost service to the poor.[18]

In general, while states can work out specific plans, hospitals will be deemed in compliance with the law if they annually provide free care in an amount equal to 10 percent of their Hill-Burton federal assistance or 3 percent of their operating costs, or if they agree not to deny admission to anyone on the basis of ability to pay and to provide services at no charge or at a charge below cost.[19] The latter option is the so-called "open door" option, and if the hospital takes this route, it may not deny admission to any patient on the basis of ability to pay.[20] Since Hill-Burton information is of public record, interested citizens may find out from the state agency designated to write the Hill-Burton state plan (usually the state department of health and/or welfare) which hospitals, if any, in a given area have agreed to this open-admissions policy.

In late 1974 a U.S. Circuit Court ruled 2-1 that a hospital's charitable status under the federal tax laws could not be revoked even if the hospital refused to agree to accept a reasonable number of nonpaying patients.[21]

Can a hospital lawfully prevent a patient from leaving?

A patient of sound mind may leave the hospital at any time he chooses, and the hospital may not prevent it. If the hospital restricts this freedom to leave, it can be sued for *false imprisonment,* which involves the intentional confinement of the patient by threat or physical barriers against the patient's will. No actual damages need be proved since the law assumes harm to the patient from this conduct.[22]

Such rules apply even if the patient has not paid the bill. In one case, for example, a patient was detained for 11 hours for not paying her bill. In concluding that she could properly sue the hospital for false imprisonment, the court said: "the fact that the bill ... had not been paid afforded no sort of excuse for detaining the [patient] against her will."[23] This rule also applies to detaining infants and children when parents have not paid the bill. Courts have found hospitals liable for interfering with the parent's right to custody of the child when discharge has been refused because of failure to pay a bill.[24]

A hospital may prevent a person of unsound mind from departing if the person is a danger to his life or the lives and property of others, provided it takes immediate steps for commitment to a mental institution[25] or at least obtains a declaration of incompetence from a qualified psychiatrist. Hospitals may also request patients to sign a "discharge against medical advice form." Patients, however, have no obligation to sign such a form as a precondition to release, and hospitals can protect themselves equally well by noting the circumstances of the patient's leaving in the medical record as well as any noncoercive attempts to persuade the patient to stay.[26] In rare cases such as contagious diseases, the public health authorities may have power to restrain a patient from leaving the premises, but this authority is generally spelled out in the state's public health laws.[27]

Under what circumstances can a patient be forced to leave the hospital against his will?

One of the more common complaints by patients is that they are discharged before they are ready to go home. This has been called the problem of "premature discharge." The general rule is that no patient may be discharged except by written order of a doctor familiar with the patient's condition.[28] If the patient disagrees with the order, he has a right to demand a consultation with another physician before the order is carried out.[29] In any event, however, the decision to discharge must be made on the basis of the patient's medical condition and *may not take into consideration the patient's nonpayment of past medical bills*.

In one case, for example, a private hospital admitted an 8-year-old boy suffering from osteomyelitis (a bone infection). The bill for treatment was $1,000, but the boy's father could only pay $349. The hospital discharged the boy for failure to pay his bills and instructed the father that the boy would be safe at home under the care of a physician. In fact, the physician was not able to provide proper care at home, and the boy's condition worsened. The court found the hospital liable for negligent and wrongful discharge.[30]

If the discharge is medically indicated, however, and the patient still refuses to leave, the hospital may take steps to forcibly remove the patient as a trespasser. All steps must, however, be reasonable, and only the minimum amount of force necessary may be used.

Does the hospital have an obligation to see to it that the patient arrives home safely?

While most hospitals do not "pick up and deliver," there is some obligation to see to it that patients with debilitating conditions are not left in the street outside the hospital. The *Hospital Law Manual* has described the hospital's liability as follows[31]:

> Discharge of a patient, apparently unable to reach home safely because of age or disability, could constitute negligence if such patient met with an injury upon leaving the hospital. The appropriate standard

of care may require that the hospital provide or arrange for a suitable escort for such a patient.

NOTES

1. This rule may have variations based on the type of hospital (e.g., governmental or private), the condition of the
   patient, and whether or not there is an existing contractual obligation to admit patients such as hospital employees. E.g., *Norwood v. Howton*, 32 Ala. App. 375, 26 So.
   2d 427 (1946). One court has said of private hospitals,
   "Harsh as this rule may sound, it is permissible for a private hospital to reject for whatever reason, or no reason
   at all, any applicant for medical and hospital services
   . . ." *Le Jeune Hospital, Inc. v. Watson*, 171 So. 2d 202,
   203 (Fla. Ct. App., 1965).
2. See generally, Cantor, *The Law and Poor People's Access
   to Health Care*, 35 LAW & CONT. PROBLEMS 901
   (1970).
3. E. Mumford, INTERNS: FROM STUDENTS TO
   PHYSICIANS, Harvard U. Press, Cambridge, Mass.,
   1970 at 179.
4. While some have argued that these restrictions would apply only to hospitals receiving any federal funding or engaged in "state action," as a practical matter these qualifications apply to almost every hospital in the United
   States. See, e.g., Civil Rights Act of 1964, Titles II and
   VI, 42 U.S.C.A. §2000 and the regulations promulgated
   thereunder, 45 C.F.R.§80. There is also case law in support of this proposition, *Simkins v. Moses H. Cone Memorial Hospital*, 323 F.2d 959 (4th Cir., 1963); *Doe v.
   General Hospital of District of Columbia*, 313 F. Supp.
   1170 (D.D.C., 1970). See generally Health Law Center,
   Hospital Law Manual, U. of Pittsburgh, Admitting &
   Discharge at 1–2 (Aug., 1973 Supp.).
5. *New York Times*, Jan. 4, 1974 at 33, col. 1.
6. *Id*. See Ch. IV, The Emergency Ward.
7. *Id*.
8. See generally on payment provisions Chapter XVI, Payment of Hospital Bills. The Medicare regulation is 20
   C.F.R.§405.10.
9. See Cantor, *supra*. note 2, at 903–907; Note, *State Action, State Law, and the Private Hospital*, 62 MICH. L.
   REV. 1433 (1964); Rose, *The Duty of Publicly Funded
   Hospitals to Provide Services to the Medically Indigent*, 3

CLEARINGHOUSE REV. 254 (1970). The argument has had some success, however, in the areas of criminal justice and voting. See *Harper v. Virginia Bd. of Elections*, 383 U.S. 663 (1966) (poll tax); and *Griffin v. Illinois*, 351 U.S. 12 (1965) (criminal appeals).

10. *Cf.* section on the effect of receiving Hill-Burton funding later in this chapter.

11. *Birmingham Baptist Hospital v. Crews*, 229 Ala. 398, 157 So. 224 (1934).

12. T. Alexander in L. Goldsmith, ed., *LIABILITY OF HOSPITALS AND HEALTH CARE FACILITIES*, Practising Law Institute, N.Y. (No. H4-2894), 1973 at 102.

13. *Le Jeune Road Hospital, Inc. v. Watson*, 171 So. 2d 202 (Fla. Ct. App., 1965).

14. *O'Neill v. Montefiore Hospital*, 11 App. Civ. 2d 132, 202 N.Y.S. 2d 436 (1970), recounted in some detail in Chapter IV, The Emergency Ward.

15. The U.S. Supreme Court recently invalidated as unconstitutional an Arizona statute that required a year's residency in a county as a condition to receiving nonemergency medical care at the county's expense. The court followed *Shapiro v. Thompson*, 394 U.S. 618 (1969) in finding that the statute created an "invidious classification" that impinged on the right of interstate travel by denying newcomers "basic necessities of life." To justify the imposition of such a requirement the court held that the state would have to demonstrate that the requirement was mandated by a "compelling state interest." Interests that were specifically found to be noncompelling by the court included cost, inhibition of immigration of indigents, dilution of the quality of services to long-time residents, discouragement of the development of modern facilities, administrative convenience, and prevention of fraud. *Memorial Hospital v. Maricopa Co.*, 94 S.Ct. 1076 (1974). On statutory requirements, see generally, *Hospital Law Manual, supra.* note 4, at 5–10.

16. 42 U.S.C.A. §291 et seq., The Hospital Construction and Survey Act of 1946.

17. For the background of these suits, see Rose, *Hospital Admission of the Poor and the Hill-Burton Act*, 3 CLEARINGHOUSE REV. 185 (1969); Rose, *The Duty of Publicly Funded Hospitals to Provide Services to the Medically Indigent*, 3 CLEARINGHOUSE REV. 254 (1970). The first case recognizing this duty was *Cook v. Ochsner Foundation Hospital*, 319 F. Supp. 603 (E.D.

La. 1970). Others include *Euresti v. Stenner*, 458 F. 2d
1115 (10th Cir. 1972), *aff'd en banc* 1972, reversing 327
F. Supp. 111 (D. Colo. 1971); *Organized Migrants in
Community Action v. James Archer Smith Hospital*, 325
F. Supp. 268 (S.D. Fla. 1971); and *Corum v. Beth Israel
Medical Center*, 359 F. Supp. 909 (S.D.N.Y. 1973).

18. See Miller, *The Hill-Burton Act and Delivery of Uncompensated Medical Services-A Brief Analysis of the Federal Regulation*, 2 *Medicolegal News* 1 (1974) (American Society of Law & Medicine, 454 Brookline Avenue, Boston, Mass. 02215).

19. *Id.* and 38 *Fed. Reg.* 16353 (1973).

20. This probably does *not* mean, however, that patients can demand admission without the referral of a doctor since there is nothing in the regulations "to imply that the admission only by a physician requirement has been superseded." *HOSPITAL LAW MANUAL, supra.,* note 4 at 4.

21. *Eastern Kentucky Welfare Rights Organization v. Shultz*, D.C. Cir., Oct. 9, 1974, reversing 370 F. Supp 325 (1973).

22. See generally, *Hospital Law Manual, supra.,* note 4, at 22.

23. *Gadsden General Hospital v. Hamilton*, 212 Ala. 531, 103 So. 553 (1925); in another case recovery was denied because the court was not convinced that the patient's apprehension that force would be used to detain her was "reasonable." *Hoffman v. Clinic Hospital*, 213 N.C. 669, 197 S.E. 161 (1938).

24. *Bedard v. Notre Dame Hospital*, 57 R.I. 195, 151 A. 2d 690 (1959).

25. *Hospital Law Manual, supra.,* note 4, at 24.

26. *Id.* at 23, Sample Form at 30.

27. E.g., tuberculosis, drug addiction, alcoholism. See generally Curran & Shapiro, *LAW, MEDICINE AND FORENSIC SCIENCES*, Little, Brown, Boston, 1970 at 687, 883–885.

28. *Hospital Law Manual, supra.* note 4, at 26. It should be noted that the decision of a hospital utilization review committee that the patient has stayed in the hospital too long *does not* relieve the patient's physician from liability for premature discharge. The committee's decision pertains only to the source of payment, not to good medical practice. *Id.* at n. 70.

29. For details see Chapter VIII, Consultation, Referral and Abandonment.

30. *Meiselman v. Crown Heights Hospital*, 34 N.E. 2d 367 (1941). *Cf. Hick vs. U.S.*, 368 F.2d 626 (4th Cir. 1966) (Dispensary physician determined that patient had harmless instead of lethal disease without properly testing for the lethal possibility. With prompt surgery the patient would have survived, instead she was was sent home and died from a high intestinal obstruction. In finding the dispensary physician liable the court said: "By releasing the patient, the dispensary physician made his diagnosis final, allowing no further opportunity for revision, and this prematurely determined final diagnosis was based on an investigation not even minimally adequate." The court went on to determine that the premature discharge of the patient was the proximate cause of death.)

31. See *supra.* note 4, at 26.

VI

Informed Consent to Treatment

Sir Henry Maine has characterized social progress as the movement from status to contract. In former times a man's status (e.g., master-slave) exclusively determined his rights. Now citizens enter into contractual relationships such as employer-employee, debtor-creditor, and buyer-seller in which their rights are determined by the terms of a contract rather than by their status. In Maine's words,[1] "It is through contract that man attains freedom. Although it appears to be the subordination of one man's will to another, the former gains more than he loses."

In the doctor-patient relationship the rights of the patient cannot be defined as subordinate to those of the doctor simply by reason of the doctor's "status." Indeed, even in the realm of contract it is said that because of his expert knowledge the doctor owes a special or "fiduciary" duty to the patient to look out for his welfare. The practical application of the principles of contract and fiduciary duty in the doctor-patient relationship are nowhere so well exemplified as in the requirement of informed consent prior to treatment. Simply stated, the doctrine is that a physician may not treat a patient until he has explained to the patient the risks and material facts concerning the treatment and its alternatives, including nontreatment, and has secured thereafter the patient's *competent, voluntary,* and *understanding* consent to proceed. The purpose is to protect the patient's right of self-determination. Because so many other patient rights are derived from the necessity to obtain informed consent, this doctrine will be dealt with in some detail. Throughout this chapter it must be remembered that *the specific legal requirements of informed consent vary from state to state.*

What is informed consent?

Most commentators begin discussions of informed consent by noting that the doctrine is difficult to define and difficult to apply.[2] While these assertions may have merit, there are significant areas of the doctrine that can be lucidly presented. First, it can be accurately stated that, as the words denote, informed consent consists of two separate elements: (1) *information* and (2) *consent.* That is, the doctor must first disclose a certain amount of information to the patient concerning the proposed treatment, its risks and alternatives, and thereafter must obtain the consent of the patient before going ahead with the treatment. Problems arise in defining the boundaries of both these elements. In general terms, however, the information conveyed must include all of the *material facts* of the treatment proposed, including risks of death or serious bodily harm, the probability of success, the *alternatives* to the treatment (including nontreatment), and their risks and probabilities of success. Courts differ on what facts are material, some leaving this to the discretion of the physician or medical community, others to the needs of the patient. Once this information is obtained, the patient's consent must be *competent, understanding,* and *voluntary.* Specifically, the patient must be legally capable of giving consent (e.g., not a minor or patient who has been adjudged legally incapable of consenting to treatment), must comprehend the information disclosed, and must not be coerced into consenting. These general rules can be illustrated by summarizing some of the cases on informed consent that have reached the courts.

What are some examples of lack of informed consent?

In a 1960 case a patient was suffering from cancer of the breast, and her breasts were surgically removed. Her doctor engaged a radiologist to administer radiation therapy to the site of the mastectomy and the surrounding areas. The radiologist did not mention any possible risks from the procedure. As a result of the radiation treatments, the patient suffered severe radiation burns and skin breakdown. The Kansas Supreme Court was asked to determine whether or not the radiologist had to inform the patient about possible risks. The court decided that he was[3]:

> obligated to make a reasonable disclosure to the patient of the *nature and probable consequences of the suggested or recommended cobalt irradiation treatment,* and he was also obligated to make a reasonable disclosure of the *dangers* within his knowledge which were incident to, or possible in, the treatment he proposed to administer. (italics mine).

The court did note, however, that if a patient knew of the risks no disclosure would be necessary. Also, in some cases, a doctor might not have to discuss risks if to do so might "so alarm the patient that it would in fact constitute bad medical practice."

In a 1972 California case a middle-aged male had consented to an operation for a duodenal ulcer. His doctor had discussed the nature of the operation with him but did not mention any of the risks of the surgery. Eight days after the operation he went into shock. During an emergency procedure it was discovered that he was bleeding internally, and his spleen had to be removed. A month later he developed a gastric ulcer that necessitated the removal of half of his stomach. At trial it was established that the loss of one's spleen occurs in about 5 percent of all such operations. The development of a subsequent ulcer was also considered an inherent risk. The court was asked to determine whether or not the doctor should have revealed these risks to the patient. The court decided, unlike the Kansas court, that the duty to disclose should not be one defined by the practice of other doctors; rather, it should be a function of "the patient's right of self-decision," measured by whatever information a reasonable patient finds *material* to making his decision.

In attempting to define informed consent, the court said that when a given procedure inherently involves a known risk of death or serious bodily harm, a medical doctor has a duty to disclose to his patient the *potential of death or serious harm* and to *explain in lay terms* the *complications* that might possibly occur. He must also disclose such additional information as a skilled practitioner of good standing would disclose under similar circumstances. In explaining the standard further, the court noted what a doctor *need not do*[4]:

> The patient's interest does not extend to a lengthy polysyllabic discourse on all possible complications. A minicourse in medical science is not required ... Second, there is no duty to discuss the relatively minor risks inherent in common procedures, when it is common knowledge that such risks ... are of very low incidence.

The drawing of blood was mentioned by the court as a procedure in which the risks are common knowledge and of low incidence.

Does the amount of information that must be disclosed depend on the elective nature of the procedure?

One can summarize the informed-consent cases by noting that the key element is self-determination and the desire to give the patient enough information so that the patient can decide how and if he is to be treated. A corollary is that the *more elective a procedure is, the more important full disclosure becomes*. If there is only one treatment available, and death is imminent, the rationale behind informed consent is less compelling. However, as is discussed in Chapter VII, Refusing Treatment, even under these circumstances patients have a right to be fully informed of their options. It also means, as discussed in Chapter IX, Experimentation, that the provision of complete information is *always* a prerequisite to using an experimental procedure since such a procedure is almost by definition elective.

In order to win a lawsuit for lack of informed consent, one must convince the jury that if one knew about the risks, one would not have undergone the procedure or operation. The more elective the procedure, the more likely the jury is to find such a decision reasonable.

What is the difference between consent and informed consent?

Traditionally, the unauthorized performance of a med-

ical or surgical procedure was dealt with by the law of
battery, as any intentional, unauthorized touching. Examples could include a punch in the face, a kiss in the
dark, or a push down the stairs. Some courts used the
terms assault and battery interchangeably. For example,
in one famous opinion Judge Cardozo said: "Every human being of adult years and sound mind has a right to
determine what shall be done with his own body; and a
surgeon who performs an operation without his patient's
consent commits an assault for which he is liable in damages."[5]

Since *battery* (sometimes called simply assault or assault and battery) connotes an *unauthorized touching*
is most applicable either when the doctor treats a patient without obtaining any consent (e.g., a young child incapable of understanding,) or when the doctor properly
obtains consent for one type of an operation but does another (e.g., when a doctor operates on the wrong leg).
The modern trend is to disgard the battery model for all
but these types of conduct (because in most other cases
the touching was in fact authorized) and to view the doctor's lack of complete disclosure to the patient as *negligence.*

Under this theory the doctor has an affirmative *duty* to
the patient, because of the doctor-patient relationship, to
disclose relevant material facts and risks of treatment. If
these are not disclosed, and if the patient suffers one of
these risks, the patient may sue the doctor in negligence.
While the distinction between suing in battery or negligence may seem to be only semantic, in most jurisdictions
a patient is still required to present expert evidence (i.e.,
a doctor) to prove how much the "average doctor of
good standing" discloses since this defines how much
the doctor should have told his patient. In a battery action, on the other hand, the failure to disclose risks and alternatives may render the consent meaningless, and any
touching therefore becomes a battery. In this view expertise becomes irrelevant since the doctor's privilege to
touch the patient ends when he exceeds the scope of the
patient's consent.[6] Whether a patient sues in battery or
negligence may also determine such things as the period of
time during which the lawsuit can be brought (statute of

limitations), and the nature and extent of the damages that can be sought.

When must the doctor or hospital obtain the patient's informed consent?

Almost always. The general rule, as noted in somewhat more detail above, is that any time there is an inherent risk of death or serious bodily injury that the patient might not know about, or when the probability of success is low, the person performing the test or treatment is required to obtain the patients' informed consent. The rule applies equally to administration of drugs orally or by hypodermic needle,[8] the performance of diagnostic tests,[9] and the performance of major or minor surgical procedures.[10] An example of a procedure that probably does not require that specific disclosures be made because the risks are both minimal and generally known is the taking of a blood sample.[11] Diagnostic tests like angiograms and myelograms, however, do require informed consent.[12]

Can complete disclosure of risks be harmful to patients?

The presumption should be that all patients are capable of dealing with complete disclosure. The informed consent requirement need not frighten patients unduly. For example, in one study conducted of patients about to undergo angiography (a procedure whereby a small tube is introduced into a blood vessel under local anesthesia and an amount of dye is injected so that the circulation can be studied), patients were asked to sign a consent form that detailed a number of serious reactions, including possible loss of an organ, a death rate of 4 in 6,500, and a complication rate of 1 in 500. Of 900 patients, over 75 percent found the information useful, and over 70 percent either felt more comfortable or were not emotionally affected. Only 1 percent decided not to go through with the procedure, and only about 25 percent felt less comfortable about the procedure.[13] The doctor who conducted this study found that "it is wise to inform the patient well in advance of the procedure. This allows the patient time to think over what is proposed, weigh the risks, and decide." He concluded with a hope that "obtaining an informed consent" would become "routine in medical practice" and that "as the public becomes aware of this practice through scientific and mass media ... apprehension will decrease."[14]

How much does a doctor have to tell a patient about a proposed treatment or procedure in order to obtain a legally valid informed consent?

As recently as 1970 a legal commentator felt certain enough of his ground to write about informed consent, "Good medical practice is good law."[15] Whatever the validity of that statement then, current reliance on it is dangerous at best. A number of recent court opinions have specifically repudiated this view and put the medical profession on notice that they can no longer rely on self-imposed standards to determine what constitutes legally sufficient disclosure for the purposes of informed consent. One of these was the California case discussed. Two others deserve specific mention.

In a case from the District of Columbia, the doctor had told both his 19-year-old patient, who was suffering from back pain, and the patient's mother that a laminectomy (an operation on the spinal column) was "no more serious than any other operation." The doctor did not mention that the procedure carried a 1 percent risk of paralysis. Following surgery and a fall from his hospital bed the youth suffered total paralysis from the waist down. The court decided that the physician was under an affirmative obligation to disclose this risk information regardless of what was "medically customary." The court held that the law, not medical custom, must define the standard of disclosure and would do so in terms of the patient's needs. In the court's words, "Respect for the *patient's right of self-determination* on particular therapy demands a standard set by law rather than one which physicians may or may not impose upon themselves."[16] (italics mine)

That case was followed by one in Rhode Island in which the patient suffered severe burns and other complications as a result of deep radiation treatments for probable cancer. In commenting on the doctor's duty to disclose such risks of therapy, the court emphasized the individual-

ity of the patient and the subjectivity of the situation. In
the court's words,[17]

> The patient's right to make up his mind should not
> be delegated to a local medical group—many of
> whom have no idea as to his informational needs.
> The doctor-patient relationship is a one-on-one affair.
> What is reasonable disclosure in one instance may
> not be reasonable in another.

These decisions currently represent the rule in a minority of states but are indicative of the modern trend.[18] That
trend is for the courts to view the doctor-patient relationship as a partnership in decision-making rather than as a
medical monopoly. Under this view the doctor is obligated
to disclose not what other doctors customarily disclose to
their patients in similar circumstances, but what the individual patient needs to know to intelligently make up his
own mind concerning the proposed treatment. "The test
for determining whether a potential peril must be divulged
is its materiality to the patient's decision."[19]

**Must the doctor make his explanation understandable to
the patient to satisfy the legal requirements of informed
consent?**
While this may seem almost a ridiculous question, there
are cases indicating that some doctors believe that the use
of medical terminology to an untrained layman is sufficient. Neither reason nor case law supports this view. As
previously noted, the California Supreme Court has made
clear that the patient's interest is not in a "lengthy poly-
syllabic discourse" but in an explanation of the relevant
risks and alternatives "in lay terms."[20]
The need for clarity is illustrated by a Pennsylvania
case in which the patient submitted to what he believed
was an "exploratory operation." The patient understood
that the doctor would make an incision for the sole purpose of diagnosis, close the incision, and then discuss further surgery with the patient after advising him of the
options. To the doctor the term meant that if any abnormality was discovered, it would be operated on immediately if possible. Such an abnormality was found, and in

an attempt to correct it, the patient was injured. The jury awarded the patient $80,000. In reinstating the jury verdict (which the judge had overruled), the court found that because of the patient's misunderstanding of the terminology used to secure his consent, the consent was invalid, and the doctor was guilty of battery.[21] Other cases are similar.[22]

Why should doctors be required to obtain informed consent from their patients before administering treatment?

The major interest being protected by the doctrine of informed consent is that of the individual's right of self-determination. Stated another way, a "person of adult years and in sound mind has the right, in the exercise of control over his own body, to determine whether or not to submit to lawful medical treatment."[23]

In order to exercise this right of self-determination the law requires that doctors obtain the consent of their patients before treating them. To be an effective consent, it must be given with a knowledge and an understanding of the relevant facts, which include risks, success probabilities, and alternatives. This can be restated as the second function of informed consent, that is, encouraging rational decision-making. Since doctors know considerably more about such things than their patients, who are generally not familiar with medical science, the patient has "an abject dependence upon the trust in his physician for the information upon which he relies during the decisional process."[24] Doctor and patient therefore are not in an equal bargaining position. On the contrary, the patient is almost completely dependent on the doctor for medical information. This gives rise to a duty on the part of the doctor that transcends normal buyer-seller contract law and obligates the doctor to make certain minimum disclosures to his patients.

Is informed consent workable in the hospital context?

One leading medical commentator has argued that the process of obtaining informed consent is no more than an "elaborate ritual," and doctors can get hospitalized patients to consent to almost anything.[25] The implication is that doctors can phrase scientific information in such a way as to predetermine the patient's decision. The response to this contention, if true, is not to abandon the doctrine of informed consent as an impractical ideal. On the contrary, this statement merely points out the inadequacies in the present method of presenting information to patients in such a way as to enable them both to understand and act intelligently on it. The solution lies in improving the ability of both the doctor and the patient to communicate with each other so the patient may regain his right of self-determination.

Is informed consent important in an outpatient clinic or doctor's office?

As previously mentioned, important as informed consent is to normal crisis-oriented medical treatment, it is even more critical to elective procedures, especially when one possibility is that the condition to be treated might become worse as a result of the treatment. This point was illustrated in a case that involved a pregnant woman who experienced skin blotches on her face. She was treated by a physician who used a procedure called dermabrasion in which he in effect sanded a layer of skin from her face. Instead of removing the blotches, they actually became more noticeable. There was evidence both that the doctor did not mention the possibility of failure and that he knew the probability of a good result was only about 50 percent. The court noted that this was "an elective thing" since "there was no emergency" and the "patient's health was not at stake." The doctor therefore was obligated to "disclose to his patient all material facts which reasonably should be known if his patient is to make an informed and intelligent decision ... Arguably, one of the facts needed ... was the percentage probability that the contemplated surgery would improve her appearance." The case was sent back for a jury determination of the sufficiency of the doctor's disclosures.[26]

Other examples of procedures that may produce results expressly contrary to those desired by the patient are plastic-surgery cases[27] and unsuccessful vasectomies.[28] In all of these instances patient knowledge of the *probability of success* is critical to an informed consent to the treatment.

When is a doctor justified in not disclosing the risks and material facts concerning a recommended treatment to a patient?

Since the major rationale for the doctrine of informed consent is the preservation and protection of individual self-determination, the exceptions to the rule should involve only those cases in which self-determination is impossible. Typical of such cases are minors (whose parents may usually make legally valid decisions concerning their treatment) and unconscious patients in emergency situations. The only other exception should probably be for patients who are found to be mentally incompetent to make decisions about their own health care.

The problem of who may consent for minors or children is dealt with in Chapter XII, and the problem of consent to emergency medical treatment is dealt with later in this chapter. The issues concerning the terminally ill patient and consent are dealt with in Chapter XIV.

Under what circumstances may a doctor withhold relevant risk information from a competent adult patient?

The first thing to remember is that no exception can be permitted to swallow up the rule, that is, the presumption must be that every adult should be fully informed, not that full information will unduly upset the average adult. Second, this exception is a very narrow one. In one case, for example, the court held that the doctor should have informed the patient about the bone fracture risks involved in electroshock and insulin shock therapy even though the patient was upset, agitated, depressed, crying, had marital problems, and had been drinking.[29] This "therapeutic privilege" exception has tentatively been stated by the Kansas court in the following terms[30]:

> It might be argued ... that to make a complete disclosure of all facts, diagnoses and alternatives or possibilities that might occur to the doctor could *so alarm the patient* that it would, in fact, constitute *bad medical practice* ... in the ordinary case there would seem to be no warrant for suppressing facts. ... (italics mine)

The California Supreme Court has put the exception in stricter terms[31]:

> A disclosure need not be made beyond that required within the medical community when a doctor can prove by a preponderance of the evidence that he relied on facts that would demonstrate to a reasonable man the disclosure would have *so seriously upset the patient* that the patient would *not have been able to dispassionately weigh the risks* of refusing to undergo the recommended treatment. (italics mine)

A better rule would be a presumption that the physician always inform the patient of all material information, but that the manner in which the information is conveyed (time, place, language used, etc.) be permitted to vary depending on the patient's circumstances.

While some doctors have argued that they might be held liable for telling too much, no court has ever held a doctor liable for giving his patient too much accurate information.

Does the patient have a right to order his doctor not to disclose information on material facts and risks to him?

The general rule is that, since individual self-determination is the critical factor, "a medical doctor need not make disclosure of risks when the patient requests that he not be so informed."[32] While at least one commentator has warned doctors not to rely on this exception,[33] it would seem safe for a doctor to follow this exception to the rule so long as he was certain that the waiver was intelligently and knowingly made. In the words of another commentator speaking to doctors[34]:

> It seems to me, an adult has full right to waive his right to know. My caution would be to be very sure indeed to make a note to this effect on the chart and have the patient sign that note ... Notes are easy to make and may save embarrassment later.

The patient should probably be asked to reaffirm this wish at periodic intervals.

What is the purpose of a written consent form?

The consent of the patient is put into writing for the same reason that most contracts are put into writing. The purpose is to preserve the exact terms of the consent in case of future disagreement. For example, should a patient sue a doctor or a hospital and allege lack of informed consent, the doctor will present the written consent form in court as evidence that consent was in fact obtained. If the form is specific in its terms, and if it was voluntarily signed by a competent and understanding patient, the patient has very little chance of winning such a lawsuit.[35]

What is a "blanket" consent form?

A blanket consent form is one that covers almost everything a doctor or a hospital might do to a patient, without mentioning anything specifically. Many hospitals continue to require patients to sign such forms on admission. A typical form will read: "I, the undersigned, hereby grant permission for the administration of any anesthetic to, and for the performance of any operation upon myself as may be deemed advisable by the surgeon in attendance at the Charity Hospital."[36]

What is the legal effect of signing a blanket consent form?

The general rule is that a blanket consent form is almost always legally inadequate. Usually, the more vague and indefinite the terms of the consent, the more specifically the form will be construed against the doctor or the hospital by a court.[37]

In one case, for example, a woman had consented only to a simple appendectomy, but the surgeon decided to also perform a total hysterectomy. She had signed the following consent form:

AUTHORITY TO OPERATE

I hereby authorize the Physician or Physicians in charge to administer such treatment and the surgeon to have administered such anesthetics as found necessary to perform this operation which is advisable in the treatment of this patient.

The court had little difficulty in deciding that this "so-called authorization is so ambiguous as to be almost completely worthless." The court determined to give it "no possible weight under the factual circumstances" of the case.[38] Some commentators have suggested that such blanket forms are properly used on admission as proof of consent to "routine hospital procedures" as long as *specific* forms are signed whenever any nonroutine procedure is contemplated.[39]

What does a typical consent form look like?

One type of consent form that is gaining popularity is one recommended by the AMA. It provides for the following[40]:

CONSENT TO OPERATION, ANESTHETICS, AND OTHER MEDICAL SERVICES

Date_____Time_____
A.M.
P.M.

1. I authorize the performance upon _____
   (myself or name of patient)

of the following operation _____
   (state nature and extent of operation)

to be performed by or under the direction of Dr. _____

2. I consent to the performance of operations and procedures in addition to or different from those now contemplated, whether or not arising from presently unforeseen conditions, which the above-named doctor or his associates or assistants may consider necessary or advisable in the course of the operation.

3. I consent to the administration of such anesthetics as may be considered necessary or advisable by the physician responsible for this service, with the exception of _____
_____ *(state "none," "spinal anesthesia," etc.)*

4. The nature and purpose of the operation, possible alternative methods of treatment, the risks involved, the possible consequences, and the possibility of complications

have been explained to me by Dr. _____ and
by _____

5. I acknowledge that no guarantee or assurance has
been given by anyone as to the results that may be obtained.

6. I consent to the photographing or televising of the
operations or procedures to be performed, including appropriate portions of my body, for medical, scientific or
educational purposes, provided my identity is not revealed
by the pictures or by descriptive texts accompanying them.

7. For the purpose of advancing medical education, I
consent to the admittance of observers to the operating
room.

8. I consent to the disposal by hospital authorities of
any tissues or body parts which may be removed.

9. I am aware that sterility may result from this operation. I know that a sterile person is incapable of becoming a parent.

10. I acknowledge that all blank spaces on this
document have been either completed or crossed off prior
to my signing.

(CROSS OUT ANY PARAGRAPHS ABOVE WHICH DO NOT APPLY)

Signed_____

*(Patient or person authorized
to consent for patient)*

Witness_____

This form has both built-in advantages and disadvan-
tages. The main advantage is that it sets forth the procedure in question and gives the patient the opportunity to
limit such things as type of anesthesia. It includes, however, a number of items not usually found in a consent
form that the patient may not be aware he is consenting
to unless he reads it carefully. For example, Item 6 is a
consent for photographing and publishing the pictures of
the procedure, Item 7 admits observers to the operating
room, and Item 8 gives the hospital the right to dispose of
tissues removed as it sees fit.[41] It also does not disclose the

patient's right to change his mind and withdraw consent at any time.[42]

It should be noted that while the patient may put some limits on a surgeon's authority in the written consent form, a surgeon who believes that the limitations are so strict that he cannot proceed with the operation in a manner consistent with good medical practice might be justified in declining to perform the procedure.[43] The surgeon has the right to have all patient-imposed conditions noted in the record with the fact that the risks of such conditions have been fully explained and consented to by the patient.

Are clauses in consent forms by which the patient agrees not to sue the hospital or doctors enforceable?

The general answer is that a patient cannot legally waive his right to sue a hospital or doctor in the event of malpractice. The leading case involved a charity patient who was admitted to a nonprofit charitable hospital. He signed a consent form that included the following clause[44]:

> RELEASE: The hospital is a non-profit, charitable institution. In consideration of the hospital and allied services to be rendered and the rates charged therefore, *the patient* or his legal representative *agrees to and hereby releases* the Regents of the University of California [the hospital was maintained by the University], and *the hospital from any and all liability for the negligent or wrongful acts or omissions of its employees,* if the hospital has used due care in selecting its employees. (italics mine)

The main issue in the case was the validity of this clause. The Supreme Court of California found that the patient was at a great disadvantage in bargaining as compared with the hospital and thus was almost forced to sign any agreement the hospital presented him with. The court found further that this agreement affected the public interest (since the hospital held itself out as one that would perform services for any person who qualified by their medical condition for service) and that requirement of such a waiver as a condition of treatment was illegal and void as against public policy. It would seem that the same reasoning would void such a clause in any hospital.

Can legal consent be given without signing a consent form?

As noted previously, the reason for a writing is only to maintain a permanent record of what was agreed to. No writing is required to make most contracts, and no written form is required to make consent to treatment valid. Consent may also be implied by actions, such as the voluntary submission to treatment.

One of the first consent cases to reach the courts in this country, for example, involved a woman who was given a smallpox vaccination. There was no explicit verbal or written consent. The court found that she consented to it by her actions of standing in the vaccination line, observing what was happening, and holding up her arm for the doctor.[45] The basis for allowing voluntary submission to imply consent is that the patient understood what was going on and should have been aware that her actions would be interpreted by a doctor as consenting to the procedure. For a more complex procedure, like electroshock, consent by mere action may never be sufficient.[46]

Treatment may also be rendered without going through the formalities of consent if the life or health of the patient is in immediate danger and obtaining consent is impossible. For example, if the victim of an automobile accident is brought in bleeding and unconscious, and no relative can be reached, treatment to save his life may be commenced immediately. While this has sometimes been justified as "implied consent," the more accurate view is that society gives doctors a "privilege" to treat patients under such extreme conditions without obtaining their consent.[47]

Is consent given under the influence of a drug valid?

As noted above, consent must be given voluntarily, competently, and with knowledge of the relevant facts. If the patient is under the influence of a drug that compromises any of these components of consent, the consent is probably invalid. In one case, for example, a patient who had been given a sleeping pill was awakened in the middle

of the night and asked to sign a consent form. The patient
testified that he could not remember the event, and the
court found that consent obtained under such circumstances was not valid.[48] The same reasoning, of course, applies to intoxicated patients.[49]

Can a patient withdraw consent after signing a consent form?

Consent must be freely given, and so given it can be
freely withdrawn at any time. While this is the general rule, there are practical limitations. For example,
once a patient is under general anesthesia and on the operating table, it is obviously too late for the patient to
change his mind! Likewise, once the dye has been injected
into the catheter during an arteriogram, it is probably too
late for the patient to decide that he does not want to
have the test performed. A written consent form in no
way affects the patient's ability to change his mind and
withdraw consent. After orally indicating one's change of
mind, it may be a good idea either to obtain and destroy
the original consent form or to execute another form—
this time a form of nonconsent to treatment, noting on it
the date and time of day.

NOTES

1. Quoted by F. Kessler & G. Gilmore, CONTRACTS:
   CASES AND MATERIALS (2d ed.) Little, Brown,
   Boston, 1970 at 3.
2. See, e.g., J. Waltz & F. Inbau, MEDICAL JURISPRU-
   DENCE, Chapter 11, "Liability for Failure to Obtain
   'Informed Consent' to Customary Therapy," MacMillan,
   New York, 1971, at 152–168; Plante, *An Analysis of
   "Informed Consent,"* 36 FORDHAM L. REV. 639 (1968);
   McCoid, *A Reappraisal of Liability for Unauthorized
   Medical Treatment*, 41 MINN L. REV. 381 (1957);
   Note, *Restructuring Informed Consent: Legal Therapy
   for the Doctor-Patient Relationship*, 79 YALE L. J. 1533
   (1970).
3. *Natanson v. Kline*, 186 Kan. 393, 350 P. 2d 1093
   (1960), *rehearing denied*, 187 Kan. 186, 354 P. 2d 670
   (1960).
4. *Cobbs v. Grant*, 8 Cal. 3d 229, 502 P. 2d 1 (1972).
   While not explicitly stated, the probability of success of

the operation would also seem to be a material fact necessary for obtained consent. A more difficult question is whether or not a doctor should be required to disclose *his own* success rate with a particular treatment of procedure. Cf. Annas, *Informed Consent: When Good Medicine May not be Good Law*, 1 *Medicolegal News* 3 (1973) (American Society of Law & Medicine, 454 Brookline Avenue, Boston, Massachusetts 02215).

5. *Schloendorff v. New York Hospital*, 211 N.Y. 127, 129, 105 N.E. 92, 93 (1914).

6. E.g., *Scott v. Wilson*, 396 S.W. 2d 532 (Tex., Civ. App., 1965).

7. E.g., *Maercklein v. Smith*, 266 P. 2d 1095 (Col. 1954) In general, the negligence statute of limitations is likely to be longer than the battery statute.

8. E.g. *Trogun v. Fruchtman*, 207 N.W. 2d 297 (Wisc. 1973).

9. E.g. *Salgo v. Leland Stanford Jr. University Board of Trustees*, 317 P. 2d 170 (Cal. App. 1957).

10. E.g. *Canterbury v. Spence*, 464 F. 2d 772 (D.C. Cir., 1972); *Cobbs v. Grant*, 502 P. 2d 1 (Cal., 1972).

11. *Cobbs, supra.* note 10.

12. Cf. *Salgo, supra.*, note 9.

13. Alfidi, Informed Consent, in Meaney et. al., eds., COMPLICATIONS AND LEGAL IMPLICATIONS OF RADIOLOGIC SPECIAL PROCEDURES, Mosby, St. Louis, 1973.

14. Id.; see also Alfidi, *Informed Consent: A Study of Patient Reaction*, 216 J.A.M.A. 1325 (1971).

15. Hagmann, *The Medical Patient's Right to Know: Report on a Medical-Legal-Ethical Empirical Study*, 17 U.C.L.A. L. REV. 758, 764 (1970).

16. *Canterbury v. Spence*, 464 F. 2d 772 (D.C. Cir. 1972).

17. *Wilkinson v. Vesey*, 295 A. 2d 676 (R.I. 1972).

18. Cf. Annas, *supra.*, note 4.

19. *Cobbs, supra.*, note 4.

20. *Id.*

21. *Gray v. Grunnel*, 423 Pa. 144, 223 A. 2d 663 (1966).

22. E.g. *Bang v. Miller*, 251 Minn. 427, 88 N.W. 2d 186 (1958) (patient unaware that prostate operation involved sterilization); *Paulsen v. Gunderson*, 218 Wis. 587, 260 N.W. 448 (1935) (consent given only for simple mastoid operation, but a radical one was performed).

23. *Cobbs, supra.*, note 10.

24. *Id.*

25. Ingelfinger, *Informed (But Uneducated) Consent,* 287 NEW. ENG. J. MED. 465, 466 (1972).

26. *Hunter v. Brown,* 4 Wash. App. 899, 484 P. 2d 1162 (1971).

27. In *Sullivan v. O'Connor,* 296 N.E. 2d 183 (Mass., 1973), for example, the patient, a female entertainer, sued her physician who she alleged guaranteed her that her nose would be gracefully shaped following surgery. In fact it became more grossly disfigured. She was awarded money damages on the theory that the doctor had entered into a contract with her to change her nose for the better and had guaranteed results.

28. In *Hackworth v. Hart,* 474 S.W. 2d 377 (Ky., 1972), the doctor had told a husband that a vasectomy was "a fool-proof thing, 100 percent," and the court held that this stated a cause of action against the doctor when husband's wife became pregnant. Here the disclosure of the *probability of success* would seem critical since the *only* purpose for having the procedure performed was *complete sterilization.* And see cases in Annot. 27 A.L.R. 3d 906.

29. *Mitchell v. Robinson,* 334 S.W. 2d 11 (Mo., 1960), cited in *Cobbs v. Grant, supra.,* note 10.

30. *Natanson v. Kline,* 186 Kan. 393, 350 P. 2d 1093 (1960).

31. *Cobbs v. Grant, supra.,* note 10.

32. *Id.*

33. Mills, *Issue of Informed Consent,* 15 Physician's Legal Brief (Jan., 1973).

34. Rosenberg, *Informed Consent—The Latest Threat?,* J. LEGAL MED. 20 (May/June, 1973).

35. E.g., *Karp v. Cooley,* 349 F. Supp. 827 (S.D. Texas, 1972) (case involved consent form for first, and to date only, artificial heart implantation).

36. The Health Law Center at the University of Pittsburgh has advised hospitals in the "Administrator's Volume" of their *Hospital Law Manual* not to use such forms for specific procedures because at a trial it will be the doctor's word against the patient's.

   Such a general consent form should not be used. Its use raises the same legal problem as reliance upon voluntary submission to prove consent. In both instances the patient is apparently permitting the physician to proceed with some treatment. In both instances there is no way of determining, without testimony, the nature of the treatment the

patient believed was going to take place. There is
no difference between a patient who is taken to an
operating room without having signed any authorization and one who has signed a written consent
to whatever surgery the physician deems advisable.
In both situations testimony would be necessary to
establish the extent of the patient's actual knowledge and understanding, for it is possible for the
patient, after treatment, to claim he never knew
the nature of the physician's treatment before it
was rendered, and it is possible that a jury will believe him and impose liability upon the physician
or hospital or both. The written general consent
form merely serves as evidence of the patient's voluntary submission to treatment, but in no way de-
clares that the patient understood the specific treatment that is to be undertaken.

"Consent to Medical or Surgical Procedures," at 16
(Feb., 1973) (loose leaf).

37. E.g., *Valdez v. Percy*, 35 Cal. App. 2d 485, 96 P. 2d 142
(1939); *Moore v. Webb*, 345 S.W. 2d 239 (Mo., 1961).

38. *Rogers v. Lumbermans' Mutual Casualty Co.*, 119 So. 2d
649 (La., 1960).

39. *Hospital Law Manual, supra.*, note 36, at 18.

40. AMA, Office of General Council, *Medicolegal Forms
with Legal Analysis*, AMA, Chicago, 1973 at 57–58
(booklet available from American Medical Association,
535 North Dearborn St., Chicago, Ill. 60610). See also
the consent form recommended by Don Harper Mills,
Whither Informed Consent?, 229 JAMA 305, 309
(1974).

41. In a recent case a patient sued a hospital upon learning
that his leg, which had been amputated in the hospital,
had been burned. He had an intense fear of fire. The
court decided in favor of the hospital, but did say that if
the patient had desired his leg treated in a special way,
he could have accomplished this by informing the hospital of his wishes prior to the operation. *Browning v. Nor-
ton Children's Hospital*, 504 S.W. 2d 713 (Ky. 1974);
See Annas, *The Amputated Limb: How Should It Be Dis-
posed Of?* 3 ORTHO. REV. 59 (Sept. 1974).

42. This is discussed in more detail in Chapter IX., Experimentation, and in a later section in this chapter.

43. *Medicolegal Forms, supra.*, note 40 at 57.

44. *Tunkl v. Regents of University of California,* 60 Cal. 2d
    92, 32 Cal. Rptr. 33, 383 P. 2d 441 (1963).
45. *O'Brien v. Cunard S.S. Co.,* 154 Mass. 272, 28 N.E. 266
    (1891).
46. E.g., *Woods v. Brumlop,* 71 N.M. 221, 377 P. 2d 520
    (1962).
47. *Hospital Law Manual, supra.,* note 36 at 71, *Kritzer v.
    Citron,* 101 Cal. App. 2d 33, 224 P. 2d 808 (1950). See
    generally Chapter IV, The Emergency Ward.
48. *Demers v. Gerety,* 515 P. 2d 645 (N.M. Ct. App., 1973).
    See also, Cahal & Cady, *Consent and the Groggy Patient,*
    40 G.P. 195 (1969).
49. *Barker v. Heaney,* 82 S.W.2d 417 (Tex. Civ. App. 1935).

VII
Refusing Treatment

This nation was founded on the concept that individuals have the right of self-determination in matters not adversely affecting the rights of others. As John Stuart Mill said in his essay *On Liberty*: "The only purpose for which power can be rightfully exercised over any member of a civilized community, against his will, is to prevent harm to others. His own good, either physical or moral, is not a sufficient warrant."[1] This general concept has gradually worked its way into the arena of medical practice. Today, as discussed in the preceding chapter, it is generally recognized that no doctor may properly treat a patient without first explaining the treatment and its risks, alternatives and success rates, and then obtaining the patient's consent. A necessary corollary to the requirement of informed consent is that without such consent a doctor cannot legally treat a patient. In short, patients have the right to refuse to submit to medical treatment. Refusal may take place in extremely varied contexts. This chapter explores some of the most frequent. Unfortunately, while the general legal rules are rather well-defined, application to individual fact situations (such as emergencies) have resulted in varying responses by the courts.

Does a hospitalized patient have the right to refuse treatment?

The general rule is that an adult patient who is both conscious and mentally competent has the legal right to refuse to allow any medical or surgical procedure to be performed on his body. The reason for this refusal may be as rational as the slim chances for success or as "irrational" as a fear of hypodermic needles. In either case the refusal is just as legally binding on the doctor and the hospital. As a leading legal textbook puts it[2]:

> The very foundation of the doctrine of informed consent is every man's right to forego treatment or even cure if it entails what *for him* are intolerable consequences or risks, however warped or perverted his sense of values may be in the eyes of the medical profession, or even of the community, so long as any distortion falls short of what the law regards as incompetency. *Individual freedom here is guaranteed only if people are given the right to make choices which would generally be regarded as foolish.* (italics mine)

Nor may "mental incompetency" be inferred from the act of refusal or even from the fact of involuntary commitment to a mental institution. In one case, for example, the court affirmed the patient's right to refuse heavy doses of a tranquilizer even though the patient was mentally ill and involuntarily confined to a mental institution.[3]

In another instance the court affirmed the right of a 60-year-old childless woman who was committed to a mental institution to refuse consent to a breast biopsy which was to be followed by surgery should cancer be found. The patient stated that she was "afraid" of the operation because her aunt had died following surgery. At a court hearing she "indicated that the operation would interfere with her genital system, affecting her ability to have babies, and would prohibit a movie career." The court found that while her reasoning was becoming increasingly delusional, she had been consistent in her opposition to surgery. The court consequently found her decision within her rights saying, "The ordinary person's refusal to accept medical advice based upon fear is commonly known and while the refusal may be irrational and foolish to an outside observer it cannot be said to be incompetent in order to permit the State to override the decision."[4]

The general rule is clear: Patients may refuse to permit any medical or surgical procedure from being performed on them regardless of the opinions of their doctors as to the advisability of the treatment. The rule applies both in and out of the hospital.

What is the hospital's duty when a patient refuses a specific treatment?

It is the obligation of the hospital, in the face of a patient's refusal, to make sure that no member of the hospital staff performs the refused procedure. If the hospital does not successfully prevent unauthorized procedures, it may be legally liable to the patient to the same extent as the doctor or other staff person who performed the procedure.[5]

The hospital is also legally obligated to continue to render the best medical care possible within the limitations imposed by the patient's refusal.[6] While a patient may refuse to consent to any treatment, it has been said by one court that the patient cannot "demand mistreatment."[7] Only if a patient consistently refuses to participate in *any* treatment program might the hospital, after making diligent attempts to verbally persuade the patient to change his mind, be justified in asking the patient to leave. Under these circumstances the hospital will probably ask the patient to sign a release form that explains the proposed treatment to the patient, sets forth his refusal to consent to it, and releases the hospital from liability for the consequences of the refusal.[8] This release form is binding on the patient. For a discussion of the problem of "premature discharge" or discharge against the patient's wishes, see Chapter V, Admission and Discharge.

Does a patient have a right to refuse life-sustaining or emergency treatment?

The general rule that a conscious, mentally competent adult may refuse treatment applies to both life-sustaining and emergency measures. In perhaps the most important case enunciating this position, the patient was suffering from internal bleeding of his stomach and intestine. An operation was recommended. The patient said he would consent to the operation only if no blood transfusions were given. The doctors testified that without the blood there was very little likelihood of recovery from the operation and that without the operation the patient would probably die. The court decided that it was "the individual who is the subject of a medical decision who has the final say." The court noted that the patient had been "completely competent" at all times while making the decision and therefore had the complete right to decline treatment. The hospital's request for an order directing treatment was denied.[9] The case was cited as authority in a 1971 Florida lower-court opinion that permitted an elderly woman who was physically and "possibly" mentally disabled to order her physicians to discontinue daily painful blood transfusions even though the doctors deemed them necessary to sustain her life.[10] She died a few days later.

While these cases support the general rule, there are instances of courts overruling the desires of even competent adult patients. In one case, for example, the court rationalized that while the patient had said that her religion forbade blood transfusions, she could not be at fault if they were ordered performed by the court. The judge accordingly ordered the transfusions to save her life.[11] In another similar case the court found that the state (New Jersey) had a "compelling interest" in preventing its citizens from committing suicide and that hospitals could not be compelled to "mistreat" patients. The court did, however, imply that if the patient had demanded to leave the hospital without being treated, this request would have had to have been honored.[12] Other cases have ordered the treatment of adults with minor children on the basis that the state has a compelling interest in making sure the children not becoming wards of the state.[13]

After reviewing all of the judicial opinions in this area, and the interests that the judges in each said they were protecting, one legal commentator has argued that "the patient's decision to refuse lifesaving treatment must be respected by the judiciary *no matter what* the reason for refusal." His conclusion was based on the patient's overriding interest in his "bodily integrity, as dictated by constitutional rights of personal privacy."[14]

What is a "living will"?

Arguing that patients used to be afraid to go to the hospital because it was a place to die, but are now afraid to go because they won't be allowed to die, Dr. Walter W.

Sackett, a physician and a member of the Florida legislature, some years ago introduced a measure called a living will. The document, termed "living" because it takes effect while the individual is still alive, directs one's doctor, family, clergyman, and lawyer to take no artificial or heroic measures to keep the individual alive if it has been determined that there is "no reasonable expectation" of recovery. The Euthanasia Educational Council of New York recommends the following form and has distributed more than a million of them:

TO MY FAMILY, MY PHYSICIAN, MY CLERGYMAN, MY LAWYER—

If the time comes when I can no longer actively take part in decisions for my own future, I wish this statement to stand as the testament of my wishes.

If there is no reasonable expectation of my recovery from physical or mental and spiritual disability, I _____, request that I be allowed to die and not be kept alive by artificial means or heroic measures. I ask also that drugs be mercifully administered to me for terminal suffering even if in relieving pain they may hasten the moment of death. I value life and the dignity of life, so that I am not asking that my life be directly taken, but that my dying not be unreasonably prolonged nor the dignity of life be destroyed.

This request is made, after careful reflection, while I am in good health and spirits. Although this document is not legally binding, you who care for me will, I hope, feel morally bound to take it into account. I recognize that it places a heavy burden of responsibility upon you, and it is with the intention of sharing this responsibility that this statement is made.

Signed_____

Date_____
Witnessed by:

_____

_____

A Harris poll taken in the spring of 1973 indicated that approximately 62 percent of Americans favored allowing the terminally ill patient to direct his doctor to "let him die rather than extend his life when no cure is in sight," and only 28 percent thought this practice was wrong.

If a patient signs such a "living will," is it binding on his doctors or the hospital?

A state statute is thought to be necessary to make such a document legally binding on doctors and hospitals because such a statement might violate "public policy" against suicide or euthanasia. No state has yet passed a law approving such a document. In the absence of such a statute, another approach would be to have the doctor *and* the patient sign the living will. In this way the document would act like a contract. As a contract, however, it would be subject to a number of challenges. For example, the terms could be said to be so vague as to make it unenforceable. An example of a far more explicit form is set out in Note 15. It could also be argued, as previously suggested, that it was an unlawful contract as undermining public policy to discourage suicide or euthanasia. As a practical matter, also, the doctor who signs it may not be the doctor treating the patient at his death. In any event, no individual doctor could ensure that another member of the hospital staff would not attempt to sustain a patient's life artificially when the doctor was not in the hospital.

All this is not to say, however, that such a document is meaningless. Indeed, if the patient had signed the document before terminal diagnosis, and after learning of the diagnosis, had reaffirmed a desire to be permitted to die, the doctor would be reasonably certain of the patient's wishes not to have heroic measures and reasonably secure in following them. The doctor might also be more successfully sued for the pain, suffering, and expense caused by unauthorized treatment by the patient or his estate should he continue treatment despite the patient's protests. Also, when such a document is signed by a terminally ill hospitalized patient, it acts as a *binding* refusal to consent to the types of treatment specified (provided, of course, that the patient is competent).[16]

Do parents have a right to refuse life-sustaining or emergency treatment for their children?

In late 1973 two doctors from the Yale-New Haven Hospital reported that of 299 deaths occurring in their special-care nursery from January 1, 1970, through June 30, 1972, 43, or 14 percent, died because treatment was

withheld from them.[17] The parents of the children participated in the decision. The major rationale was that the
physical and/or neurological problems of these infants
were so great that their chance to lead any meaningful life
was slim. The doctors, who had purposely not sought legal
advice, wrote: "If working out these dilemmas in ways
such as we suggest is in violation of the law, we believe
the law should be changed."[18] The report not only raises
the problem of withholding treatment from infants with
severe medical problems, but also points to another phenomenon in the major medical center: a cavalier disregard
of the law when it is perceived as inconsistent with the
desires of the medical staff.

One problem with infant euthanasia, even when confined to the severely deformed or retarded, is that once established as permissible the indicationes for its use are
likely to expand. In Nazi Germany, for example, even after Hitler had put a stop to the adult euthanasia program,
the killing of "defective" children continued, the age limit
being raised from 3, to 8, to 12, and, in some cases, to 16
or 17.[19] The counter argument is that the United States is
far different from prewar and World War II Germany,
and sufficient safeguards could be built in to prevent such
abuses. The purpose here is not to debate the merits of
such a program but to outline the current status of the
law.

Parents in the United States, unlike those of ancient
Rome, do not have life and death authority over their
children.[20] Since the early 1960s all of the states have
adopted child-abuse statutes, and many put a legal obligation on parents to provide medical care for their children. While parents and doctors may be able to make decisions to withhold treatment in the "privacy" of major
hospitals, when the issue reaches the courts, it is likely to
be found that such decisions, if based on a "quality of
life" rationale, are against the law and constitute child
neglect. Unfortunately, there is only one lower-court case
specifically on the subject.[21]

In early 1974 a hospital in Maine sought an order to
proceed with the treatment of an infant born with no left
eye, a rudimentary left ear with no ear canal, a malformed thumb, and a tracheal-esophageal fistula (which

prevented eating by mouth and complicated breathing).
The treatment recommended and objected to by the parents was repair of the fistula to permit normal eating and breathing. Before the case got to the court, the child's mental condition had also been affected and was deteriorating. At a court hearing the doctors joined in a recommendation that treatment not be undertaken and the child be allowed to die. The court noted that "the most basic right enjoyed by every human being is the right to life itself."
The court then went on to make the following rulings[22]:

> Where the condition of a child does not involve serious risk of life and where treatment involves a considerable risk, parents have a considerable degree of discretion in refusing treatment and the courts will not intervene.

> A doctor's opinion that a child's life is not worth preserving because of the probable quality of that life is irrelevant since it is not legally within the scope of his expertise.

> Where corrective life-saving surgery is medically necessary and medically feasible, parents have no right to withhold it from their children and to do so constitutes neglect in the legal sense.

The court accordingly ordered the treatment performed. The child died within a week after the operation. While the authority of one lower court in Maine is not great, it is likely that most courts faced with a similar fact situation would reach a similar conclusion.[23]

Situations need not be life and death for the court to overrule the parents' refusal. In one leading case, for example, a 15-year-old child was suffering from Von Recklinghausen's disease, which had caused a massive deformity on the right side of his face and neck. The disease was progressing and was having a detrimental effect on his psychological development. Surgery was recommended even though it entailed substantial risk. The mother, a Jehovah's Witness, refused to consent to the surgery unless it was done without blood transfusions. The surgeons refused to operate under this condition. The court, finding the procedure necessary "to insure the physical, mental and emotional well-being" of the child, ordered the operation performed with the necessary blood transfusions.[24] The basis for the court's intervention was again the state's child-neglect statute. The main authority cited was a statement by the U.S. Supreme Court when it considered an analogous problem: "Parents may be free to become martyrs themselves. But it does not follow they are free, in identical circumstances, to make martyrs of their children before they have reached the age of full and legal discretion when they can make that choice for themselves."[25]

It can probably be concluded, however, that it is only in *extreme* cases involving the potential of death or permanent disability to the child, that courts are likely to overrule a parent's refusal of treatment for a child.

NOTES

1. J. S. Mill, ON LIBERTY, Parker, London, 1859 at 22.
2. Harper & James, *THE LAW OF TORTS* (1968 Supp.) §17.1 at 61.
3. The patient's refusal in this case was founded upon religious objections. *Winters v. Miller*, 306 F. Supp. 1158 (E.D.N.Y. 1969), *reversed on other grounds*, 446 F. 2d 65 (2d Cir. 1971), *cert. denied*, 404 U.S. 985 (1971).
4. *In re Yedder*, Northampton Co. Orphans Court, Pa., No. 1973–533 (June 6, 1973) (Unreported opinion, Judge Alfred T. Williams, Jr.).
5. Health Law Center, *Hospital Law Manual*, U. of Pittsburgh, Pittsburgh, Consents at 77 (Feb. 1973 Supp.).
6. *Id.*
7. *John F. Kennedy Hospital v. Heston*, 58 N.J. 576, 279 A. 2d 670 (1970).
8. A typical release form will read:
    I, ——————————, refuse to allow anyone to ——————————. The risks attendant to my refusal have been fully explained to me, and I fully understand, that I will in all probability need——————————, and that if the same is not done, my chances for regaining normal health are seriously reduced, and that in all probability, my refusal for such treatment or procedure will seriously imperil my life. I hereby release the Hospital, its nurses and employees, together with all physicians in any way connected with me as a patient,

from liability for respecting and following my express wishes and direction.

The form will also contain a clause setting forth religious objections if that is the basis for the patient's refusal.

9. *Erickson v. Dilgard*, 44 Misc. 2d 27, 252 N.Y.S. 2d 705 (Sup. Ct. 1962). Accord *In re Brook's Estate*, 32 Ill. 2d 361, 205 N.E. 2d 435 (1965); *In re Osborne*, 294 A. 2d 372 (D.C. Ct. App. 1972).

10. *Palm Springs General Hospital v. Martinez*, Dade Co. 11th Circuit Ct., Fla., No. 71–12687 (July 2, 1971) (Unreported opinion, Judge David Popper).

11. *In re Application of the President and Directors of Georgetown College, Inc.*, 331 F. 2d 1000 (D.C. Cir., 1964); Accord, *Powell v. Columbia-Presbyterian Medical Center*, 49 Misc. 2d 215, 267 N.Y.S. 2d 450 (1965). Both cases involved Jehovah's Witnesses.

12. *John F. Kennedy Memorial Hospital v. Heston*, 58 N.J. 576, 279 A. 2d 670 (1970).

13. See Cantor, *A Patient's Decision to Decline Life-Saving Medical Treatment: Bodily Integrity versus the Preservation of Life*, 26 RUTGERS L. REV. 228 (1973).

14. *Id.* at 263.

15. Dr. Walter Modell has recently published an explicit "living will" which one of his patients gave him in 1962 and which he "advised her that a physician could follow without fear of violation of his Hippocratic Oath (290 NEW ENG. J. MED. 906, 907 (1974):

Statement of Intent in case I am incapacitated from making such a decision at the time that a decision is called for

I believe that in each age it is appropriate to rethink the responsibilities which each individual carries in regard to his own life and the life of others. In this present age we have reached a crisis because medical advances have outdistanced our expected forms of ethical behavior. Before the development of modern medical techniques the will to live, the will to recover, could be seen as part of an individual's struggle to live as complete and responsible a life as possible. But today there are many forms of intervention which have not yet been absorbed into the individual's consciousness of when a determination to live on is appropriate. I believe it is, therefore, wise to establish an order of preference which can be used to guide those physicians who care for me in any instance where through accident, illness or mental illness I am not fully conscious and am not able to make a conscious decision at the time. This document is essentially a recital of choices which I would wish to be able to make.

If I become involved in any illness or accident where intervention of any kind, which a patient would be able to accept or refuse, if taken, involves a risk that I would survive with any sort of decreased mental efficiency of any kind, brain damage, amnesia, cognitive loss of any kind, I do not wish those measures taken unless I am fully conscious at the time and able to make a conscious decision and do so decide.

If intervention involves the loss either of a receiving sense or a form of communication with the rest of the world I wish this to be considered in the following way: I would be willing to risk intervention which might involve my continuing to live blind, alone *or* deaf alone, *or* incapable of movement of the lower half of my body. If further impairment were risked, I would be willing to live blind if I were able to hear and to speak, or deaf if I were able to see and to write. In other words I would want to be certain of being able to receive communications from others and of communicating with others in appropriately related ways.

I also understand that I can legally designate someone to act as a responsible friend in my affairs. I believe that it is always dangerous to play God and that there might be an occasion, which it is impossible for me to foresee in a document such as this, where doubt of the completeness and responsibility of my attempt to forecast events would occur or where my competence to make a decision at the time might be in doubt. In such case I empower my friend and literary executor [. . .] to over-ride the relevant item in this statement, and to make whatever decision is more congruent with my general intent, which I have communicated to her in full.

By intervention I mean all positive medical and surgical procedures and nursing procedures which tend to preserve my life, operations on the brain, intravenous feeding, blood transfusions, tube feeding, implantation of radium, amputation, etc.

These decisions are taken in the full knowledge that I can rely on the love and care of my relatives and friends, colleagues and students, in affection for them and thankfulness that they will understand my reasons. In our present culture I am the only one who can make such a decision and I do not wish to impose on others the burden of carrying out measures which they know I would not have chosen but which they would have no way of choosing against. It is my belief that a decision not to live when one has ceased to be oneself can be taken in full responsibility and with love for those whom one leaves behind.

At all times and under all circumstances I wish to be told the full truth about any physical condition without any protective evasions or optimisms whatsoever. If I am to have a limited and definite period before death, I wish to use such a period responsibly and constructively.

16. In December, 1973 the Judicial Council of the AMA took the following position on the "living will": "The end of the use of extraordinary means to prolong life when there is irrefutable evidence that biological death is imminent is the decision of the patient and the immediate family. The advice and judgment of the physician should be freely available to the patient and his family." *Medical World News,* Dec. 28, 1973. For a discussion of the legal issues involved in euthanasia, see Survey, *Euthanasia: Criminal, Tort, Constitutional and Legislative Considerations,* 48 NOTRE DAME LAW. 1202 (1973); and works cited in note 20 *infra.*

17. Duff & Campbell, *Moral and Ethical Dilemmas in the Special Care Nursery,* 289 NEW ENG. J. MED. 891 (1973).

18. *Id.* at 894. *Cf.* Shaw, *Dilemmas of Informed Consent in Children,* 289 NEW ENG. J. MED. 886 (1973); Engelhardt, *Euthanasia and Children: The Injury of Continued Existence,* 83 J. PEDIATR. 170 (1973).

19. Mitscherlich & Meilke, *DOCTORS OF INFAMY* (1949) at 114–116. Cited in Kamisar. *Euthanasia Legislation: Some Non-Religious Objections* in Downing, ed., EUTHANASIA AND THE RIGHT TO DEATH, Nash, Los Angeles, 1970, at 85, 111. Cf. Fletcher, *Attitudes Toward Defective Newborns,* 2 Hastings Center Studies 21 (1974). The general issue of euthanasia is beyond the scope of this book.

20. See generally Chapter XII, Children.

21. See generally Note, *Judicial Power to Order Medical Treatment for Minors over Objections of Their Guardians,* 14 SYR. L. REV. 84 (1962); Sharpe & Hargest, *Lifesaving Treatment for Unwilling Patients,* 36 FORDHAM L. REV. 695 (1968); Note, *Unauthorized Rendi-*

tion of Lifesaving Treatment, 53 CAL. L. REV. 860 (1965); Note, *The Right to Die,* 7 HOUS. L. REV. 654 (1970); and Cantor, *supra.* note 13.

22. *Maine Medical Center v. House,* Sup. Ct. Cumberland Co., Maine, No. 74–145 (Feb. 14, 1974) (Unreported opinion, Judge David Roberts). Case noted in Knox, Defective Newborns: Life or Death Issue, *Boston Sunday Globe,* March 10, 1974 at A-1.

23. See Robertson, *Involuntary Euthanasia of Defective Newborns: A Legal Analysis,* 27 STAN. L. REV. 213 (1975).

24. *In re Sampson,* 317 N.Y.S. 2d 641 (1970). It is possible to read this case as one in which the court took into account the child's potential for living "a normal, useful life" in making its decision. One could thus argue that it opens the door for these types of considerations in other cases, e.g., deciding that parents are justified in refusing treatment on the grounds that no "normal, useful life" is possible with or without the treatment. See also discussion of this case at pages 138–139.

25. *Prince v. Massachusetts,* 321 U.S. 158 (1943).

VIII

Consultation, Referral and Abandonment

When a patient is in a teaching hospital, he or she is generally seen by many physicians, including interns, residents, and specialists. In such a situation consultations and referrals take place almost as a matter of course. In non-teaching hospitals, however, the patient may have only one physician who is responsible for his or her care. In this situation, questions concerning the duty of that physician to obtain a consultation or to refer the patient to a specialist may be of critical importance to the patient and his family. These questions, as well as the question of when a doctor may properly discharge a patient from a hospital, are dealt with in this chapter.

Does a doctor ever have a duty to refer the patient to a specialist or to seek a consultation with a specialist?
The general rule is that if a doctor knows or should know that the patient's ailment is beyond his knowledge, technical skill, ability or capacity to treat with a likelihood of reasonable success, he is obligated to either disclose this to his patient or advise him of the necessity of other or different treatment.[1]

Section 8 of the AMA's Principles of Medical Ethics states: "A physician should seek consultation upon request; in doubtful or difficult cases; or whenever it appears that the quality of medical services may be enhanced thereby."

Not only must the general practitioner call in a specialist, but the specialist must also call in a specialist in another field when indicated. If a reasonably careful and skillful attending physician would have suggested calling in a specialist, a doctor may be found negligent for not making such a suggestion.[2] In a circumcision case, for example, an infant boy's penis had to be amputated. Evidence showed that prior to the infant's release from the hospital a black spot appeared on his penis which continued to grow when he was at home. Upon return to the hospital the following day, both a pediatric specialist and a urology specialist were called in. They concluded that the spot was caused by gangrene, but that it was too late to do anything about it. The court found the evidence sufficient to warrant a finding by the jury that the circumcising physician should have called in a specialist prior to the child's discharge from the hospital, when something might have been done to save the child's penis.[3]

Does the hospital have a duty to ensure that doctors practicing in the hospital seek and obtain indicated consultation?

It can be said in general that hospitals have recognized such a duty. Perhaps the best-known case dealing with this issue was decided in Illinois in 1965. In that case an 18-year-old boy broke his leg while playing college football. He was treated by a general practitioner in the hospital's emergency ward. The doctor applied a plaster cast to the leg. Over the period of the next two weeks the boy almost continuously complained of severe pain and pressure. His leg turned a grayish color, and the smell in his room was terrible. He was finally taken out of the hospital by his parents, and his leg, having been found to be gangrenous, had to be amputated. One of the major issues considered by the court was whether the hospital itself could be found negligent for failure "to require consultation with or examination by members of the hospital surgical staff skilled in such treatment; or to review the treatment rendered to the plaintiff and to require consultants to be called in as needed." The court concluded on the basis of the evidence—which included the state's public-health licensing regulations, the Standards for Hospital Accreditation of the JCAH, and the bylaws of the hopsital—that the jury could properly have found that the hospital was negligent in failing to require a consultation.[4]

It is likely that in cases like this, and in similar cases when the need for consultation in view of the patient's worsening condition should be apparent to the doctor, the hospital will be found liable for failure to ensure that such consultation is obtained.[5]

Must a doctor refer a patient to a specialist or seek a consultation upon request by a patient?

As indicated above, the AMA's Principles of Medical Ethics require physicians to respond to such patient requests. While this is an ethical, not a legal guideline, a member of the AMA's legal staff has advised doctors that refusal of such a patient request "is an invitation to a malpractice suit if the attending physician turns out to be wrong [in suggesting to the patient that a consultation is not necessary]."[6]

One case in which a request for consultation was refused involved an 11-year-old boy who was brought to an air force dispensary with severe abdominal pain and vomiting. The doctor took some tests and referred the patient to the U.S. Naval Hospital with a diagnosis of "possible appendicitis." At the emergency ward of the hospital the boy was seen by another doctor who performed no lab tests and did a cursory physical examination. He concluded that it was not appendicitis and asked that the child be taken home. The child's mother asked that another physician be called in to look at the child, but the doctor refused. At approximately 1:00 A.M. the following morning the child started crying and rolling around in extreme pain. He was again taken to the emergency ward and seen by an intern who ordered no lab tests but gave the child pain medication and sent him home. The next day the boy returned to the dispensary. After delays at both the dispensary and the hospital, the surgery was finally performed the following day, *after* the boy's appendix had ruptured. As a result of the delay peritonitis developed, and the child not only had to spend an additional 3 weeks in the hospital but suffered permanent internal damage. Citing the AMA Principles, the emergency ward policy, the U.S. Government's Medical Department Manual, and the Standards of the JCAH, the court concluded that both doctors seen in the emergency ward, and therefore the hospital, could be found negligent for failure to seek consultation.[7]

It is safe to conclude that a doctor who refuses a patient's request for a consultation or referral does so at his own peril, and if the doctor is wrong in reassuring the patient that he is treating him properly, he may be found negligent for failure to meet the patient's request.

Who is responsible for paying for a consultation or a second opinion?

Like almost everything else that happens to a patient in a hospital, the patient is responsible for paying the bills. Almost all insurance policies, however, cover indicated consultations since they are recognized as an integral part of good medical care.[8]

May a doctor refuse to continue to see a patient without obtaining the services of another doctor for the patient?

The general rule is that once a doctor-patient relationship is established, it continues until:

1. it is terminated by the consent of both doctor and patient;
2. it is revoked by the patient;
3. the doctor's services are no longer needed; or
4. the physician withdraws from the case *after* reasonable notice to the patient.[9]

Abandonment occurs when the physician severs the doctor-patient relationship without the consent of the patient. If injury results to the patient because of the abandonment, the patient may successfully sue the doctor for damages. If the treatment is in a critical stage at which abandonment might be harmful to the patient, nonpayment of bills by the patient cannot be used as a jusitification for refusal by the physician to extend further aid.[10] This rule, of course, should also apply to the hospital.

A Virginia case illustrates how abandonment can occur. The doctor properly set a fracture and applied a cast to a child's leg. However, when the patient later complained of pain and the doctor was called, he failed to respond. The doctor then left town. When the child's parents were unable to locate the doctor, they called in another physician who cut the cast to relieve the pressure and noted evidence of an infection. When the doctor returned to town, he again refused to see the patient in the hospital and instead discharged the patient. At home the pain continued, and another physician was called who observed necrotic (dead) spots on the child's leg, which had to be amputated. In upholding a jury verdict for the patient, the court restated the general rule[11]:

> After a physician has accepted employment in a case it is his duty to continue his services as long as they are necessary. He cannot voluntarily abandon his patient. Even if personal attention is no longer necessary in the treatment of an injured limb, the physician must, if the case calls for it, furnish the patient with instructions as to its care. . . .

If a physician discharges a patient from the hospital, and the patient has a relapse and calls the physician for help, the physician has an obligation to take steps to help the patient or face a charge of abandonment unless another physician has taken over the patient's care.

Can a patient recover damages from a doctor or a hospital for premature discharge?

As two noted medicolegal commentators have stated, "It is uniformly held by the courts that the premature discharge of a patient constitutes abandonment."[12] These commentators also note that "unfortunately, instances of premature discharge abound in the reported cases."[13]

Premature discharge can be illustrated by a particularly gruesome case. The doctor involved had performed an unskillful operation on the patient for a strangulated hernia. After an improper incision, he closed, without attempting to relieve the obstructed bowel, and informed the patient that she was going to die. He then ordered the patient sent home in a hearse and refused thereafter to see her at home in spite of her calls. The Rhode Island Supreme

Court had no difficulty in holding that the doctor was liable to pay damages to the patient for abandonment.[14]

Should a person routinely seek a consultation before entering the hospital or agreeing to elective surgery?

Accumulating evidence of unnecessary surgery indicates that this may be advisable. In a recent preliminary study of elective procedures in which patients for whom surgery had been recommended were examined by a specialist, over one-fourth of the recommended operations were found to be unnecessary. The rate of unnecessary surgical recommendations among the 1356 patients was lowest in ear, nose and throat (16%) and highest in orthopedics (40%) and urology (36%). Specific procedures most frequently found not to be necessary included hysterectomy, dilatation and currettage, breast operations, and gall bladder removals.[15]

NOTES

1. Annot., 132 A.L.R. 392; *Manion v. Tweedy,* 100 N.W. 2d 124, 128 (Minn., 1957); and See Annot., 57 A.L.R. 2d 440. A doctor does *not,* however, become liable for the negligent acts of another physician merely by recommending the specialist. *Dill v. Scaka,* 175 F. Supp. 26, 29 (E.D. Pa. 1959).

2. O'Hern, *Duty to Refer to Medical Specialist,* in AMA, BEST OF LAW & MEDICINE, 1968–1970 (1970) at 25–26; *Graham v. St. Luke's Hospital,* 196 N.E. 2d 355 (Ill. App. 1964).

3. *Valentine v. Kaiser Foundation Hospitals,* 15 Cal. Rptr. 26 (Cal. App. 1961).

4. *Darling v. Charleston Community Memorial Hospital,* 33 Ill. 2d 326, 211 N.E. 2d 253 (1965), cert. denied, 383 U.S. 946 (1966).

5. See generally, Southwick, *The Hospital's New Responsibility,* 17 CLEV.-MAR. L. REV. 146 (1968); Note, *Hospital Liability—A New Duty of Care,* 19 ME. L. REV. 102 (1967); Mueller, *Expanding Duty of the Hospital to the Patient,* 47 NEB. L. REV. 337 (1968); see also, Chapter III.

6. Holder, *Referral to a Specialist,* in AMA, BEST OF LAW & MEDICINE, 1968–1970 (1970) at 27.

7. *Steeves v. U.S.*, 294 F. Supp. 446 (D.C. So. Car., 1968).

8. See generally Chapter XVI.

9. Comment, *The Action of Abandonment in Medical Mal-practice Litigation*, 36 TULANE L. REV. 834, 835 (1962).

10. *Id.* at 841; E.g., *Becker v. Janinski*, 15 N.Y.S. 675 (App. Div. N.Y., 1891); *Ricks v. Budge*, 91 Utah 307, 64 P.2d 208 (1937). The physician may, however, properly terminate the doctor-patient relationship for refusal to pay if he gives the patient enough notice so that the patient can obtain other medical attention. *Burnett v. Layman*, 133 Tenn. 323, 181 S.W. 157 (1915).

11. *Vann v. Harden*, 187 Va. 555, 47 S.E. 2d 314 (1948).

12. Jon R. Waltz & Fred E. Inbau, MEDICAL JURIS-PRUDENCE, Macmillan, New York, 1971 at 146.

13. *Id.;* see also *Mucci v. Houghton*, 57 N.W. 305 (Iowa, 1894); *Reed v. Laughlin*, 58 S.W. 2d 440 (Mo. 1933); *Meiselman v. Crown Heights Hospital*, 34 N.E. 2d 367 (Ct. App. N.Y. 1941).

14. *Morrell v. Lalonde*, 120 A. 435 (1923).

15. McCarthy & Widmer, *Effects of Screening by Consultants on Recommended Elective Surgical Procedures*, 291 NEW ENG. J. MED. 1331–1335 (1974). See also discussion of unnecessary surgery on women at pages 153–156.

IX
Human Experimentation

The history of medical progress is to a large extent the history of medical experimentation. While few wish to extinguish the practice of experimentation, there is a growing awareness that individual rights have often been trampled on in the process and that steps must be taken to protect hospital patients from overzealous researchers. Many of the most blatant abuses of human beings for the purpose of medical experimentation have taken place in prisons, mental institutions, and residences for the retarded. While all of these are important, this chapter will deal only with human experimentation in the hospital context.[1]

Even in hospitals there have been some abuses. As early as the 1880s a doctor was innoculating the eyes of infants with gonorrhea to see what effect it would have.[2] Other researchers purposely infected unknowing patients with syphilis to test both the degree of contagiousness and the immunity factors.[3] The justification for such human experimentation was that animals could not be made to contract the disease. These and other experiments were cited by the defendants at the Nuremberg trials to attempt to demonstrate that the types of experiments they performed on Jews and prisoners of war during World War II had long been accepted practice in the medical profession.[4] While we have probably come a long way since then, the rights of patients can only be guaranteed by continued vigilance against potential abuses. The purpose of this chapter is to provide the patient with sufficient information to protect himself.

Nothing in this chapter should be read to suggest that

there is a significant percentage of unethical or illegal human experimentation presently going on. Indeed, all the evidence available is that the majority of researchers in hospitals are highly ethical and very concerned about both informing their subjects and preventing them from being harmed. On the other hand, what abuses there are should be eliminated. An informed patient population will aid in this goal.

What is medical experimentation?

No single definition of medical experimentation is entirely satisfactory. Some doctors have argued, for example, that every time any patient is treated, a therapeutic experiment is taking place since that particular patient has never been treated at that particular time in that particular way.[5] Perhaps the most distinguishing aspect of experimentation is uncertainty as to outcome. For the purposes of this chapter a doctor is engaged in experimentation on a patient when he or she *departs from standard medical practice* in treating a patient for the *purpose of obtaining new knowledge* or testing a hypothesis.

It should be emphasized that experimentation in humans, undertaken after careful and successful animal work, and with the informed consent of the patient-subject, is a completely legitimate and important scientific endeavor. It is usually only when departures from standard practice are extreme, or when the informed consent of the patient is not obtained, that abuses occur.[5]

Who is likely to be experimented on in the hospital setting?

While many doctors argue that all persons in any teaching hospital are candidates for experimentation, what empirical data we have suggest that the poor are more likely to be experimented on than the rich. One recent study of a major teaching hospital concluded that while private patients may not be much better off, "the ignorant, the poor, and the ethnically despised are more likely to be used as subjects, partly just because they are more often ward and clinic patients, but partly also because their handicaps make them more available."[6] In a specific instance, only one of three clinic patients in a study of a new drug for the induction of labor in childbirth knew they were experimental subjects. Also, instead of being told that an experimental drug was being used on them, they had been informed that a "new" (implying "better") drug was being used.[7]

One medical commentator has argued that the hospital patient is the most "at risk" for experimentation and that the doctrine of informed consent cannot protect patients adequately. In his words[8]:

> Volunteers for experiments will usually be influenced by hopes of obtaining better grades, earlier parole, more substantial egos, or just mundane cash. These pressures, however, are but fractional shadows of those enclosing the patient-subject. *Incapacitated and hospitalized because of illness, frightened by strange and impersonal routines, and fearful for his health and perhaps life, he is far from exercising a free power of choice* when the person to whom he anchors all his hopes asks, "Say, you wouldn't mind, would you, if you joined some of the other patients on this floor and helped us to carry out some very important research we are doing?" When "informed consent" is obtained, it is not the student, the destitute bum, or the prisoner to whom, by virtue of his condition, the thumb screws of coercion are most relentlessly applied; it is *the most used and useful of all experimental subjects, the patient with disease.* (italics mine)

In one of the most widely publicized cases of abuse, terminally ill patients at the Jewish Chronic Disease Hospital in Brooklyn, New York, were injected with live cancer cells to test their immune responses. They were told only that they were getting a "skin test."[9] In 1958 a study on the treatment of staphylococcus infection among premature babies was conducted at the Los Angeles County Hospital. According to a Congressional investigation, 45 infants who received a treatment that had been recognized as potentially dangerous since 1951 (chloramphenicol) died during the experiments.[10] In 1966 Dr. Henry Beecher of Harvard University reported in the *New England Journal of Medicine*[11] on 22 unethical experiments involving human beings. Examples included the withholding of penicillin from sufferers of streptococcal infection (even though this standard treatment was known to prevent rheumatic fever) and the transplantation of a cancer tumor from a daughter to her mother to see if it would produce cancer in the mother. It did.

The list could be lengthened, but the point is better made by the comment of a young intern who was questioned about the private life, problems, and aspirations of one of the patients under his care.

He replied: "I cannot answer your questions. You're interested in patients. I'm interested in the disease in the body in the bed."[12]

The tensions are the same—between learning and caring and between advancement of knowledge and protection of human rights.

How is human experimentation monitored in the hospital?

All hospitals in which research is being conducted with the financial support of the National Institutes of Health (NIH) of HEW have been required since 1966 to take certain measures designed for the protection of patients. While these measures are only required to be taken for research actually funded by NIH, most hospitals in fact require that all research proposals go through these procedures.[13]

Specifically, the NIH Guidelines require that before an experiment involving human beings can be carried out in a hospital setting, the experiment *must be reviewed by a hospital committee* (usually consisting mostly of doctors, but having other members like lawyers, community representatives, and chaplains). This committee is charged with ensuring that (1) the research design is sound, (2) the benefits anticipated outweigh the risks involved, and (3) that the patient-subjects give an informed consent.

Emphasis is generally placed on the provisions for *informed consent*, which have been defined by NIH as requiring the following 6 elements[14]:

1. A fair explanation of the procedures to be followed, including an identification of those which are experimental;
2. A description of the attendant discomforts and risks;

3. A description of the benefits to be expected;
4. A disclosure of appropriate alternative procedures that would be advantageous for the subject;
5. An offer to answer any inquiries concerning the procedures;
6. An instruction that the subject is free to withdraw his consent and to discontinue participation in the project or activity at any time.

These elements must be incorporated into a written consent form that must be signed by the patient. Moreover, no language may appear in the form by which the subject waives or appears to waive his right to sue the experimenter or the hospital for malpractice.[15]

While these regulations ostensibly cover almost all hospital experimentation, one recent study found that even in hospitals that had agreed to review *all* experimentation regardless of funding source, 9 percent of medical research workers volunteered the information that they were doing research on patients that had not been so reviewed.[16] And even when the research is reviewed, other problems may arise. For example, the review committee is likely to be heavily weighted on the side of the medical researcher, with little or no patient-population representation. Also, after a project is approved, there is generally little or no follow-up to make sure that it is conducted in the manner proposed or that the rights of subjects are actually being protected.[17] It was primarily with these problems in mind that NIH recently proposed much more stringent review and monitoring guidelines for research involving fetuses, children, the institutionalized mental patient, and prisoners.[18]

Can a patient be legally experimented on without his informed consent?

One doctor has argued: "When society confers the degree of physician on a man, it instructs him to experiment on his fellow. . . . When a patient goes to a modern physician for treatment . . . he is also unconsciously presenting himself for the purpose of experimentation."[19]

While physicians may well have a duty to continue to improve their skills through experimentation, it is clearly against the law to experiment on a patient without obtaining his informed consent. This concept was articulated in relatively complete terms in the Nuremberg decision that concerned the Nazi experiments during World War II. The judges there found that such experiments *violated natural law*, which bound all men. Among the principles they found that "must be observed in order to satisfy moral, ethical and legal concepts" was that of informed consent. In the words of the court[20]:

> The *voluntary* consent of the human subject is absolutely essential. This means that the person involved should have *legal capacity* to give consent; should be so situated as to be able to exercise *free power of choice*. . . ; and should have sufficient *knowledge and comprehension* of the elements of the subject matter involved as to enable him to make an *understanding* and enlightened decision . . . there should be made known to him the nature, duration, and purpose of the experiment; the method and means by which it is to be conducted; all inconveniences and hazards reasonably to be expected; and the effects upon his health or person which may possibly come from his participation in the experiment. (italics mine)

These principles have been recognized by the courts of this country[21] and have been incorporated into declarations like the AHA's Patient Bill of Rights. As noted in the preceeding section, the obtaining of informed consent is also a requirement of the federal government in facilities that use NIH research funds.

Is the informed consent of a patient all that is legally required before a doctor or researcher may experiment on a patient?

Because it is recognized that even informed patients might consent to anything if their plight is desperate enough, the consent of the patient has generally been held to be a *necessary but not sufficient* precondition for lawful experimentation.

The first U.S. case was decided in 1871 and involved a device used to straighten a broken limb. The court found that where a surgeon departs from what has come to be a recognized course of treatment, he must be "prepared to take the risk of establishing, by his success, the propriety and safety of his experiment."[22] In other words, the experimenting doctor was to be held to be an ensurer of a good result and absolutely liable for any injuries caused by the experiment to the patient.

While in some states courts might hold a doctor absolutely liable in an experimental setting, most courts would probably use the two-tier test: (1) Was the use of the experimental procedure *reasonable under* the circumstances; and if so, (2) did the patient give his *informed consent* to it? In other words, doctors are generally required to refrain from radically departing from accepted practice unless they had compelling reasons (e.g., extensive successful animal testing) for doing so. Only if the procedure can be considered medically reasonable does the patient's informed consent become relevant. If the procedure is medically unreasonable under the circumstances, the patient *cannot* lawfully consent to it no matter how informed he is.

The reason informed consent cannot be relied on exclusively can be illustrated by some examples from the medical literature. In one study involving how kidney donors made up their minds to give a kidney to a relative, 14 of 20 said that they had made their decision "immediately" on hearing of the need over the telephone. The others said they could not recall exactly when they made the decision but that it was not based on any medical information they received from the doctors. The authors concluded that even though all donors were subjected to intensive instruction in the medical aspects of transplantation, their "decision-making process was immediate and 'irrational' and could not meet the requirements adopted by the American Medical Association to be accepted as an 'informed consent.' "[23] Heart transplant recipients reported making similar split-second decisions.[24] In Brazil doctors took the next "logical" step, that is, if informed consent is impossible, don't even try. A heart recipient was not even told that a transplant was going to take place and did not find out until he saw himself on television a week later in his hospital room. The doctors explained, "If a man is incapable of understanding an operation he vitally needs, there is no choice but to proceed ... the patient was psychologically better off not knowing and worrying about his risks."[25]

While one may conclude that in life-death decision-making informed consent may have little meaning to either doctor or patient, the proper response would seem to be to supplement it rather than abandon it. Additional mechanisms like multidisciplinary review committees, for example, may be needed to protect the patient.[26]

Can parents give legal authorization for medical experiments to be performed on their children?

There are a number of ways of classifying experiments. For the purposes of this question, the most useful is the following:

1. An experimental treatment or procedure aimed at curing the child's condition.

2. An experimental procedure aimed at finding out more about the child's condition.

3. An experimental procedure designed to learn more about the disease from which the child is suffering.

4. An experimental procedure designed to learn something that might benefit others but will not benefit the child.[27]

The first two types of experiments can be consented to by parents. Under proper conditions, the third might also be consented to, if, for example, there is no known cure or treatment for a disease, and experimenting on children suffering from it is the only way to develop one. It is within the fourth area that decisions are the most difficult. It is arguable, for example, that parents have no legal right to subject their children to experiments that cannot be of benefit to the children.[28] In another context, the U.S. Supreme Court has said that while parents are free to become martyrs themselves, they are not free to make martyrs of their children.[29]

Case law on this subject has been somewhat difficult to decipher. The leading case is a 1941 opinion from the District of Columbia. A 15-year-old black youth consented to the formation of a "tube of flesh" from his armpit to his waist, which was attached to his severely burned cousin in an attempt to form a skin graft. The experiment failed and the child lost some skin and much blood. The court decided that the child's consent alone was not sufficient since no benefit to the child was involved, but that his mother's consent was also necessary.[30]

There are other cases that conclude that even with the consent of both the child and the child's parents, only a court of law can sanction the experiment, even when some benefit to the child, usually psychological, is alleged. This has been the major thrust of cases dealing with kidney transplants involving minors, for example.[31] One court has gone so far as to say that no one, not even the court, could authorize the taking of a kidney from a child.[32] The better view would appear to be that the only time experimentation on children not designed for their benefit should be permitted is under the supervision of a court with a court-appointed guardian. The duty of the guardian would be to represent the interests of the children in the experiment and call a halt to it whenever their health was in danger.[33]

Should indemnification for injury to subjects in human experimentation be made mandatory?

Indemnification, or paying the subject of a medical experiment for injuries suffered because of his participation in the experiment, is not now currently required either by statute or by state or federal regulations. There are, however, many compelling reasons why either the investigator, the institution in which the research is being conducted, the sponsor of the research, or the federal government should be required to provide their research subjects with an insurance policy to cover their risks as subjects. This suggestion was made in early 1973 by the Secretary of HEW's Commission on Medical Malpractice.[34] Others have also made it. Dr. Henry K. Beecher of Harvard Medical School has argued[35]:

> Even if all reasonable precautions have been taken to protect both the subject and the investigator from physical damage as well as from unethical practices, the possibility for injury still remains. It is unreasonable to expect that the society which profits actually or potentially should not share in the responsibility for what was done.

A leading legal commentator, Professor Clark Havighurst, has argued similarly that requiring the research agencies to bear the financial risk of adverse or unexpected effects would be in the public interest[36]:

> The principle of societal responsibility makes not only humanitarian but economic sense, for the research industry will undertake fewer projects that are not justified by a balancing of risks (and other costs) against potential benefits if all of the potential costs are taken into account . . . balancing risks and benefits lacks needed indices and incentives—and thus sacrifices precision—unless dollar costs must be contended with. Whatever compensation system is devised must not only compensate the unlucky subject but also place the burden on those best able to evaluate and control the risks attending the experiment.[36]

Under the Public Health Service's grant policy funds can be provided to researchers to purchase such indemnification insurance. However, few, if any, researchers have ever applied for such funds.[37] I would argue that experimentation on human beings which involves potential serious risks should almost never be allowed unless provision is made to compensate the subject for adverse effects.[38]

NOTES

1. See generally J. Katz, EXPERIMENTATION WITH HUMAN BEINGS, Russell Sage Foundation, New York, 1972; *Ethical Aspects of Experimentation with Human Subjects,* 98 DAEDALUS 219 (Spring, 1969); M. H. Pappworth, HUMAN GUINEA PIGS, Beacon Press, Boston, 1967; Bryant, *The Burgeoning Law of Medical Experimentation Involving Human Subjects,* 8 JOHN MARSHALL J. PRAC. & PROC. 19 (1974).
2. Katz, *supra.* note 1, at 285.
3. E.g., Wallace, *Clinical Lectures on Venereal Diseases,* ii LANCET 535 (1836–1837).
4. Katz, *supra.,* note 1, at 300 (closing brief for defendant Siegfried Ruff).
5. Oral remarks at a Symposium on "The Semi-Artificial Person," Boston University Law School, March 2, 1974 (sponsored by Boston University's Center for Law and

Health Sciences, 209 Bay State Road, Boston, Ma. 02215).

6. Prepared Statement by Professor Bernard Barber for House Subcommittee on Health, Protection of Human Subjects Act, Sept. 28, 1973 at 2.

7. Study of Prof. Bradford Gray quoted by B. Barber in a book review, *Experimentation on Human Beings: Another Problem of Civil Rights?*, 11 MINERVA 415, 418 (1973).

8. Ingelfinger, *Informed (But Uneducated) Consent*, 287 NEW ENG. J. MED. 465, 466 (1972).

9. Many of the legal documents in this case are reprinted in Katz, *supra.*, note 1, at 10–65. See *Hyman v. Jewish Chronic Disease Hospital*, 15 N.Y. 2d 317, 206 N.E. 2d 338 (1965).

10. *Human Experiments Criticized*, Drug File, 9 *TRIAL* 33 (Jan.–Feb., 1973).

11. Beecher, *Ethics and Clinical Research*, 274 NEW ENG. J. MED. 1354 (1966). Beecher originally submitted 50 unethical studies, but the editors cut it to 22 "for reasons of space."

12. R. Duff & A. Hollingshead, SICKNESS AND SOCIETY, Harper & Row, New York, 1968, cited by Katz, *supra.*, note 1 at 212.

13. B. Barber et. al., RESEARCH ON HUMAN SUBJECTS: PROBLEMS OF SOCIAL CONTROL IN MEDICAL EXPERIMENTATION, Russell Sage Foundation, New York, 1973.

14. See *The Institutional Guide to DHEW Policy on Protection of Human Subjects*, U.S. Dept. H.E.W. (Pub. No. NIH 72–102), U.S. Gov. Printing Office, Washington, D.C., 1971 at 7. (For sale through Superintendent of Documents, Washington, D.C. 20402 for 25 cents; stock #1740–0326).

15. *Id.*

16. Barber, *supra.* note 13; Barber, *supra.* note 7, at 417.

17. *Id.*

18. 38 *Fed. Reg.* 31738–31749 (Nov. 16, 1973) 39 *Fed. Reg.* 18914–18920 (May 30, 1974); 39 *Fed. Reg.* 30648–30657 (Aug. 23, 1974).

19. Modell, *Editorial*, 3 CLINICAL PHARM. & THER. 145, 146 (1962).

20. *U.S. v. Karl Brandt*, portions reprinted in Katz, *supra.*, note 1 at 305–306.

21. See generally Chapter VI, Informed Consent to Treatment.

110 THE RIGHTS OF HOSPITAL PATIENTS

22. *Carpenter v. Blake*, 60 Barb. 488 (N.Y. Sup. Ct., 1871), *reversed on other grounds*, 50 N.Y. 696 (1872). A British case involving similar facts had implied that such an experiment might be conducted if previous research had indicated it would not be a "rash" decision, and if the patient gave his knowlegable consent. *Slater v. Baker & Stapleton*, C.B., 95 Eng. Rep. 860 (1767).

23. Fellner & Marshall, *Kidney Donors-The Myth of Informed Consent*, 126 AM. J. PSYCHIATRY 1245 (1970).

24. E.g., Philip Blaiberg as he recounts his decision in LOOKING AT MY HEART, Stein & Day, New York, 1968 at 69.

25. He Had a New Heart for a Week and Didn't Know It, *Med. World News*, July 12, 1968 at 9–10.

26. This has become a popularly espoused position for control of potential abuses in brain surgery designed to modify behavior, or "psychosurgery." For a discussion of the legal problems involved in attempting to control surgical innovation, see Annas & Glantz, *Psychosurgery: The Law's Response*, 54 B.U.L. REV. 249 (1974).

27. Each of these can be further subdivided by comparing potential risks to potential benefits.

28. A lawsuit making this argument has recently been filed in the courts of California. "Is Research on Children Illegal?" *Med. World News*, Sept. 28, 1973 at 40.

29. *Prince v. Massachusetts*, 321 U.S. 158, 170 (1943).

30. *Bonner v. Moran*, 126 F. 2d 121 (D.C. Cir., 1941). For a discussion of this case see, Curran & Beecher, *Experimentation in Children*, 210 JAMA 77 (1969).

31. See, e.g., *Strunk v. Strunk*, 445 S.W. 2d 145 (Ky. 1969); Savage, *Organ Transplantation With an Incompetent Donor: Kentucky Resolves the Dilemma Of Strunk v. Strunk*, 58 KY. L. REV. 129 (1970); Curran, *A Problem of Consent: Kidney Transplantation in Minors*, 34 N.Y.U. L. REV. 891 (1959) (articles discusses first three such cases in Massachusetts); Curran, *Kidney Transplantation in Identical Twin Minors—Justice is Done in Connecticut*, 287 NEW ENG. J. MED 26 (1972). See also *Howard v. The Fulton-DeKalb Hospital Authority*, (Ga. 1973) 42 U.S.L.W. 2322 (court may sanction the donation of a kidney by a 15-year-old moderately retarded child to her mother). This same court procedure to sanction consent is currently being used in Massachusetts in bone-marrow transplant cases involving minor donors.

32. *In re Richardson*, 284 So. 2d 185 (La. Ct. App., 1973)

(Neither the child's parents nor the courts may authorize the removal of a kidney from a 17 year old retarded youth for transplantation to his 32 year old sister.)

33. See generally Chapter XVIII, The Patient Rights Advocate. This person has a critical role to play whenever the interests of parent and child may not be the same in regard to proposed medical treatment.

34. *Medical Malpractice: Report of the Secretary's Commission on Medical Malpractice,* (DHEW Pub. No. OS 73–88), 1973 at 79.

35. Beecher, *Human Studies,* 164 SCIENCE 1256, 1257 (1969)

36. Havighurst, *Compensating Persons Injured in Human Experimentation,* 169 SCIENCE 153, 154 (1970)

37. U.S. Public Health Service, *Grants Policy Statement* (DHEW) Pub. No. OS 74–50,000) (July 1, 1974), at 15, and 57.

38. See also, Calabresi, *Reflections on Medical Experimentation in Humans, DAEDALUS* (Fall, 1969) 387, 398; and Ladimer, *Clinical Research Insurance* (ed.), 16 J. CHRON. DIS. 1229, 1233 (1963). This issue was raised in a Massachusetts bone-marrow case, but insurance was not compelled because no private insurance company was able to come up with a satisfactory policy. See *Nathan v. Farinelli,* S.J.C., Civil Action, 74–87 (July 3, 1974).

X
Hospital Records

From the moment the patient enters the hospital, various records begin to accumulate. Those dealing with medical care rather than payment will be discussed in this chapter. The purposes of the medical record are[1]:

to serve as a basis for planning and continuity of care;

to provide a means of communication among the members of the health care team;

to document the course of the patient's illness and treatment;

to serve as a basis for review of quality of care;

to protect legal interests of patient, doctor and hospital;

to provide a data base for research and education.

While each hospital may have its own particular rules relating to hospital records, the minimum standards promulgated by the JCAH are followed by almost every hospital, and thus much uniformity can be anticipated.

What does a patient's hospital record contain?

The JCAH requires that all hospital records contain at least the following data: (1) identification information and consent forms; (2) medical history of the patient; (3) report of the patient's physical examination and laboratory tests; (4) diagnostic and therapeutic orders; (5) observations of patient condition, including progress notes; (6) reports of actions and findings, including all treatments, consultations, preoperative, operative, and post-operative reports; and (7) conclusions, including the provisional diagnosis, primary and secondary final diagnoses, clinical resumé, and necropsy reports.[2] Minimum record content may also be required by state statute or regulation.

Some large teaching hospitals are using a relatively new type of record called a "problem-oriented record." It is designed to improve patient care, clinical training, and data retrieval. The patient's history, physical examination, and laboratory test results are put in a section labeled "data base." The next section contains a list of the patient's medical "problems." The record is then divided on the basis of these problem areas. Under each individual problem will first appear a list of the initial plans to deal with the patient's condition (diagnostic, therapeutic, and patient education) and then a series of progress notes that will be written chronologically during treatment by all members of the health-care team. In this type of record all intern, resident, and attending-physician communications will appear on the record, as well as all nurses' notes on the patient's condition and progress.[3] In both types of records the last document will be a final or discharge summary that, as the name implies, summarizes what happened to the patient while in the hospital.

In some teaching hospitals interns and residents communicate with the attending physician on a separate sheet of paper (sometimes called the "green" or "yellow sheet"). On this, doctors discuss proposed treatments, communicate orders, and state their reasons for orders. The sheet is usually *not* part of the permanent record. Also, in some states like Massachusetts, nurses' notes are not made part of the permanent record but are destroyed.[4] Both of these are records that patients injured by possible malpractice would like to have—the former to prove deviation from standard practice, the latter to better document patient condition and pain and suffering.

Why might a patient want to see his medical record?

The primary reason a patient might want to see his medical record is to gain a better understanding of his medical condition so that he can better cooperate in his treatment. Other reasons include checking the accuracy of family and personal histories, to be better informed when asked to consent to diagnostic and therapeutic procedures, to better understand the role his physician is taking in his care, and to appreciate more fully the state of his health so that he might be able to prevent a recurrence of his disease or condition in the future. In general, the record can be a powerful means of health education that can benefit the patient both during his stay in the hospital and after discharge.

If a patient is moving out of town, out of the country, or going on a long trip, he may also have a good reason to take a copy of his record or at least the discharge summary of his latest hospital visit with him.

All of this implies that there are many parts of the record (which could cover hundreds of pages), like laboratory reports, in which the patient may have no interest. In having copies made, therefore, the patient should probably review the entire record first and get copies only of those documents he needs to answer his specific questions.

If a patient sees his medical record, will he be able to understand it without the help of a doctor?

If you can make out the handwriting in the record, know the meanings of the abbreviations being used,[5] and have a good medical dictionary,[6] you can get some important information out of the record.

In reading the handwriting, even a doctor may not be able to help. It is common practice among doctors and epidemiologists who do studies on the basis of past medical records, to hire someone to interpret and type them out before the study is conducted.[7] You should, however, be able to check the accuracy of the history you related, the diagnosis, test results, and treatments prescribed. All of this is easier if a "problem-oriented record" is being maintained since you can then refer directly to the problem that concerns you most. Any detailed record analysis, however, requires consultation with an experienced medical practitioner.

Who owns a patient's hospital record?

Under the standards of the JCAH and the law of all 50 states, "the medical record is the property of the hospital."[8] Although the hospital is the owner of the rec-

ord by virtue of custom, and owns the paper on which
the record is printed, this still does not mean that it can
do whatever it wants with the record. Indeed, there is
case authority establishing that while the hospital has a
property right in the record, the patient has a property
right in the information contained in the record and cannot be denied access to that information.[9] How access can
be obtained is discussed below.

Who owns a patient's x-rays?

In the absence of any agreement to the contrary, x-rays
are universally held to be the property of the physician or
facility that takes the x-ray.[10] The rationale is that the patient sought an expert diagnosis of his medical condition
by consenting to x-rays, not a photograph for his own
use.[11] If for any reason, therefore, the patient wants copies
of the x-rays taken of his body, he should execute a written agreement with the head of the x-ray department to
this effect before the x-rays are taken. Without this agreement, a patient probably has no right either to see or copy
his x-rays. The patient could, however, legally refuse to
consent to further treatment until he is shown his x-rays.[12]

Who has access to a patient's medical records?

While you are in the hospital you have given permission
by implication for all hospital personnel directly involved
in your treatment to see your medical records. Your records may also be viewed by hospital committees involved
in monitoring quality of care. With some specific exceptions noted below, no other person has a legal right to see
your records without your written permission.

Certain information in your medical record is considered "non-confidential" and may be released to the police,
public agencies, or the press *unless* you *specifically deny,
orally or in writing,* the hospital the right to release it. This
information includes your name, address, age, marital
status, date of admission, and other similar information.[13]
Other information that may be available to the police or
public agencies, whether you consent or not, includes, for
example, reports of dangerous diseases, acute poisoning,
child abuse, motor vehicle accident, and firearm and knife
wounds. In certain states public health officials may also

be informed of venereal disease, illegitimate births, birth defects and deformities, cerebral palsy cases, industrial accidents, and chronic drug addiction.[14] If you are receiving public assistance or Medicaid, the state agency administering the program may also have access to your records for the purpose of monitoring quality of care and cost.

In addition, the state licensing authority and medical researchers are usually granted access to records but should not be shown records on which the patient's name appears. You may specifically forbid the hospital to use any of your medical records for education or research.

Outside of these exceptions, the general rule is that no one can see your medical records without your express written permission. The authorization will look something like this:

> I hereby authorize X hospital to furnish a copy of my hospital records covering the period of———— to——, to Mr., Ms., or Dr. Y, or to allow said records to be inspected or copied by Mr., Ms., Dr. Y. I hereby release X hospital from all legal responsibility or liability that may arise from this act.
>
> Signed:————— Date:—————

If you want to specifically limit the *use* to which the authorized party may put your medical records, this must be written into the form to be effective (e.g., "not to be computerized under any circumstances"). Most hospitals will retain a complete copy of your medical record for at least 20 years. All retain it until the statute of limitations runs out (2 to 3 years for malpractice, 6 years or more for contracts).

For a more detailed discussion of the confidentiality of medical records, see Chapter XI, Privacy and Confidentiality.

Can a patient see and copy his medical record?

While medical records are the property of the hospital, like other forms of personal property they are subject to court subpoena. In 41 states the only legal right you have to see your medical record is by instituting a lawsuit against the hospital or doctor involved in your care and having the records subpoenaed for evidence.[15] This procedure has been severely criticized by the Report of the Secretary's Commission on Medical Malpractice as needlessly increasing the number of malpractice claims filed.[16] It is possible that you may be permitted to view and copy your records without instituting suit if you persuade the hospital that you will sue if you are not given your record. Also, almost all hospitals will make a copy of your medical record available to the doctor of your choice upon your written authorization without any resort to the courts.

Only nine states have laws that give the patient or his attorney the right to inspect hospital records. Of these, California, Illinois, and Utah limit access to the patient's attorney.[17] In the other six states, Massachusetts, Wisconsin, New Jersey, Louisiana, Mississippi, and Connecticut, patients may have direct access to their records under various circumstances.[18] Perhaps the most liberal statute, that of Massachusetts, provides that the patient's medical records "may be inspected by the patient to whom they relate ... and a copy shall be furnished upon his request and a payment of a reasonable fee."[19] Even in this state, however, it is common hospital policy that records never be given to patients without the knowledge and consent of their doctor, even though this is a clear violation of the law.[20]

The medical profession's major objection to permitting patients to see their medical records is that they are not equipped to understand them and may become unreasonably alarmed by what they contain if a physician is not available to explain it to them. The inherent weakness of this position has prompted some doctors to advocate giving all patients, in and out of hospitals, a carbon copy of their medical record as it is written.[21] The advantages of this system would include: (1) increased patient information and education; (2) continuity of records as patients move or transfer physicians; (3) an added criterion on which patients may base physician selection; (4) improvement in the doctor-patient relationship by making it more open; (5) an added way for physicians to monitor quality care; (6) increased responsiveness to consumer needs.[22]

The AMA has taken the position that only a patient's

doctor should decide what portions of a record a patient can see.[23]

While a patient's access to his medical record is now generally limited to his doctor's good graces and the legal subpoena, we are likely to see moves in the near future to make the medical record more easily available to patients both as hospital policy and as good medical practice. A recent court decision in Illinois, for example, determined that both hospitals and physicians must disclose the information on a patient's medical record to the patient without requiring that the patient go to court.[24] And in Vermont, initial studies have indicated that when patients at the Medical Center Hospital of Vermont were routinely given a complete copy of their medical records, cooperation was stimulated, anxiety reduced, and no adverse effects were noted.[25] In the meantime, patients do have a legal right to demand to see any part or all of their hospital record and have it explained before consenting to any operation or treatment.[26] As unsatisfactory as it may seem, one's only recourse to a denial of medical information may be to either simply refuse to have the procedure performed or to change doctors if that is feasible.

NOTES

1. Joint Commission on Accreditation of Hospitals, ACCREDITATION MANUAL FOR HOSPITALS, Medical Records Services (July, 1973 Supp.).
2. Id., see generally, E. Hayt & J. Hayt, LEGAL ASPECTS OF MEDICAL RECORDS, Physicians' Record Co., Berwyn, Ill., 1964; and W. J. Curran & E. D. Shapiro, LAW, MEDICINE AND FORENSIC SCIENCES, Little, Brown, Boston, 1970 at 68-85.
3. See generally J. W. Hurst & H. K. Walker, THE PROBLEM-ORIENTED SYSTEM, Medcom, Inc., New York, 1972; L. L. Weed, MEDICAL RECORDS, MEDICAL EDUCATION, AND PATIENT CARE: THE PROBLEM-ORIENTED RECORD AS A BASIC TOOL, Case Western Reserve University Press, Cleveland, 1969; Goldfinger, *The Problem-Oriented Record: A Critique From a Believer*, 288 NEW ENG. J. MED. 606-608 (1973).
4. See. IIC 1-5, *Licensure Rules and Regulations for Hospi-*

tals and Sanatoria in Massachusetts, Dept. of Public Health. Authorized by 1968 Mass. Op. Att'y Gen. 40.

5. Abbreviations may vary from one hospital to another, and in the same hospital, from one year to another. See, e.g., *supra*. note 2, Curran & Shapiro at 44-46.

6. STEDMAN'S MEDICAL DICTIONARY (22nd ed), Williams & Williams, Baltimore: 1972.

7. E.g., Brook & Appel, *Choosing a Method for Peer Review*, 288 NEW ENG. J. MED. 1323 (1973).

8. See *supra*., note 1. The laws of all 50 states relating to medical records are set out in Helfman, Harrett, Lutzker, Schneider & Stein, *Access to Medical Records*, APPENDIX, H.E.W. SECRETARY'S COMMISSION REPORT ON MEDICAL MALPRACTICE, U.S. Gov. Print. Office, Jan., 1973 at 177, 186-213.

9. See generally Fleisher, *Ownership of Hospital Records and Roentgenograms*, 4 ILL. CONTINUING LEGAL ED. 73 (1966); *Wallace v. University Hospitals of Cleveland*, 164 N.E. 2d 917 (Ohio, 1959), *mod. on othr. grds.*, 170 N.E. 2d 259 (1960), *app. dism.*, 172 N.E. 2d 469 (1961); *Pyramid Life Ins. Co. v. Masonic Hospital Ass'n*., 191 F. Supp. 51 (W.D. Okla. 1961).

10. Fleisher, *supra*. note 5, at 82.

11. Id. at 81. Donaldson, *Medicolegal Considerations of X-Rays*, 19 RADIOLOGY 388, 391 (1933); see *McGarry v. Mercier*, 272 Mich. 501, 262 N.W. 296 (1935).

12. See ch. 6, Informed Consent to Treatment

13. HOSPITAL LAW MANUAL: ADMINISTRATORS VOLUME, "Medical Records," Health Law Center, Pittsburgh 1959 at 11.

14. See generally, Curran, Stearns & Kaplan, *Confidentiality and Other Legal Considerations in the Establishment of a Centralized Health Data System*, 281 NEW ENG. J. MED. 241 (1969).

15. See Holfman et al. *supra*. note 4.

16. REPORT OF THE SECRETARY'S COMMISSION ON MEDICAL MALPRACTICE, HEW Pub. No. (OS) 73-88, 1973, at 75.

17. *Access to Medical Records, supra*. note 8 at 181.

18. *Id.*

19. Mass. Gen. Laws, ch. 111, §70.

20. Survey of 16 largest hospitals in Boston area conducted by the Center for Law and Health Sciences of Boston University School of Law. Results published in *Boston Evening Globe*, March 1, 1974 at 1, col. 1. Only one hospital responding, Boston Hospital for Woman, indi-

cated that their policy was to obey the law with regard to allowing patients to see their hospital records.

21. Shenkin & Warner, *Giving the Patient his Medical Record: A Proposal to Improve the System*, 289 NEW ENG. J. MED. 688 (1973).
22. *Id.* at 689. See also, Letters to the Editor in response to the proposal, 290 NEW ENG. J. MED. 287-288 (1974).
23. See, e.g., Holder, *Physician's Records and the Chiropractor*, 244 JAMA 1071 (1973).
24. *Cannell v. Medical & Surgical Clinic*, 315 N.E. 2d 278 (Ill. App. 1974). *See also Emmett v. Eastern Dispensary & Casualty Hospital*, 396 F.2d 931 (U.S. App. D.C. 1967). *Contra., Gotkin v. Miller*, 379 F. Supp. 859 (E.D.N.Y. 1974).
25. *Medical World News*, Jan. 13, 1975 at 48.
26. See generally, Chapter VI, Informed Consent to Treatment.

XI
Confidentiality and Privacy

As society becomes increasingly complex and organized, individuals are subjected to more and more governmental questions. Questioners range from the Bureau of Census to the Internal Revenue Service, from the Social Security Administration (SSA) to the Selective Service System. Similarly, as medicine becomes more organized and complex, records on individual patients tend to proliferate. Patients believe that they have (or should have) a right to their "privacy" in medical matters, and that the doctor-patient relationship is one of "confidentiality." In order for a patient to protect medical information he does not want disclosed, however, it is essential that he understand how the law defines these concepts, and what steps he can take to safeguard medical information about himself.

What is meant by "confidentiality"?

In common speech, to tell someone something in confidence means that the person will not repeat what you said to anyone. Confidentiality thus presupposes that something will be told to the doctor that the patient does not want repeated. Relationships such as attorney-client, priest-penitent, and doctor-patient are said to be confidential relationships. When one uses the term confidential in the doctor-patient context, it is descriptive of an express or implied agreement that the doctor will not disclose the information received from the patient to anyone not directly involved in the care and treatment of the patient. Disclosure of such information would be a breach of confidentiality and may give rise to a legal cause of action against the doctor or hospital as discussed below.

121

What is meant by a "privileged communication" or the "testimonial privilege"?

The testimonial privilege refers to a legal rule of evidence and applies *only* in the courtroom or in court-related proceedings. It simply states that a doctor may not disclose information he has learned in confidence from his patient in a court of law without the patient's permission. Unlike the attorney-client privilege, the doctor-patient privilege is not recognized as common law and therefore exists only in those states that have a statute establishing it. Twelve states do not currently recognize the doctor-paient testimonial privilege,[1] and in these states doctors must answer questions about communications with their patients or be faced with a contempt of court finding.

When the privilege exists, it is for the protection of the patient, not the doctor. Its purpose is to encourage the patient to be completely open and frank with the doctor so that the doctor will be better able to care for him. The privilege has been severely criticized by evidence experts, including Dean John Henry Wigmore and Charles T. McCormick, as tending to keep the truth from the courts.[2] In practice, however, there are many exceptions to the rule that allow the doctor to testify to confidential information under certain circumstances.

When can the doctor testify in court about confidential medical information without the patient's consent?

The most important *exceptions* to the privilege rule are[3]:

1. communications made to a doctor when no doctor-patient relationship exists.
2. communications made to a doctor that are not for the purposes of diagnosis and treatment or are not necessary to the purposes of diagnosis and treatment (e.g., who inflicted the gunshot wound and why).
3. in actions involving commitment proceedings, issues as to wills, actions on insurance policies.
4. in actions in which the patient brings his physical or mental condition into question (e.g., personal injury suit for damages, raising an insanity defense, malpractice action against a doctor or hospital).
5. reports required by state statutes (e.g., gunshot

wounds, acute poisoning, child abuse, motor vehicle accidents, and, in some states, venereal disease).
6. information given to the doctor in the presence of another not related professionally to the doctor or known by the patient.

Are psychiatric records treated differently?

Some hospitals keep psychiatric records separately, and some state statutes provide that they be less accessible than other medical records. Psychiatric records are generally viewed both by the law and the medical profession as being more sensitive than general medical records, to the extent that in some states patients may be legally barred from viewing them altogether, and in many states special statutes may require that hospitals or mental institutions make special efforts to keep this information from getting into the hands of unauthorized persons. You should know both the law of your state and the practice of the hospital involved.

What legal action can the patient take if the doctor discloses confidential information?

The patient's main remedy is to sue the doctor for a breach of confidentiality. While much lip service is paid to this type of lawsuit, no American appellate case has been found in which the patient has been able to recover money damages from a doctor due to an alleged breach of confidentiality. Courts have, however, recognized that doctors do have a duty to keep the confidences of their patients. In a 1920 case, for example, a doctor was permitted to disclose to a hotel manager that a patient of his had syphilis only by demonstrating to the court that the disease was "dangerously contagious" and that his disclosures were limited in nature and made only "to such persons as necessary to prevent the spread of the disease."[4] A much more recent case involved disclosure by a doctor to a patient's employer of certain information acquired in the course of a doctor-patient relationship. The court permitted the patient to sue the doctor on three separate grounds[5]:
1. breach of a common law duty on the part of the doctor not to reveal confidences obtained through the

doctor-patient relationship unless prompted by some supervening interest of society;

2. invasion of the patient's right to privacy by unauthorized disclosure of intimate details of the patient's health; and

3. breach of an implied contract to keep confidential all personal information given to the doctor by his patient.

It is likely that most courts in this country would recognize at least one, and perhaps all, of these bases for a suit for breach of confidence.

Can a doctor disclose confidential information to a patient's spouse?

While the AMA contends that "reporting to one spouse information about the medical condition of the other is not a breach of confidentiality,"[6] only two cases have been found that support this proposition, and each is of dubious value. The first is a 1963 Louisiana case that rested on the proposition that the husband had a right to know about his wife's condition because "he is head and master of the family and responsible for its debts."[7] The only other case is a 1966 memorandum opinion of the New York Supreme Court sitting in Nassau County. This case also involved disclosure to a husband, and the court cited the Louisiana case in denying liability. As if unsure of his position, however, Judge Paul J. Widlitz added: "At any rate, a physician who reveals the nature of the condition of the patient to the patient's husband may hardly be charged with reprehensible conduct."[8]

The better rule is that no disclosures to spouses be permitted without the patient's consent. If the patient is worried about this possibility, an agreement should be made with the physician prior to consultation that no disclosure will be made to the spouse without the patient's consent. The problem of such disclosures to spouses and near relatives, discussed in greater detail in Chapter XIV, The Terminally Ill, involves more than the concept of confidentiality. There is the additional danger that a doctor who tells a relative is unlikely to inform the patient about the condition he has diagnosed.

Does the doctor have an ethical duty not to disclose confidential information?

With exceptions similar to those listed under privilege above, the answer is clearly yes. The Hippocratic Oath, while not a legal document, first set out this duty in the following words:

> *Whatsoever things I see or hear* concerning the life of man, in any attendance on the sick or even apart therefrom *which ought not to be noised about, I will keep silent thereon,* counting such things to be professional secrets. (Italics mine)

This oath has been reinterpreted in the current formulation of the AMA's Principles of Ethics[9]:

> A physician *may not reveal the confidences entrusted to him in the course of medical attendance,* or the deficiencies he may observe in the character of patients, unless he is required to do so by law or unless it becomes necessary in order to protect the welfare of the individual or the community. (Italics mine)

At least one case has recently held that a physician may be found legally negligent for violating the canon, and thus a plaintiff may base a suit for breach of confidentiality on this ethical pronouncement.[10]

Who may read the patient's hospital record?

The general rule is that only those persons directly involved in your care may read your record without your permission. This means that your doctor, the nurses on the floor, and those working for your doctor (this may include residents, interns, and medical students) may have access to your record. As previously noted, however, the AHA Bill of Rights demands that anyone viewing your record solely for teaching or learning purposes *must* have your *express* permission before doing so.[11]

What are the advantages of storing medical records in a centralized computer?

There are several advantages to the centralized computerization of medical records. The first is that these records would, unlike present records, be legible.[12] The second is that they would be quickly retrievable from a central source. Thus, if a person living in New York needs emergency care in Massachusetts, the record could be retrieved quickly from the central computer by the Massachusetts hospital. Third, all the patient's medical information could be located in one place instead of in several hospitals in different areas. Fourth, it would prevent the loss of medical records. Finally, it would facilitate the gathering of medical statistics and epidemiological studies.[13]

Why might a patient be concerned about having his records stored in a centralized computer?

The primary danger to the patient from computerization of medical records is that unauthorized persons might obtain access to them. This might be accomplished through intentional theft or negligent handling of the record files. This may be important to patients since those persons obtaining the patient's record may be in a position to make important decisions about the patient on the basis of the record.

These agencies or persons would include life and health insurance companies, present and potential employers, banks and lending institutions, and the press. Serious risks arise, for example, when individuals are rejected for jobs, promotions, credit, loans, or insurance coverage without being told the reason. Medical records might also fall into the hands of an unidentified source that might circulate them to the groups mentioned without either informing the patient or giving the patient the opportunity to challenge, amend, or amplify the contents of his medical record.

Information may also be inaccurate. One expert in the field of computerization of medical records estimated that in the system employed on a trial basis at Kaiser-Permanente Health Plan, some 10 percent of patient records contained errors. His hope was to someday reduce that figure to 3 percent, a no-error system being considered "prohibitively costly and probably not possible."[14]

The major disadvantage of the computerization and centralization of medical records is that it facilitates unauthorized access to patient records. One advantage of the inefficiency of the present system is that it is not very easy to find all the medical records generated about an individual over the years. To obtain these records one would probably have to go to several hospitals, often located in several states, as well as to numerous doctors. In a computerized system all the records could be stored in one place.

Before concluding that this risk of unauthorized access is overwhelming, however, one must ask, "How secure is the present system?" The answer is, "Not very." Once an individual's records are located, only a locked filing cabinet stands between them and their misappropriation. As the recent cases of Dr. Daniel Ellsberg, Senator Thomas Eagleton, and New York District Attorney Frank S. Hogan demonstrate, the present security of medical records leaves much to be desired.

There are several ways to protect the information stored in computers. One is to utilize the numerous electronic safeguards that exist to prevent unauthorized access to the files, such as those developed by the government, industry, and the military to guard their highly sensitive and classified information.[15] Another is to pass strong laws that would punish the unauthorized disclosure, use, or receipt of medical records.

Has there been any centralized computer storage of medical records?

There have been a number of attempts to build such systems. The largest and best known is the Medical Information Bureau, (M.I.B.) located in Greenwich, Connecticut. It is run and paid for by 700 insurance companies and contains medical data on 11 to 12 million people. Their $8 million computer supplies information to the insurance companies that supposedly allows them to determine bad risks. The files not only contain purely medical information, but also data about the sex lives, drinking habits, and dangerous hobbies of individuals. The information is from member insurance companies who get it from doctors, hospitals, credit examinations, company examinations of their employees, government files, police and court records, newspaper accounts, informers, and information supplied by applicants for insurance policies.[16]

One way information gets into the system is when a policy holder files a claim for benefits. In order to receive benefits, the patient must release all relevant medical information to his insurance company. The insurance company then sends this information to M.I.B. to be filed in its computer for the use of all the other participating insurance companies.

One of the few comprehensive health-information systems that presently exists is on an Indian reservation in the Southwest. Developed by HEW, it contains the records of 14,000 people. This population is considered to have severe health problems, and the computerized record-keeping system is designed to enable it to benefit from the comprehensive medical services available. Besides the record-keeping aspect of the system, it is also used to gather statistical information concerning the incidence of certain diseases. In addition, it has a "surveillance" function as it can determine whether or not a patient has had certain scheduled tests for the purpose of discovering incipient medical problems. This system demonstrates the possible future uses of computers in medicine under prepaid health plans or full scale National Health Insurance.[17]

A large governmental computer bank is maintained by the Medicare system. Its computer in Baltimore receives information, which is protected by a federal statute, on 5 million people annually.

Major problems with private medical-data banks are that the individual does not have access to his records, and that much of the information may be inaccurate. Under these circumstances an individual cannot intelligently consent either to have information added to his file or to have the information in the file viewed by anyone. Unless and until complete access to one's file is given to an individual with the ability to have inaccurate information changed, no consent should ever be given which allows one's medical record to be placed in a centralized computer. At present the operation of such computers is completely unregulated.[18]

Should the patient's social security number be used to identify his hospital records?

Because use of such a number greatly increases the possibility of "arbitrary or uncontrolled linkage of records about people, particularly between government and government-support automated personal data systems," the Secretary of HEW's Advisory Committee on Automated Personal Data Systems recommended in July 1973 that any universal identifier such as the Social Security number not be used for record identification.[19]

The committee specifically recommended that:

—Uses of the social security number be limited to those necessary for carrying out requirements imposed by the Federal government;

—Federal agencies not require or promote use of the social security number except where specifically mandated by Congress;

—Congress should be sparing in such mandates and not make any without complete public hearings aimed at safeguarding the automated personal data;

—When the social security number is used outside the framework of a congressional mandate, no individual should be coerced into providing his social security number, nor should it be used without his informed consent;

—An individual should be fully and fairly informed of his rights and responsibilities relative to uses of his social security number.

Can I refuse to disclose my social security number to the hospital if the hospital uses it as a patient-record identifier?

While existing laws are silent on this question, as a practical matter disclosure of one's social-security number has almost universally survived legal challenge in such diverse areas as motor vehicle licenses, public utility companies, high schools, colleges, and credit unions. No case has been located regarding a hospital. The Secretary's Advisory Committee proposed specific pre-emptive federal legislation providing the individual with a right to refuse to disclose his social security number to any person or organization that does not have specific authority provided by Federal statute to request it, and including legal remedies for the individual should any benefits be denied him as a result of his refusal to disclose the information. As the Advisory Committee noted, such legislation is needed if the social security number is "to be stopped from becoming a *de facto* standard universal identifier."[20] Currently, all that can be said is that the patient has as much of a right to refuse to disclose his social security number as the hospital has to demand it.[21]

Are hospitals likely to increase the use of social security numbers for identification in the future?

Hopefully not. The AHA has recently advised hospitals *not* to use these numbers. Only one of the 12 reasons cited involved protecting the confidentiality of patient records. The others all dealt with practicalities. The AHA noted, for example, that over 45 percent of patients admitted to hospitals either do not have a social security number or cannot give it at the time of admission. Four million Americans have two or more social security numbers, and over 2.5 million corrections are made annually in social security's master file. Also, social security will not confirm numbers for hospitals, and a nine-digit number is thought to be too long and could lead to many errors in transcribing and reading.[22]

What is meant by the "right of privacy"?

There are at least two senses in which this term is generally used. The first describes a *constitutional* right of privacy. This right, while not found directly enunciated in the constitution, was the basis for decisions by the U.S. Supreme Court limiting state interference with birth control and abortion.[23] This right is said to be one of *personal* privacy and involves the ability of an individual to make decisions regarding his body. At least one lower court case has extended it to permit decisions to refuse life-sustaining treatment.[24]

In the more traditional sense the term has been defined as "the right to be let alone, to be free of prying, peeping and snooping,"[25] and as "the right of someone to keep information about himself or access to his personality inaccessible to others."[26] In both of these senses this concept is based more on property interests than on bodily-control interests. As a property right, this right usually requires a state statute to recognize it before it will be enforced.[27] The typical right of privacy action in this category will allege: (1) intrusion of physical solitude, (2) publication of private facts, or (3) appropriation of name or likeness for commercial use.

In the hospital context the law implies consent to those invasions of privacy that any reasonable person would view as essential to proper diagnosis and treatment of the patient.[28] For example, a physical examination requires a certain amount of disrobing and record keeping, but it does not import observation via closed-circuit television, the presence of persons not directly involved in the examination, the taking of pictures, or the publication of results in any manner.[29] None of these latter activities can be performed legally without obtaining the patient's prior consent.

What are some examples of rights encompassed in the "right of privacy"?

As a patient in a hospital you have the following rights based on the right of privacy:

1. to refuse to see any or all visitors;
2. to refuse to see anyone not officially connected with the hospital;
3. to refuse to see persons officially connected with the hospital who are not directly involved in your care and treatment;
4. to refuse to see social workers and to forbid them to view your records;
5. to wear your own bedclothes so long as they do not interfere with your treatment;
6. to wear religious medals, etc.;
7. to have a person of your own sex present during a physical examination of yourself by a medical professional of the opposite sex;
8. not to remain disrobed any longer than is necessary for accomplishing the medical purpose for which you were asked to disrobe;

9. not to have your case discussed openly in the hospital;

10. to have your medical records read only by those directly involved in your treatment or the monitoring of its quality;

11. to insist on being transferred to another room if the person sharing it with you will not let you alone or is disturbing you unreasonably by smoking or other actions.

Can a patient's problems be discussed at teaching rounds without his permission?

While the answer to this question is no, practice in most hospitals is probably not to tell the patient that his case is being presented. A recent issue of the community publications of a major hospital, for example, contained the following opening to a story about their Tumor Clinic[30]:

> He didn't know it, but he had 26 doctors free of charge. There were four pathologists, a diagnostic radiologist and a radiological therapist, perhaps half a dozen or more surgeons, several medical specialists . . . and ten house officers. For half an hour, they all concentrated on his problem and what to do about it.

Doctors in teaching hospitals often tend to believe that when they discuss a case with the house staff or at grand rounds, they are *de facto* helping the patient. Medically, of course, this may be true. Indeed, one of the great advantages of being in a teaching hospital is that the patient is exposed to such a diversity of medical professionals. Such an advantage may, however, be properly considered a major disadvantage by patients who are not told what is occurring and why.

Under the AHA Bill of Rights a patient's case may not be presented to "outsiders" in this manner without his express permission. More serious cases occur when the patient is wheeled into a large amphitheater to be put on display to a hundred or more people. In all cases the patient has an absolute right to refuse to participate in such teaching activities.

NOTES

1. The states that do not recognize the physician-patient privilege are Alabama, Connecticut, Delaware, Florida, Georgia, Maryland, Massachusetts, Rhode Island, South Carolina, Tennessee, Texas, and Vermont. McCormick, EVIDENCE, §98 (2d ed.) 1972.

2. Waltz & Inbau, MEDICAL JURISPRUDENCE, MacMillan, New York, 1971 at 252.

3. Tortorella, "Physician-Patient Privileged Communications: When Can a Doctor Speak?" *Trial*, March/April, 1973 at 59, and C. Dewitt, PRIVILEGED COMMUNICATIONS BETWEEN PHYSICIAN AND PATIENT, Thomas, Springfield, Ill., 1958.

4. *Simonsen v. Swenson*, 177 N.W. 831 (Neb., 1920). *And see Tarasoff v. U. Cal.*, Cal. Sup. Ct. Dec. 23, 1974 (43 USLW 2289, Jan. 14, 1975) (psychotherapist has a duty to warn third party of a patient's threat against her life).

5. *Horne v. Patton*, 287 So. 2d 824 (Ala., 1973). In a leading New Zealand case both the plaintiff and her husband had been regular patients of the defendant psychiatrist. The psychiatrist, upon the request of the husband and his lawyer, issued a report on the wife correctly stating that she was deluded, had accused her husband of cruelty and violence, and exhibited symptoms of paranoia. Treatment was recommended. A year later, in connection with the wife's application for separate support, the husband's lawyer produced the report while cross-examining the wife. She had not known of the report, and it caused her great mental distress. She sued the psychiatrist and recovered a substantial verdict on the ground that the psychiatrist should have foreseen that this disclosure would have caused the wife harm. The court intimated that faced with the proper case it would hold that the doctor's duty should always be to "preserve a patient's secrets," citing both the Hippocratic Oath and the Code of Ethics of the British Medical Association. *Furniss v. Fitchett*, 1958 N.Z.L.R. 396, 404 (Barrowclough, C.J.).

6. *Disclosure of Confidential Information*, 216 JAMA 385 (1971).

7. *Pennison v. Provident Life & Accident Ins Co.*, 154 So. 2d 617, 618 (La. Ct. App., 1963).

8. *Curry v. Corn*, 277 N.Y. S. 2d 470, 472, 52 Misc. 2d 1035 (1966).

9. AMA Principles of Medical Ethics, 1957, §9.
10. *Steeves v. U.S.*, 294 F. Supp. 446 (D.C. So. Car. 1968).
11. See §5 of the A.H.A. Bill of Rights, reprinted in its entirety in Chapter III.
12. See Chapter X, Hospital Records.
13. See generally Freed, *A Legal Structure for a National Medical Data Center*, 49 *B.U.L. REV.* 79 (1969), and Freed, *Legal Aspects of Computer Use in Medicine*, 32 LAW & CONTEM. PROB. 674 (1967).
14. Dr. Morris Collen quoted in A. Westin et al, DATABANKS IN A FREE SOCIETY, New York Times Book Co., New York, 1973 at 210.
15. Specific safeguards, recommended by Richard I. Miller in his *Invasion of Privacy by Computer*, 5 LEX ET SCIENTIA 18, 23 (1968) include:

> (1) Some sort of minimal cryptographic protection for transmission lines which carry personal data could be devised so that eavesdropping may be a bit more complicated and expensive than tapping a telephone line is today. (2) Personal data should never be filed in a 'clear' state, so that a simple access-deposit box in the vault at once. (3) Auditing of access to storage will, in a sense, open every safety computer programs which store personal data, to be certain that no programmer has deliberately or inadvertently short circuited access routes, should become as standard as the audit of bank records. (4) Recording devices should be built into computers which will verify and record the source of requests for personal information interrogatories ... notice should be given to individuals that such data is being collected about them and access afforded for the purposes of verification.

Roy N. Freed adds to this list the restricting of access to only certain individuals, such as licensed physicians, the restriction of the number of terminals from which access to the central files can be had, the use of authorized input-output devices, such as personal wafers, to identify qualified users, strict security control over the computer premises, and security clearance of individuals working with the computer. *Id.* 49 B. U. L. REV. 79, 87-88.

16. *New York Times*, October 7, 1973 at E3; *Computerworld*, June 7, 1972 at 1, *Medical World News*, June 1, 1973 at 18. *And See* Stern, *Medical Information Bureau:*

The Life Insurer's Databank, 4 RUTGERS J. COMPUTERS & LAW 1 (1974).

17. RECORDS, COMPUTERS AND THE RIGHTS OF CITIZENS, Report of the Secretary's Advisory Committee on Automated Personal Data Systems, U.S. Dept. HEW, DHEW Pub. No. (OS) 73-94, U.S. Gov. Print Office Stock No. 1700-00116, July, 1973 at 24-25.

18. *Id.* See also, Ware, *Security and Privacy in Computer Systems,* Proceedings of the AFIPS 1967 Spring Joint Computer Conference, 1967, at 279.

19. See *supra,* note 16 at 122.

20. *Id.* at 123-124.

21. Cf. Chapter XVI, Payment of Hospital Bills. The social security number is the Medicare and Medicaid identifier, and some Blue Cross plans use it. In this case the patient doesn't even have the option of giving a false number.

22. 48 *Hospitals, JAHA* 124 (1974).

23. *Eisenstadt v. Baird,* 405 U.S. 438 (1972) (contraception), *Roe v. Wade,* 93 S. Ct. 705 (1973) (abortion). *See also Loving v. Virginia,* 388 U.S. 1 (marriage); *Skinner v. Oklahoma,* 316 U.S. 535 (procreation).

24. *In re Yedder,* Northampton Co. Orphans Court, Pa., No. 1973-533 (June 6, 1973) (Unreported opinion, Judge Alfred T. Williams, Jr.).

25. Miller, *supra* note 14, at 21.

26. Curran, Stearns & Kaplan, *Confidentiality and Other Legal Considerations in the Establishment of a Centralized Health-Data System,* 281 NEW ENG. J. MED. 241 (1969).

27. The "right to privacy" was first articulated in an 1890 law review article by Louis Brandeis and Samuel Warren. *The Right to Privacy,* 4 HARV. L. REV. 193 (1890). Since that time many states have passed laws expressly recognizing the right. In those that have not, or have passed limited laws, some courts have recognized the right of privacy, and some have refused to uphold an action based on this right in the absence of a state statute.

28. Waltz & Inbau, *supra,* note 2 at 278.

29. *Id.* at 279.

30. 4 NEWTON-WELLESLEY Q. 17 (June, 1973).

XII
Children

The Romans gave fathers the power of life and death over their children. Even today, parents have almost complete control over their children, limited only by such measures as child abuse statutes and compulsory education laws. Thus, when we speak of the rights of hospitalized children, we are more often than not speaking of the rights of the parents of hospitalized children. This tension—between the rights of the child as a patient and the rights of the parent of the child—is a theme that runs through this entire chapter. There are also, of course, children who live apart from both their parents—3 million of them under the age of 18 in the United States. Their problems can be especially difficult for the hospital to deal with in the face of a legal tradition that looks to parents as the sole source of support and welfare of the child. For material on parents refusing to consent to the treatment of their child see Chapter VII, on experimentation on children, Chapter IX, and on abortion, Chapter XIII.

How is a "child" or "minor" defined by law?

Under English and American common law an individual was a minor until he reached the age of 21.[1] Until he attained adult status, the minor or child owed his services and earnings to his parents and had to obey his parents' demands. In return his parents were obligated to support him.

The theory on which the age of majority was based was that minors needed special protection. As Blackstone put it[2]:

Infants have various privileges, and various disabilities; but their very disabilities are privileges; in order to secure them from hurting themselves by their own improvident acts.

Today, the age of majority is governed by state statute and cases and therefore varies from state to state. There is a strong trend in the United States toward lowering the age of majority to 18 or 19. Since 1970 at least 44 states have taken action in this direction.[8]

The age of majority is relevant in the area of consent to treatment. Touching a person without his consent is a battery. A minor is legally incapable of giving consent, and therefore any touching of a minor by a doctor or health worker even with his consent is a technical battery. In general, the parent or guardian of a minor is the only person legally capable of giving consent to medical treatment.

Can a child ever consent to medical treatment for himself?

Many state statutes list *specific diseases* or *conditions* that a minor can consent to have treated. For example, in Massachusetts a minor can consent to treatment for venereal disease. Or a minor who is at least 12 years old and is drug dependent may consent to the treatment of the drug dependency.[5] Other conditions dealt with by statutes in many states include pregnancy, contraception, blood transfusion, alcoholism, and contagious diseases. Reference should be made to the statutes of the state in question.[6]

In an *emergency situation* a doctor can also treat a minor without parental consent. If an adult is brought to an emergency room unconscious or delirious and requires immediate care, the doctor may treat him without obtaining consent. It is often said the consent is "implied," although it is probably more accurate to say the doctor is privileged due to the situation.[7] As with adults, if a minor needs emergency treatment, he can be treated without consent. Some states have codified this doctrine. For example, in Massachusetts a doctor can treat a minor without parental consent if a delay in treatment will "endanger the life, limb or mental well-being" of the patient.[8] Similar laws have been enacted in Maryland,[9] Mississippi,[10] and Pennsylvania.[11]

Some jurisdictions allow *emancipated minors* to consent to their own medical care.[12] A child who is emancipated is free from the care, custody, control, and services of his parents.[13] It is generally agreed that married minors and minors in the armed forces are emancipated.[14]

Other states have adopted what is referred to as the *mature minor rule*. The Mississippi statute states that "any unemancipated minor of sufficient intelligence to understand and appreciate the consequences of the proposed surgical or medical treatment or procedure . . ." may consent to such treatment.[15] In New York this doctrine is recognized by the courts.[16] That there are no reported cases of doctors or hospitals being held liable for the performance of an accepted therapeutic procedure on a minor over the age of 15 tends to support the view that judges and juries believe that "mature minors" should be permitted to consent to treatment under ordinary circumstances.

If a parent refuses to consent to the treatment of his child, can the hospital treat the child?

There are certain cases when a hospital can treat a child although the parent refuses to consent. When a child's life is endangered and the parents will not permit treatment, the courts will authorize treatment. The hospital must go to court and have someone (usually a member of its staff) appointed the guardian of the child for the purpose of consenting to the treatment.

In most of these cases the parents refuse to consent on the basis of their religious convictions. In one case, for example, the parents were Jehovah's Witnesses and refused to grant permission for the necessary blood transfusions in the treatment of their infant son's heart abnormality. The hospital went to court and had the superintendent of the hospital appointed guardian. The superintendent then consented to the transfusion.[17]

In one unusual case, a court ordered an operation to correct a condition that did not endanger the life of the minor. A 15-year-old boy was suffering from Von Recklinghausen's disease, which caused a severe facial deformity. The mother, a Jehovah's Witness, would not consent to the blood transfusion necessary to effect the performance of the operation. The court permitted the operation to proceed without the mother's consent.[18] More commonly the courts will not interfere in a non-life-threatening parental decision. In *Matter of Seiferth*, for example, the court would not override a father's refusal to consent to a surgical procedure necessary to repair his son's harelip and cleft palate.[19]

Who is liable for the payment of a minor's medical bills?

One of the advantages of minority is the right to disaffirm or refuse to go ahead with one's contract. This means that a minor may be able to avoid his obligation to pay for services rendered in a hospital.[20] One exception to this rule is that minors are "liable for the reasonable value of necessaries furnished him."[21] Necessaries include what is reasonably needed for the minor's subsistence. Examples of necessaries would include food, lodging, and education. Legally doctor and dentist fees, and bills for medicines, are considered necessaries, and thus even a minor is obligated to pay for them.[22]

In some instances, the minor's parent might also be liable for the cost of necessaries supplied to an unemancipated minor.[23] But a parent is not liable for the necessaries of emancipated minors. In any event, for a parent to be liable for the medical bills of an unemancipated minor, it must be shown that the parent negligently failed to provide such services, although he knew they were necessary to the well-being of the child.[24]

If a parent does consent, can a child refuse to undergo the treatment?

In answering this question, there is very little law that can be relied on. In one case, a mother wanted to force her 16 year-old, unmarried, pregnant daughter to have an abortion over the minor's objections. The state had a statute that gave a minor the same capacity to consent to medical treatment as an adult when the minor seeks treatment concerning pregnancy. The court found that medical treatment concerning pregnancy included abortion and held[25]:

> ... the minor, having the same capacity to consent as an adult, is emancipated from control of the parents with respect to medical treatment within the contemplation of the statute. We think it follows that if a minor may consent to medical treatment as an adult upon seeking treatment or advice concerning pregnancy, the minor, and particularly a minor over 16 years of age, may not be forced, more than an adult, to accept treatment or advice concerning pregnancy ... the one consenting has the right to forbid.

If other states follow this court's opinion, any minor who can consent to medical treatment due to a statute or court decision should have the right to refuse medical treatment.

An extension of the concept of the minor's right to refuse treatment may come from HEW's proposed guidelines for the protection of human subjects. Under these proposals an experimenter would have to obtain the consent of all minors 7 years of age or older as well as their parents or guardians before he could use them as subjects in an experiment.[26] The proposal gives the child the power to refuse to participate in experimental treatments irrespective of his parents' wishes.

May a doctor or hospital tell a child's parents about the child's condition or treatment against the child's will?

As stated in the chapter on confidentiality and privacy, the doctor has an ethical duty and probably a legal duty not to disclose information he receives from the patient or the type of treatment provided. Is there anything in the parent-child relationship that should work to deprive the minor of confidential dealings with the doctor?

The parent is generally the consenting party, and in order for the parent to be able to give informed consent, he or she needs complete information from the doctor. Thus, if the parent must give the informed consent, the parent must be provided with the medical information essential to provide an *informed consent*.

On the other hand, it would seem that anyone who

could consent to his own care has a right to a confidential relationship with his doctor. In a jurisdiction in which an older minor can consent to his own care, the parents would not need the information for consent purposes, and the doctor should not supply it—or at best should not solicit it without telling the child in advance that he is going to disclose whatever he learns to the child's parents. The purpose for confidentiality or testimonial privilege is to encourage the patient to disclose all relevant information without worrying about embarrassing information being disseminated. A child who can consent for himself has a legal right to refuse to speak to a doctor or to submit to examination or treatment until the doctor agrees not to tell his parents anything about the examination or treatment.

Some states do have statutes permitting certain disclosures to parents. For example, in Massachusetts, a doctor who knows or has reason to know that a minor is infected with venereal disease may, but is not required to, disclose this fact to the minors' parents.[27]

May a hospital prevent or restrict visits to children by their parents?

In general, if the law or the hospital requires the parent's consent for treatment of the child, the hospital cannot prevent or restrict parents from being with their children while in the hospital.

Before antibiotics, the possibility of the introduction and spread of infection meant that parents were generally not allowed to be with their children in hospitals. By the 1950s some in the medical profession started to view as paradoxical the fact that "when a young child needs his mother most, when he is ill and perhaps in pain, she is generally not allowed to be with him for more than brief visits."[28] Since then, moves have continued toward the liberalizing of the visiting hours in pediatric wards and hospitals.[29]

In Boston a consumer group called "Children in Hospitals" has been organized to support parents who want to stay with their children in the hospital and to encourage hospitals to broaden their visiting policies.[30] It was founded by a mother who demanded and was granted the right to stay with her 10-month-old daughter during a hospitalization. At one point a nurse put some drops in the child's eye and left. The baby started screaming and would not open her eyes. Twice the mother carried the child out to the nursing station and was given no satisfaction. After a third try she persuaded the nurse to check to be sure the right drops had been administered. The nurse discovered that the iodine drops were for the baby to drink prior to a brain-wave test. Her eyes were immediately flushed out, and luckily no permanent damage was done.[31]

The legal right to be with one's children derives from the doctrine of informed consent. Parents may not be able to give fully informed consent for their children if they are not able to be with them constantly to monitor their reactions (which they can interpret better than anyone else because of their experience with their children). Also, parents have the right to withdraw their consent to treatment at any time, and this right can only be meaningfully exercised if the parent is continuously present with the child to determine that circumstances have changed to such an extent that consent should be withdrawn. Parents whose requests to stay with their children are refused can always condition any consent they are asked to give, or form they are asked to sign, with being permitted to stay with their children. If they are thereafter denied the right, their consent terminates, and the hospital can no longer legally treat their child.[32]

I would argue that the only reasonable limits a hospital can probably place on parental visitation would involve actual interference with the hospital's ability to care for other patients (not the parent's child, since the parents and not the hospital have the ultimate treatment authority).[33] This would mean that parents, if they so desired, have the legal right to stay with their children during all tests and procedures, the administration of anesthesia, and be present in the recovery room.

What can parents do to make hospitals more responsive to their desires?

1. Question hospital policy before your child is admitted.

2. Select the doctor and hospital best able to make the arrangements you desire.

3. Negotiate directly with the chief of pediatrics or the chief of anesthesia, never with admissions offices or floor nurses.

4. Publicize your experiences, both favorable and unfavorable.

5. Form parent groups to work for the changes you desire.

NOTES

1. I. W. Blackstone, COMMENTARIES (1904 Sharswood ed.) at 463.
2. *Id.* at 464.
3. Katz, Schroeder & Sidman, *Emancipating Our Children—Coming of Legal Age in America,* 7 FAMILY L.Q. 211, 213 (1973).
4. Mass. Gen. Laws Ann. c. 111 §117.
5. Mass. Gen. Laws Ann. c. 112 §12E.
6. The laws of the 50 states regarding specific conditions under which doctors may treat minors without parental consent are summarized in C. Rosenberg, *When Can You Treat Minors Without Parental Consent?* MED. ECONOMICS, July 9, 1973, 77, 80-81.
7. Prosser, TORTS, 104 (3rd ed., 1964).
8. Mass. Gen. Laws Ann. ch. 112 §12F (1970).
9. Md. Ann. Code, art. 43, §135 (1971).
10. Miss. Code Ann. §7129-81 (1966).
11. Pa. Stat., tit. 35, §10104 (1969).
12. In addition to states in which minority status terminates upon marriage, there are at least 14 states that allow emancipated and/or married minors to consent to medical treatment: Ariz. Rev. Stat. Ann. §44-132 (1967 Supp.); Cal. Civ. Code §25.6 (1967 Supp.); Del. Code Ann. title 13, §707 (1970 Supp.); Fla. Stat. Ann. §743.01 (1971); Ida. Code Ann. §32-101 (1963); Ind. Ann. Stat. §35-4407 et seq. (1968 Supp.); Ill. Ann. Stat. §§18.1-18.2; Minn. S.F. No. 1496, ch. 544, §144.341, 144.342; Miss. Code Ann. §7129-81 (1966); Mont. Rev. Codes Ann. §69-6101 (1970); Neb. Rev. Stat. §38-101 (1969); Nev. Rev. Stat. 129.030 (1967 Supp.); N.J. Stat.

Ann. §9:17A-1 (1967 Supp.); N.M. Stat. Ann. §12-12-1 et seq. (1967 Supp.); N.C. Gen. Stat. §90-21.5 (1971); Pa. Stat. tit. 35, §10101 (1969); Va. Code Ann. §32-137 (1970); See also Kan. Stat. Ann. §38-122 (1967 Supp.) regarding minor parents.

13. See generally, Cohen v. Delaware L. & W.R.R., 150 Misc. 450 (S. Ct. N.Y., 1934), Lowell v. Inhabitants of Newport, 66 Me. 78 (1876), and Dunks v. Grey, 3 F. 862 (1880).

14. Eg. Bach v. L.I. Jewish Hospital, 49 Misc. 2d 207 (S.Ct. Nassau Co., 1966), In Re Palumbo, 172 Misc. 155 (Dom. Rel. CT., 1939).

15. Miss. Code Ann. §41-41-3(h).

16. Bach v. L.I. Jewish Hospital, 49 Misc. 2d 207 (S.Ct. Nassau Co., 1966).

17. State v. Perricone, 37 N.J. 463, 181 A.2d 751 (1962).

18. In re Sampson, 317 N.Y. S 2d 641 (1970) aff'd. 29 N.Y. 2d 900, 328 N.Y.S. 2d 686, 278 N.E. 2d 918 (1972).

19. 309 N.Y. 80, 127 N.E. 2d 820 (1955).

20. Simpson, CONTRACTS §105.

21. Id. at §104.

22. 2 Williston, CONTRACTS §241 (1959).

23. 59 Am. Jur. 2d, Parent and Child §87.

24. Id.

25. Matter of Smith, 16 Md. App. 209, 295 A. 2d 238-246 (1972).

26. 38 Fed. Reg. 31738 (Nov. 16, 1973).

27. Mass. Gen. Laws Ann. ch. 112 §12.

28. See Robertson, YOUNG CHILDREN IN HOSPITALS, Basic Books, New York, 1958.

29. See generally, Mason, The Hospitalized Child-His Emotional Needs, 272 NEW ENG. J. MED. 406 (1965), which summarizes the medical arguments for allowing parents unlimited visitation with their hospitalized children.

30. For further information write Children in Hospitals, 31 Wilshire Park, Needham, Massachusetts.

31. Fager, Hospital: Keep Out of Reach of Children, The Real Paper (Boston), Sept. 12, 1973, at 6.

32. See generally Chapter VI, Informed Consent to Treatment.

33. Potentially contrary to this view is the case of Hulit v. St. Vincent's Hospital, 520 P.2d 99 (Mont. 1974) (hospital regulation denying father admission to labor and delivery rooms within administration's discretion). This case is discussed in the following chapter.

XIII
Women

It is impossible to write an apolitical chapter about the legal rights of women in hospitals. By including a special chapter on women, one's immediate assumption must be that women are more "at risk" concerning their human rights in a hospital setting. The two women[1] who have helped me research this chapter share this view, and the facts seem to support them.[2] More than 90 percent of all physicians in this country are men—most of them white and upper-middle class. This group tends to subscribe to many myths about women that are reinforced by medical school training and by the attitudes exhibited by the actions of their clinical instructors toward their female patients. Traditional psychoanalytic theory as practiced in most medical schools, for example, teaches both that the ambitious woman is neurotically rejecting her femininity and that the housewife who willingly accepts her role is "infantile."[3] Most medical journals are filled with advertisements for mood-altering drugs depicting a neurotic or distressed woman as the likely patient. Their success can be measured by the fact that 67 percent of such drugs are prescribed for women.[4]

It is also apparent that women are becoming more and more dependent on the obstetrics-gynecology specialist for all of their health care needs. This is both because of the shortage of general practitioners, and because of the practice of the G.P.'s that do exist of referring women to these specialists. It has been argued that, to the extent that this speciality is isolated from all of the other specialties in medicine, and to the extent that women are dependent upon this one group for most of their care, they are the most uninformed medical consumer group and the group least able to "shop around" for medical care.

A number of women commentators have argued persuasively that the women's movement toward health rights should not concentrate its efforts on medical practices rooted in female anatomy such as menstruation, childbirth, and menopause. Rather, they argue that the movement should aim at taking control of the social context within which services important to women are rendered, from "the availability of abortion at one end [to] day care at the other."[5] The purpose of this chapter is to outline areas in which the law may be a help (or possibly a hindrance) to the women's movement for equal rights in hospital care.[6] While the legal rights of women in the hospital are not essentially different from other patients, women are at greater risk of certain violations of their rights, especially in the area of reproduction. This chapter therefore necessarily concentrates on areas such as abortion, childbirth, hysterectomies, and breast cancer.

In reading this chapter the reader should remember at all times that the author is a lawyer, not a doctor. *The medical data presented herein is used simply to illustrate points of law, not to make any judgments on the medical advisability of the practices discussed.*

Is the husband's consent legally necessary for any type of treatment of a married woman?

The consent of a husband is never legally necessary for the treatment of a conscious, competent, and consenting married woman.[7] This has been consistently affirmed by the courts. Specific cases considered in the context of a husband suing the doctor for treating his wife without his consent have included both sterilization and pregnancy care.[8] The husband's consent was determined not to be necessary. This finding, of course, works both ways, that is, the wife's consent is not required for any type of medical treatment of her husband.[9]

The question of whether a doctor may discuss what he has learned about a woman's condition with her husband without her consent is discussed in Chapter XI, Confidentiality and Privacy.

Does a patient being examined by a doctor of the opposite sex have a right to have another person of the patient's sex present in the examining room during the examination?

Approximately 95 percent of all specialists in obstetrics and gynecology are men. Most routinely have a female nurse with them during all physical examinations. The reason generally given is to protect themselves from a possible charge by the woman patient of improper advances. If the doctor's practice is not to have another female present, however, a woman does have the right to demand that another female be present during the examination if she so desires. If the doctor refuses this request in the hospital context, his method of practice is open to serious ethical question, and his conduct should be reported immediately to the chief of his service. The name and phone number of his chief can be obtained from one of the nurses or through the hospital administration. In the context of a private office, the woman's remedy is probably limited to walking out, informing the local medical society, and going to another doctor.

Increasingly, feminists are advising women to "bring a friend" with them on visits to the doctor for psychological support. Such a person can also act as a witness to what goes on and remind the patient to ask certain questions that are bothering her. No ethical doctor should object to this request.

Does a woman have a right to refuse to be examined by medical students, interns, or residents in a hospital setting?

All patients have a right to refuse to be examined by *anyone* in the hospital setting.[10] When a woman is asked, "Do you mind if these other doctors look at you also?" she has every right to say, "*Yes*, I do mind," and refuse to permit them to examine her. One should be especially wary when the phrase "young doctor" is used since this almost always means medical student—usually a first or second-year one. In some hospitals, medical students are also referred to simply as "doctors," even though the patient has a right to know both what the extent of their training is and the purpose of their proposed examination.

In one court case from the 1930's a woman objected to being examined by a medical student just before she was due to give birth. Thereupon an older doctor came in, performed a rectal and vaginal examination, and then had the same examination performed two or three times each by "ten or twelve young men who she took to be students." She protested repeatedly and testified, "Whenever I screamed and protested they just laughed, told me to shut up." She experienced both emotional and physical damages from the delivery. The court had no difficulty in finding this conduct "revolting" and an assault on the patient. In the court's words, "A physician or a medical student has no more right to needlessly and rudely lay hands upon a patient against her will than has a layman." The court also found, over 30 years before the *Darling* case (discussed elsewhere in this book[11]), that the hospital in which this event took place could be held liable for permitting "unlicensed students to experiment on the patient and treat her without her consent."[12]

The lesson is not only that the medical students themselves but also the attending physician *and* the hospital are liable to the patient for any unauthorized examination or treatment. It goes almost without saying that consent by a patient based on a belief that the person examining her is a doctor is consent achieved by fraud or misrepresentation and as such is not legally valid if the examiner is not a doctor.

Does a woman have a legal right to an abortion?

The 1973 U.S. Supreme Court's abortion decisions[13] placed the primary decision-making power concerning abortion in the hands of the pregnant woman. This is not, however, tantamount to saying that the court sanctioned "abortion on demand," something the court specifically said it was not doing.[14] Abortion laws are still the province of state governments and as such vary from state to state. What the Supreme Court decided is that while states may make and enforce laws limiting abortions, there are some things these state laws may not prohibit. Specifically, a state may not prohibit a woman from obtaining an abortion from a physician, in or out of the hospital, during the first trimester of pregnancy. Second, during the second trimester, all state laws relating to abortions must be based *only* on protection of the health of the woman. (E.g., a state may lawfully require all second trimester abortions to be performed in hospitals in order to protect the life and health of the woman.) After the sixth month, the state may constitutionally prohibit nontherapeutic abortions from being performed altogether because at this point the state may have a "compelling reason" for such a restriction. The reason is protection of a potentially viable fetus that may be able to live independently of the pregnant woman. The idea is that protection by the state of this potential life becomes more important than the woman's right to control her own body once there is a possibility that the fetus may survive outside the womb.

While some have argued that the court was giving the doctor the authority to decide about abortion *with* the woman, letting the doctor or the medical profession have a veto power over the decision of the individual woman would undermine the very constitutional basis on which the Supreme Court decided the case.[15] On the other hand, the argument that one need not be a physician to perform an abortion during the first trimester is also inconsistent with the emphasis throughout the case on the "health and safety of the woman."

As a practical matter, under the medical practice statutes of most, if not all, of the states, only a doctor is authorized to perform an abortion. Moreover, no individual doctor can legally be forced to perform an abortion against his will. In addition, many states have passed new abortion laws that, while they will probably eventually be declared unconstitutional, may still deter doctors and hospitals in the particular state from complying with the Supreme Court rulings as outlined above. Under these circumstances, access to abortion to which the woman now has a limited constitutional right may become the critical question.

Under what circumstances must a hospital provide abortion services?

While an argument can be made that the government has an affirmative obligation to make abortion services available to those who cannot afford them (because not to do so would effectively deny the poor the right to exercise a constitutional right), no court in the U.S. has yet gone this far.[16] The court decisions to date do provide, however, that *Medicaid must pay for abortions* and that *governmental hospitals or private hospitals with sufficient governmental involvement*[17] *must allow their facilities to be used for abortion services* for those doctors and their women patients who request them.[18] As to private hospitals that have not become sufficiently involved with governmental activity, they need not make their facilities available for the performance of abortions. While strong arguments exist for the establishment of a right to use these facilities for abortion, it is likely to take some time before the question reaches the U.S. Supreme Court.[19]

Under what circumstances must a hospital provide sterilization services?

A governmental hospital, or one sufficiently involved in governmental activities,[20] cannot permit certain surgical procedures and, at the same time, ban others involving reproduction that involve no greater risk or demand on staff and facilities. A municipal hospital's ban on the performance of sterilizations, for example, has been found to be illegal as a violation of the equal protection clause of the 14th Amendment.[21] Likewise, these hospitals could not prevent qualified staff physicians from performing abortions in the hospital.

Can a hospital require the husband's consent as a prerequisite for a married woman's abortion?

Because of the state's asserted interest in the family, a number of state statutes require the husband's consent for an abortion.[22] The U.S. Supreme Court specifically declined to determine whether or not this practice was constitutionally prohibited in their 1973 abortion decisions,[23] but in early 1975 the court refused to enforce a Pennsylvania statute restricting the use of public funds to abortions consented to by spouses or parents during the time the statute's constitutionality was being challenged in lower courts. Only a few other cases on this issue have reached the courts. A Florida court refused to permit the father of an illegitimate fetus to intervene to prevent an abortion, and the Massachusetts Supreme Judicial Court refused to allow a husband separated from his wife to prohibit her from obtaining an abortion.[24] If a hospital refuses to perform an abortion on you without your husband's permission, you should see a lawyer immediately. Legal challenges to this practice will probably be successful.

Where can a woman locate a doctor, hospital, or clinic that performs sterilization procedures and/or abortions?

This can be a critical question since, as noted previously, one usually needs a physician to get into a hospital to have these procedures performed. Referral to competent physicians or clinics can often be obtained through the local office of Planned Parenthood or some similar organization. A listing of a number of sources of information on referrals, state laws, medical practices, and insurance coverages for abortion and sterilization is contained in Note 25.

An excellent periodical on the current status of the law in this area, *Family Planning / Population Reporter,* is published by the Planned Parenthood Federation of America, Inc., and is available from the Center for Family Planning Program Development, 1666 K Street, N.W., Suite 903, Washington, D.C. 20006.

What are a woman's rights concerning childbirth in a hospital?

While more than 98 percent of all births in the United States take place in a hospital, a woman might want to have her child at home. While most obstetricians will concede that 85 to 95 percent of all births are normal and uncomplicated enough not to require any obstetrical intervention, the medical profession strongly discourages people from having their children at home. Few doctors will deliver children at home, and the competency, training, and legal status of independent midwives is spotty.[26] Some women have also reported having trouble getting prenatal care if they tell their doctor that they intend to have their child at home. Without taking sides on the merits of home delivery, one can observe that with decreasing birth rates, the medical profession, and especially obstetricians, have a strong financial and professional interest in maintaining hospital-based deliveries as the societal norm.

Inside the hospital, the woman in labor has all the rights of any other hospital patient. As such she cannot be given any specific types of treatment without her consent and has the right to refuse specifically recommended procedures.[27] She has, for example, the right to refuse any and all drugs before and during delivery or to fully participate in deciding which drugs will be used on her, at what time, and in what doses.[28]

No one not directly concerned with the medical care and treatment of the mother may be present in the delivery room without the consent of the mother.[29] The harder question concerns her ability to have someone not on the hospital staff with her during the delivery. This problem is discussed in the following section.

In general, in dealing with hospitals on issues concerning birth, political pressure in the form of community organization aimed directly at the hospital administration on specific issues is likely to be most effective in producing long-term changes. Dr. Kenneth Ryan of the Boston Hospital for Women, the site of more than 6,000 deliveries annually, has asserted that his hospital is "receptive to any change that makes sense. I think that all of us subscribe to the idea of patients' rights and any responsible physician will only be delighted by a well-informed patient."[30] Consumer-patients who desire changes in the way hospitals handle certain conditions must take people like Dr. Ryan up on this and similar assertions by presenting cogent cases for change. In this way what are currently political rights can be transformed into legal rights by being written into hospital policy.[31] The importance of this type of pressure is well illustrated by Dr. Ryan's hospital. Historically, it has usually been the last hospital in the Boston area to change its methods and the most ardent proponent of the use of specialists during childbirth. If consumers are not able to make the community aware of what actually happens in this and other large, specialty-oriented teaching hospitals, the possibility of consumer-influenced change is minimal. Consumers should also have positions on all hospital policy-making boards and committees.

Does a woman have a right to have the father of the child present during the delivery if she so desires?

Thirteen years ago a young man in California handcuffed himself to his wife in order to witness the birth of their child.[32] Since then much has changed, and many, perhaps most, hospitals now admit husbands into the labor and delivery rooms. Once a hospital adopts a policy of permitting this practice, it may not arbitrarily deny access to a particular husband or father on an unconstitutional basis such as race, religion, or national origin. In terms of the woman's psychological needs, it is probably even more important for her to have someone with her during labor and delivery if she is unmarried (e.g., child's father, her brother or sister, her mother, etc.). The choice of who this person is should, of course, be the woman's.

Only one case has reached a state supreme court on this subject, and that was in Montana. In that case the court decided that a Catholic hospital could reasonably deny fathers access to labor and delivery rooms on the grounds that this practice might increase the possibility of infection, increase the number of malpractice suits, disturb doctors in the doctors' locker room, increase costs, make nurses in the delivery room nervous, invade the privacy of other women in the delivery rooms, and create harmony problems among a staff of physicians who did not all ascribe to the natural childbirth method.[33] In my view the court in this case took a far too narrow view of its role, gave the hospital far too much discretion, and did not adequately deal with the rights of the physician, the woman, or her husband. The case can be attacked on these and other grounds and should not be taken as the final word on this subject. At present, however, having the father in the delivery room is a "political" right that will most probably become a legal right only through community pressure on individual institutions to adopt desired practices.

How can a woman determine if a recommended hysterectomy is really necessary?

This question can be asked about many surgical procedures. It is especially appropriate for this particular one, nonetheless, because it is, after appendectomies, the most common operation performed on women in the United

States. Compared with England and Wales, more than twice as many hysterectomies per 100,000 women are performed in this country.[34] An argument can be made that many of these operations are performed not because of medical necessity but because of our overabundance of surgeons and hospital beds. It has been said that doctors will think twice about orchiectomy (removal of a testicle) but rarely hesitate to remove an ovary.[35] Some doctors call unnecessary operations "hip-pocket hysterectomies," because the only beneficiary is often the doctor's pocketbook.[36]

Whatever one's view of the general desirability of routinely having one's uterus removed, the fact remains that a lot of unnecessary surgery is performed in the United States, probably as many as 2 million unnecessary procedures a year of all kinds. A 1953 study revealed that over half of the hysterectomies performed in Los Angeles were unnecessary and a 1974 New York-based study put the figure at between 25 and 34%.[37] While there is no absolutely certain way to avoid having unnecessary surgery performed on oneself, one good protection is to *insist on another opinion* from a board-certified surgeon or internist not associated with the doctor recommending surgery.[38] Much unnecessary surgery can be directly attributed not to doctors but to patients who are overeager to be operated on. As former Pennsylvania Insurance Commissioner Herbert S. Denenberg warns in his *Shopper's Guide to Surgery*, "Don't be so eager for surgery that you prescribe your own unnecessary operation."[39]

Does a woman have a right to be informed about the medical alternatives available for the treatment of breast cancer before a biopsy is performed?

As dealt with at length in Chapter VI, Informed Consent to Treatment, a frank and full discussion of the alternatives available and their risks and probabilities of success is a legal prerequisite to obtaining the informed consent of the patient. Since the medical literature, some of which is cited in Note 40, indicates that there are a number of alternatives that range from no surgery to radical surgery with radiation, women have a legal right to be informed about these before being asked to consent to treatment.

Since the procedure undergone by Mrs. Betty Ford, however, women will probably have a difficult time arguing
that they had no information about alternative procedures.
That a woman's physician believes one or the other of
these treatments is clearly superior in terms of results does
not relieve him of his duty of information.[41]

One leading surgeon has argued that the only thing all
surgeons agree on in the controversial area of breast
cancer is that "there is no proof that any of the treatments, varying from local excision with or without irradia-
tion to ultraradical mastectomy with or without irradia-
tion, result in a higher rate of survival than any of the
others."[42] He has gone on to argue that if survival is a
woman's most important consideration, she should not be
misled into believing that her odds are considerably better
if she accepts the deformity and dysfunction associated
with a radical operation.[43] Other doctors strongly disagree,
and none have apparently been able to duplicate his results. The purpose here is not to take sides in a medical
dispute but merely to point out that women should have
access to this type of medical information when they are
asked to make surgery decisions.

While most of the initial discussion probably occurs in
the doctor's private office, the hospital is the place where
the biopsy and the surgery are performed. Apparently
many doctors still require women to sign a consent to a
radical mastectomy as a prerequisite to a biopsy.[44] The biopsy is then done under general anesthesia, the woman in
this case wakes up to learn either that she does not have
cancer or that a breast and some muscles are missing.
Some have argued that this prodecure was devised primarily for the benefit of the physician. The argument runs as
follows. First, general anesthesia is dangerous. Second,
over 90 percent of all cysts prove to be benign and require
no additional surgery; thus, the general anesthesia risk was
medically unnecessary for the vast majority.[45] Third, even
those women who do require some further treatment
should have the opportunity to think about and discuss
their options with the knowledge that they *do* have cancer
rather than in the context of hoping (and believing?) that
they do not. There is also no proof that delaying surgery
for a day or two affects the patient's survival probabili-

ties.[46] Counterarguments are that this type of biopsy may
be inadequate to locate a malignancy, that if general anesthesia is used at biopsy, it is not worth risking a second
general anesthesia so soon if surgery is indicated.

The legal answer is that no patient can be compelled to
either sign a consent form for surgery prior to knowing
what the diagnosis is or to have a biopsy done under general anesthesia against her will. The problem, however, is
one of available alternatives within the community. Some
things that can be done to locate surgeons who will ac-
commodate patients' desires are to contact all the chiefs of
surgery in the hospitals in the area, local and state medical
societies, local women's organizations, local medical
schools, and your state department of public health. If
doctors are not responsive to patients in this important
area, a series of malpractice suits alleging failure to obtain
informed consent may be the patient's only resort.

NOTES

1. Susan Shalhoub of Boston University School of Law and
   Donna McFadden of Tufts Medical School.
2. See generally, on the history of women in medicine,
   Ehrenreich & English, WITCHES, MIDWIVES AND
   NURSES: A HISTORY OF WOMEN HEALERS,
   The Feminist Press, New York, 1973; and Ehrenreich &
   English COMPLAINTS AND DISORDERS: THE SEX-
   UAL POLITICS OF SICKNESS, the Feminist Press,
   New York, 1973. Both are available from The Feminist
   Press, Box 334, Old Westbury, New York 11568. Sim-
   ilar views are expressed in Barbara Seaman, FREE AND
   FEMALE, Fawcett Greenwich, Conn., 1973; and Ellen
   Frankfort, VAGINAL POLITICS, Quadrangle Books,
   New York, 1972.
3. COMPLAINTS AND DISORDERS, supra. note 1 at 80
   and see Willson, Beecham & Carrington. OBSTETRICS &
   GYNECOLOGY, (4th ed.), Mosby, St. Louis, 1971 at
   43-45.
4. Boston Globe, August 20, 1973. At least 100,000 more
   women than men seek psychiatric treatment. This trend
   has caused a number of organizations to be set up whose
   sole function is to refer women to feminine therapists.
   Examples in New York City include: The Women's
   Psychotherapy Referral Service, Inc., 29 Fifth Ave. (964-

0400); The Consultation Center for Women, 145 Fourth Avenue (343-5858); The Feminist Therapy Referral Collective (787-4600), and The New York Association of Feminist Therapists (228-2278). *New York Times,* March 5, 1974 at 24.

5. *COMPLAINTS AND DISORDERS, supra.* note 1 at 88–89.

6. The most complete book on the general subject of women and their health-care system is the Boston Women's Book Collective, OUR BODIES, OURSELVES, Simon & Schuster, New York, 1971. On the legal rights of women in general see another book in this series, Susan Ross, THE RIGHTS OF WOMEN, Avon, New York, 1973.

7. See Chapter VI, Informed Consent to Treatment. *Murray v. Vandevander,* 522 P. 2d 302 (Okla. App. 1974).

8. *Kritzer v. Citron,* 101 Cal. App. 33, 224 P. 2d 808 (1950); *Rosenberg v. Feigin,* 119 Cal. App. 2d 783, 260 P. 2d 143 (1953); *Burroughs v. Crichton,* 48 App. D.C. 596, 4 ALR 1529 (1919) (breast surgery); *State v. Housekeeper,* 16 A. 382 (Md., 1889); *Rytkonen v. Lojacono,* 257 N.W. 703 (Mich., 1934).

9. Nor will the husband's lack of consent relieve him from any liability he may have for paying the wife's hospital or doctor's bills. *McClalle v. Adams,* 36 Mass. 333 (1837). Cf. *Karp v. Cooley,* 349 F. Supp. 827, 835 (S.D., Texas, 1972).

10. See Chapter VII, Refusing Treatment.

11. See Chapter III, Rules the Hospital Must Follow.

12. *Inderbitzen v. Lane Hospital,* 124 Cal. App. 462, 12 P. 2d 744 (1932).

13. *Roe v. Wade,* 93 Sup. Ct. 705 (1973), and *Doe v. Bolton,* 93 Sup. Ct. 739 (1973).

14. *Id.* at 727.

15. See L. Tribe, *Toward a Model of Roles in the Due Process of Life and Law,* 87 HARV. L. REV. 1, 37 (1973). In Professor Tribe's words:

> Any notion that the doctor ... is in a better position than the woman ... to make the final choice with respect to whether the family should have and raise a child, amounts to nothing more than a denial of the underlying First Amendment premise that groups should ordinarily have the role of making their own ultimate associational choices, informed and perhaps influenced, but not forced, by others.

16. Professor Tribe suggests, for example, that *Boddie v. Connecticut*, 401 U.S. 371 (1971) (government cannot withhold from those too poor to afford the filing fees for a divorce the means to dissolve a marital relationship) might provide the proper analogy to withholding abortion based on ability to pay. *Id.* at 46-50. *See also Klein v. Nassau Co. Medical Center*, 347 F. Supp. 496 (E.D.N.Y., 1972) (state policy of withholding Medicaid assistance for nontherapeutic abortions on the grounds that elective termination of pregnancy is not "necessary medically indicated care" held to be unconstitutional).

17. Defining just what constitutes "sufficient" governmental involvement has proved rather difficult. Some courts have held that the receipt of federal Hill-Burton construction funds is sufficient, *e.g., Simkins v. Moses H. Cone Memorial Hospital*, 323 F. 2d 959 (4th Cir., 1963), *cert. denied*, 376 U.S. 938 (1964); *Sams v. Ohio Valley General Hospital*, 413 F. 2d 826 (4th Cir., 1969); *Citta v. Delaware Valley Hospital*, 313 F. Supp. 301 (E.D. Pa., 1970); while others have looked to the character and to use to which the funds were put by the hospital to decide. See *Stanturf v. Sipes*, 335 F. 2d 224 (8th Cir., 1964), *cert. denied*, 379 U.S. 977 (1965); *Doe v. Bellin*, 479 F. 2d 756 (7th Cir., 1973) (involving the specific question of abortion). The U.S. Congress also specifically indicated in The Health Programs Extensions Act of 1973 (P.L. 93-45, June 18, 1973), 42 U.S.C. §300 a-7, that receipt of federal funds under various programs, including Hill-Burton, *did not* authorize involvement of the government, through the courts, in the sterilization or abortion policies of *private* hospitals. See *Taylor v. St. Vincent's Hospital*, Civil No. 1090, Oct. 26, 1973 (D. Montana). On Medicaid, *Klein v. Nassau Co., supra.*, note 16.

18. *Nyberg v. City of Virginia*, 361 F. Supp. 932, 938-939. (D. Minn., 1973).

19. See generally, Gutman, *Can Hospitals Constitutionally Refuse to Permit Abortions and Sterilizations?* 2 FAMILY PLANNING/POPULATION REPORTER 146 (Dec., 1973). Many states have also passed statutes allowing private hospitals to have a policy of not doing abortions.

20. *Hathaway v. Worcester City Hospital*, 475 F. 2d 701 (1st Cir. 1973).

22. As of Jan. 1974 these included Colorado, Florida, Idaho,

Nevada, Oregon, South Carolina, Utah, Virginia, and
Washington.

23. See *supra.* note 13 at 733, n. 67. And see Gilbert, *Abortion: The Father's Rights*, 42 U. CINN. L. REV. 441
(1973).

24. *Doe v. Doe*, 314 N.E.2d 128 (Mass. 1974).

25. M. Edbon, EVERYWOMAN'S GUIDE TO ABORTION, Pocket Books, New York, 1971; Abortions in
New York, What You Need to Know, *New York Magazine*, July, 1972 (Reprints from Dept. H., *New York
Magazine*, 207 E. 32nd St., New York, N.Y. 10016,
$1.25); Family Planning Information Service, 300 Park
Avenue, So., New York, N.Y. 10010 (212-677-3040).
This service is operated by Planned Parenthood of New
York City. For other areas of the country contact the
National Clergy Consultation Service (NCCS), 55 Washington Square South, New York, N.Y. 10012 (212-477-
0034) or your local NCCS chapter.

   The following publications are available from the Center for Family Planning Program Development, 515 Madison Avenue, New York, N.Y. 10022 (order by number and
enclose check or money order for proper amount made
payable to Planned Parenthood Federation of America,
Inc.): Muller, *Health Insurance for Abortion Costs*, No.
C1173 (50¢) (nationwide survey of all major health insurance plans and their coverage of abortion costs);
Weinberg, *State Administration and Financing of Family
Planning Services*, No. C1292 (35¢) (analyzes financing
and staffing of family planning programs in each of the
states); Fisher & Rosoff, *How States Are Using Title IV-
A to Finance Family Planning Services*, No. C1333
(35¢) (analysis of the use of Title IV-A monies by ten
family planning programs).

26. See Stern, *Midwives, Male-Midwives and Nurse-Midwives*, 39 OBSTET. & GYN. 308 (1972); Levy et al, *Reducing Neonatal Mortality Rate with Nurse Midwives*,
109 AM. J. OBSTET. GYN. 50 (1971).

27. See Chapter VII, Refusing Treatment.

28. For a discussion of the types of drugs used see OUR
BODIES, OURSELVES, *supra.*, note 6 at 192-195.

29. See Chapter XI, Confidentiality and Privacy. *Cf. DeMay
v. Roberts*, 9 N.W. 146 (1881) (woman had a right to
privacy during childbirth, and no one had a right to intrude unless invited).

30. *Boston Globe*, Feb. 17, 1974 at B-1, B-9, col. 7.

31. See Ch. III, Rules the Hospital Must Follow.

32. *Supra.* note 30 at col. 3.

33. *Hulit v. St. Vincent's Hospital,* 520 P.2d 99 (Mont. 1974).

34. Bunker, *Surgical Manpower: A Comparison of Operations and Surgeons in the United States and in England and Wales,* 282 NEW ENG. J. MED. 135, 137 (1970). In a more recent study of physician's wives, Bunker found that they underwent more hysterectomies than the rest of the population and concluded: "It is apparent that physicians and their wives do place a high value on hysterectomy." Bunker & Brown, *The Physician-Patient as an Informed Consumer of Surgical Services,* 290 NEW ENG. J. MED. 1051, 1054 (1974).

35. Buruchian, *Every Tissue Committee Needs Women Physicians,* MED. ECONOMICS, Sept. 13, 1971 at 176.

36. E.g., Dr. Norman S. Miller of U. of Michigan quoted in *Free and Female,* supra., note 2 at 184.

37. Doyle, *Unnecessary Hysterectomies,* JAMA (Jan. 31, 1953); cited by McCleery et al, ONE LIFE—ONE PHYSICIAN, Public Affairs Press, Washington, D.C., 1971 at 14. McCarthy & Widmer, *Effects of Screening by Consultants on Recommended Elective Surgical Procedures,* 291 NEW ENG. J. MED. 1331-1335 (1974).

38. See generally Chapter VIII, Consultation, Referral, and Abandonment.

39. This Guide is available for $1.00 from Consumer Insurance, 813 National Press Building, Washington, D.C. Its full title is *Shopper's Guide to Surgery: Fourteen Rules on How to Avoid Unnecessary Surgery.*

40. *Proceedings, First National Conference on Breast Cancer,* 24 CANCER 1101 (1969) (contains 56 short articles on various aspects of the disease; *Surgical Treatment of Early Breast Cancer,* 15 THE MEDICAL LETTER 19 (Feb. 16, 1973); Fisher, *Breast Cancer,* 172 ANN. SURGERY 711 (1970); Crile, *Conservative Treatment of Advanced Breast Cancer,* 126 AM. J. SURGERY 343 (1973); Crile et al., *A New Look at Biopsy of the Breast,* AM J. SURGERY 117 (1973); Crile, *Treatment of Cancer of the Breast: Past, Present and Future,* 38 CLEV. CLINIC Q. 47 (1971); Crile, et al, *Partial Mastectomy for Carcinoma of the Breast,* 136 SURGERY, GYN & OBSTET. 929 (1973) ("In a properly performed partial mastectomy, not only the tumor is removed but at least two centimeters and usually three centimeters or more of breast tissue around it are removed" at 930); Taylor et al, *Sector Mastectomy in Se-*

lected Cases of Breast Cancer, 58 BRIT. J. SURGERY 161 (1971).

41. See Chapter VI, Informed Consent to Treatment.

42. Crile, *Breast Cancer and Informed Consent*, 39 CLEV. CLINIC. Q. 58 (1972).

43. *Id.*

44. See, e.g., *Boston Globe*, Feb. 26, 1974 at 17 col. 4.

45. See *Proceedings, supra.* note 40.

46. Gray, *Role of the Physician in Diagnosis of Breast Cancer, Proceedings, supra* note 40 at 1183, 1184. A typical doctor will argue against this position as follows:

> The temptation to accede to the patient's convenience or concern by agreeing to perform the biopsy in the hospital on an in-and-out basis, or even worse, as an office procedure, should be dismissed. The patient should be admitted as a routine surgical case, with routine preoperative studies, and prepared for a general anesthesia. Coffey, *Biopsy—Indications and Technique, Proceedings, supra.* note 40 at 1280, 1281.

XIV
The Terminally Ill

When a patient is categorized as terminal, he is often simultaneously deprived of both his right to know the truth
and his right to privacy, as well as his right to consent to
treatment and to exercise discretion in choosing a place
and time to die. Between 70 and 80 percent of all Americans now die in hospitals or nursing homes, making the
problems of the terminally ill in these institutions extremely important. Doctors frequently define the terminally ill patient as "one I can't do anything for," and often
use this as a justification for depriving the patient of what
the doctor would otherwise consider basic human rights.
This chapter will examine the unique problems of a patient who has been categorized as terminally ill. Questions
concerning refusing treatment and the "living will" are
dealt with in Chapter VII, and issues concerning organ
donation and autopsy are dealt with in chapter XV.

**Does the terminally ill patient have a right to know his
diagnosis?**
In this respect there is no legal justification for treating
the terminally ill patient differently than any other patient.
The first thing a physician usually tells a non-terminal patient is his diagnosis. This, however, is the last thing a
physician usually tells a terminal patient. While the limited
studies done on this subject can by no means be considered invulnerable, they indicate that about 90 percent of
all patients desire to know their diagnosis even if terminal,[1] whereas between 60 and 90 percent of all physicians
prefer to withhold a diagnosis of a terminal illness.[2] There
is also an indication in the literature that when patients

are told of a terminal disease diagnosis, they often express relief that the subject is out in the open.[3] That a patient may have a will to write or property to get in order before his death are only two reasons patients should be told the truth about their condition in all but the rarest of cases.

While some physicians rationalize their preference for withholding a terminal diagnosis on the basis that such a decision can only be made by considering "individual circumstances," such a stance is usually translated into a policy of almost never telling, especially if the patient has a family onto which the physician can unburden his knowledge.[4] A second rationale often advanced is that "the patient knows anyway."[5] If this is true, not telling him only forces both him and those around him to live the lie, increasing the patient's conflict and anxiety.

A final argument is that the patient should not be forced to abandon hope.[6] While hope may be essential, it is not true that the only rational hope a person may harbor is that he will live forever. A cancer patient may begin by hoping he does not have cancer, then hope it will not be too painful, then hope he will live to see his daughter graduate, etc.[7] Telling a patient he is dying is, therefore, not the same thing as denying him all hope. To help the patient accept the diagnosis, the physician must, however, continue to attend the patient, talk with him openly about his condition, and assure him that all that is medically possible will be done to keep him comfortable. These requirements have led many physicians to conclude that they do not have time for such "treatment," and therefore either the chaplain should talk with the patient about death, or no one should. This is as unique in medical practice as it is unjustified. In no other instance would the physician share such confidential information with a third party. Giving the task of transmitting prognostic information to the chaplain is the symbolic way a physician "hands over" his patient, saying in effect, "There is no longer anything I can do for this patient."

While right implies duty, it also implies option. In the case of a patient who clearly expresses a desire not to be told his diagnosis, it would seem proper for his physician to inquire as to who should be told, and tell that person instead.

Does the terminally ill patient have a right to demand that no one in his family be told of his diagnosis?

While physicians generally do not like to tell dying patients about their condition, most do feel compelled to tell someone, and usually the family is informed.[8] When this is done, the patient is deprived not only of his right to know the truth but also of his rights of confidentiality and privacy.[9] It would seem to follow, therefore, that a patient has the right to both make such a demand and expect his physician to respect it. A civil damage suit for breach of confidentiality would probably be the main legal action a patient could take against a doctor who refused to respect such a demand.[10]

One possible explanation for physicians telling families instead of patients is that once the patient is labeled terminal, the physician ceases to treat the individual alone and begins to treat the family unit as his patient. Cynics would say that this is perfectly natural since it is now the family to whom he will have to look for payment of his bills, and it is the family members who will spread his reputation and be his future sources of income. Whatever the motive, the physician's reluctance to candidly discuss his diagnosis with his patient makes his concentration on the family almost inevitable. The tragedy is that it has the result of isolating the patient both from the truth and from his family. Both patient and family try to pretend all is well, while each knows better. Visits are uncomfortable for family members, who try to talk of trivialities like the weather or football, and almost unbearable for the patient whose impending death is transformed into a mockery.

Can a terminally ill patient give informed consent to treatment if he doesn't know that his doctor considers his condition terminal?

The answer to this question is implicit in it. If the patient lacks this vital piece of information, his main motive to consenting to any medical procedure, the belief that it will help him regain his health, is based on misinformation. Any consent given without the knowledge of one's terminal diagnosis can be considered consent given upon false and misleading information, therefore no consent at all.[11]

Rationales for treating without telling vary from, "If I don't do something, he'll turn to quacks," to, "He's going to die soon, anyway, so he won't be able to sue me," to, "I will perform this experimental treatment for the good of society and the advancement of medicine even though I know it will not help him." Such lines of reasoning are easily predictable. When the physician determines, "I have done all I can for you," his perception may change to: "Now, what can you do for me?" The patient loses all his rights as a person in this instance. He becomes little more than a passive object to be used as a "sample" in a medical experiment. Worse than being told nothing, he may be told that a proposed experimental treatment will help him.[12]

Do terminally ill patients have a right to know a hospital's cardiac resuscitation policy?

Most hospitals have a cardiac code or procedure for dealing with cardiac arrest. It would seem that at a minimum the patient should be informed as to what the procedure is and be given the option of directing his doctor to write "no code" (meaning, do not resuscitate this patient in case of a heart attack) on his chart and order card.[18] Such a procedure has at least two major points to recommend it. It fulfills the patient's right to consent to treatment and eliminates the covertly penciled "no code" notations that are erased after the patient has died, a procedure that only intensifies public distrust of the medical profession. In one Boston area hospital the practice is to place a silver dot on the patient's chart to indicate that the staff should not resuscitate. Such a policy is completely inexcusable since any person with access to the record could place a dot on it for any reason. The only acceptable procedure is for the person making such an order to first discuss it with the patient, if possible, or the patient's family, if communication with the patient is not possible, obtain consent, and write the order and the reason for it in the record, and *sign* the order.

Does the patient have a right to die at home?

Since the patient initiates the admission to the hospital and, while competent, retains the ability to sign out of the hospital, even against medical advice, the theoretical answer is yes. However, as a practical matter, society has made it extremely difficult to die at home.

Although most would prefer to, few Americans in fact die at home.[15] To do so requires not only the strong resolve of the dying patient but also the cooperation of his family or the person or persons with whom he or she is living. Cooperation of the medical profession is also important since without it pain-relieving drugs and other medications cannot be obtained.

Does the dying patient have a right to use narcotic drugs for pain relief?

The general answer is that while there is no legal right, as a matter of public policy, narcotic and psychedelic drugs should be made freely available to dying patients. Experience demonstrates that to be effective in pain relief, doses need not be so high as to distort reality.[16] Also, notions that these drugs should be denied terminally ill patients because they might become addicted or their chromosomes might be damaged are almost always ridiculous on their face. In places in which drugs have been used, much success has been reported, for example, by patients on LSD, who report learning to accept death as a natural event.[17] When he was dying of cancer, columnist Stewart Alsop wrote eloquently of the experience and suggested that the patients be allowed "to *decide for themselves* how much pain-killing drug they will take—it is, after all, they, not the doctors, who are suffering the agonies."[18] This "right" is another example of a political right that patients can only translate into a legal right or institutional policy by exerting political pressure.

How can a patient get his doctor to tell him about a terminal diagnosis?

It can probably be argued that no diagnosis is absolutely certain until death actually occurs. This is obviously too long to wait for a patient who wishes to prepare for

death in any way. It is also obvious, however, that a dead
person cannot sue for failure to disclose pertinent medical
information to him while he was alive. The administrator
of his estate is unlikely to bring such a suit unless it could
be demonstrated that had the person known about his impending death, he would have made certain financial arrangements that would have saved his estate money.

All this means that the threat of a lawsuit is not going
to be very persuasive, especially if the doctor has informed the family, since the family is probably estopped
from suing the doctor for withholding a diagnosis that
they knew and also withheld. If the surveys are right and
patients really do desire to know their terminal diagnoses,
they must insist that their doctor give them this information and obtain and read all of their medical records if
their doctor is not open with them.[19] As some legal commentators have argued persuasively, "the law should concentrate on developing a duty to inform patients carefully
of material information, even if it is distressing. Requiring
tactful disclosure would provide the patient with the information necessary to make an informed decision while
avoiding excessive discomfort in the patient."[20]

NOTES

Being Told Their Diagnosis, 1 BRIT. MED. J. 783
(1959); Branch, *Psychiatric Aspects of Malignant Disease*, 6 BULL. CANCER PROG. 102 (1950); Kelly &

1. Aitken-Swan & Eassen, *Reactions of Cancer Patients on
Friesen, Do Cancer Patients Want to be Told?*, 27 SUR-
GERY 825 (1950); Samp & Currieri, *Questionnaire Sur-
vey on Public Cancer Education Obtained from Cancer
Patients and Their Families*, 10 CANCER 382 (1957).

2. Fitts & Ravdin, *What Philadelphia Physicians Tell Patients with Cancer*, 153 JAMA 901 (1953); Oken, *What
to Tell Cancer Patients*, 175 JAMA 86 (1961); Rennick,
What Should Physicians Tell Cancer Patients?, 2 NEW
MED. MATERIA 51 (1960).

3. E. Kubler-Ross, ON DEATH AND DYING, MacMillan,
New York, 1969; and *infra*, note 7.

4. Martin, *The Role of the Surgeon in the Prospect of
Death from Cancer*, 164 ANN. N.Y. ACAD. SCI. 739
(1969); Ginsberg, *Should the Elderly Cancer Patient Be
Told?*, 4 GERIATRICS 106 (1949); Piatt, *Physician and
the Cancer Patient*, 42 OHIO ST. MED. J. 801 (1947).

 5. Meyer, *Comment*, 164 ANN N.Y. ACAD. SCI. 742
    (1969).
 6. See Oken, *supra.*, note 2 and Kubler-Ross, *supra*, note 3.
 7. Conversation with Dr. Ned Cassem, December 10, 1971.
    And see Cassem, *What You Can Do For Dying Patients*,
    MED. DIMENSIONS, Oct. 1973 at 29.
 8. See notes 1 and 2 *supra.*
 9. See generally Chapter XI, Privacy and Confidentiality.
10. *Id.*
11. See generally Chapter VI, Informed Consent to Treat-
    ment.
12. Sudnow, *Dying in a Public Hospital*, in O.G. BRIM,
    THE DYING PATIENT, Russell Sage Foundation, New
    York, 1970; and Jonas, *Philosophical Reflections on Ex-
    perimenting with Human Subjects*. 98 DAEDALUS: *Eth-
    ical Aspects of Experimentation with Human Subjects*,
    219 (1969); and *see generally* Chapter IX, Experimenta-
    tion.
13. Symmers, *Now Allowed to Die*, 1 BRIT. MED. J. 442
    (1968).
14. See Chapter VII, Refusing Treatment.
15. Fulton & Geis, DEATH AND IDENTITY, Wiley, New
    York, 1965 at 2.
16. Saunder, *A Death in the Family: A professional View*, 2
    BRIT. MED. J. 30 (1973). Dr. Saunder is director of St.
    Christopher's Hospice near London, England. There the
    family and the dying patient are drawn closer together.
    Death is openly discussed, heroin is freely used, no he-
    roic resuscitations are undertaken, and no respirators or
    other life-lengthening technologies are available.
17. Avorn, Beyond Dying: Experiments Using Psychedelic
    Drugs to Ease the Transition from Life, *Harper's*,
    March 1973 at 56. In the U.S., however, LSD is a Sched-
    ule I drug under the Comprehensive Drug Abuse and
    Control Act of 1970 and so is not available for use in
    treatment programs and can be used in clinical research
    only with FDA approval. It is suggested that an excep-
    tion to this law should be made for the terminally ill in
    light of the evidence that its use can be beneficial. And
    see E. Kast, *LSD and the Dying Patient*, 26 CHICAGO
    MED. SCH. Q. 80 (1966).
18. Alsop, The Right to Die with Dignity, *Good Housekeep-
    ing*, Aug., 1974, 69, 130.

19. On obtaining medical records see Chapter X, Hospital Records.

20. Note, *Informed Consent and the Dying Patient*, 83 YALE L.J. 1632, 1655 (1974). Courts have given physicians much latitude in deciding what to disclose and not disclose to a terminally ill patient. In one particularly strange case, for example, the court found that a doctor was justified because of his "therapeutic privilege" in not disclosing a terminal diagnosis to a patient because it might unduly upset him, and further that because the patient was competent, no disclosure of his condition had to be made to his family! *Nishi v. Hartwell*, 473 P. 2d 116 (Ha. 1970) A better rule would seem to be to require disclosure to the family in those rare cases where disclosure to the competent patient is found to be psychiatrically contraindicated.

XV
Organ Donation and Autopsy

Because many of the problems involved are analogous, a new procedure, organ donation, and an old procedure, autopsy, are discussed together in this chapter. Autopsies and the use of cadavers for the advancement of medical knowledge and education are at least 200 years old. Because of the shortage of cadavers in the early nineteenth century doctors purchased cadavers from grave robbers or "resurrectionists." As a reaction to such practices, laws were passed. Some made grave robbing a crime. Others provided for the use of unclaimed bodies for medical education. With the rise of the technological ability to transplant organs like the kidney and heart and tissues like the cornea, there was a need to develop procedures that both made such organs available and protected the rights of the donor and his family. One answer has come in the form of the Uniform Anatomical Gift Act, which has been enacted in one form or another in all 50 states during the past 6 years. Many of the questions posed in this chapter can be answered by reference to the Anatomical Gift Act of the state in which the patient is located.

How can an individual donate organs to others so that they may have them upon the individual's death?

Under the Uniform Anatomical Gift Act, any person 18 years or older and of sound mind may make a gift of all or any part of his body to the following persons for the following purposes[1]:

   (1) any hospital, surgeon, or physician, for medical or dental education, research, advancement of

    medical or dental science, therapy or transplan-
    tation; or

(2) any accredited medical or dental school, college
    or university for education, research, advance-
    ment of medical or dental science or therapy; or

(3) any bank or storage facility, for medical or
    dental education, research, advancement of medi-
    cal or dental science, therapy or transplantation;
    or

(4) any specified individual for therapy or trans-
    plantation needed by him.

The gift can be made by a provision in a will (the donation provisions take effect immediately upon death without the necessity of probate) or by signing a card like the
following in the presence of two witnesses;

UNIFORM DONOR CARD

OF_____
                        Print or type name of donor
In the hope that I may help others, I hereby make this
anatomical gift, if medically acceptable, to take effect upon
my death. The words and marks below indicate my desires.
I give:

      (a)_____any needed organs or parts
      (b)_____only the following organs or parts

_____
             Specify the organ(s) or part(s)
for the purposes of transplantation, therapy, medical
research or education;
      (c)_____my body for anatomical study if needed.
Limitations or
special wishes, if any:_____

This card is usually carried by the person signing it at all
times.[2] In most states the gift can be revoked either by
destroying the card or an oral revocation in the presence
of two witnesses.

**Can an individual place conditions on the organ do-
nation?**
Yes. As the above form indicates, you can specify

which organs are to be donated and the person or institution to whom they are to be donated. You may also specify how your body is to be buried following its medical use. The donee may accept or reject the gift. If accepted, and if only part of the body is donated, that part must be removed without unnecessary mutilation and the remainder of the body turned over to the surviving spouse or other person responsible for burial.[3] The next of kin may also consent to organ donation following death.

Can a relative override a person's wishes about donation of one's body or organs after a person dies?

Not if the person has followed the provisions of the Uniform Anatomical Gift Act of the state of which he is a resident. The gift legally takes effect immediately upon death and is binding on the relatives. Few hospitals will, however follow the deceased's wishes over strong objections from the family.

Why are autopsies performed?

An autopsy is a comprehensive study of a dead body performed by a trained physician employing recognized dissection procedures and techniques. The most common purpose of autopsies is to determine the cause of death, but they also serve valuable educational functions.[4] Usually only the thoracic, abdominal and cranial cavities are opened during an autopsy and neither the face nor the hands are cut or in any way disfigured.

Why would a hospital want to perform an autopsy on a deceased patient?

Teaching hospitals view the percentage of autopsies performed as a measure of the adequacy of their teaching program. Autopsies can confirm the suspected cause of death, help train doctors, and be useful in research projects. To be approved for internships and residencies by the AMA's Council on Medical Education, a hospital must provide proper facilities for post-mortem examinations and maintain a high percentage of autopsies. "A hospital which does not maintain an autopsy rate of at least 25% of its deaths, exclusive of still births and cases related to legal authorities, may not be approved."[5]

What is a legal or official autopsy?

This is a type of autopsy performed to determine the cause of a person's death when foul play may have contributed to it. The circircumstances under which such autopsies are performed are set out in the medical examiner or coroner statute of the state. If the state official who is responsible for performing such autopsies deems one necessary (e.g., suspected homicide, suicide, violent death or accidental death, etc.) no permission of the family is necessary nor can the family prevent the autopsy from being performed.

An official autopsy may also be called for if the patient dies in the hospital before a diagnosis can be established. As one judge put it, "If a hospital leaves uncertain or indifferently explained how a patient entrusted to its care dies, it is manifestly the duty of the medical examiner in the public interest to find out if he can."[6]

Perhaps the most famous case of such an official autopsy occurred following the assassination of President John F. Kennedy. The autopsy was performed under exceptionally poor conditions, with incomplete knowledge of prior medical treatment, and some of the original records were destroyed. Much of the continuing controversy over the possibility of a conspiracy in the assassination stems directly from the autopsy findings.[7]

Who is responsible for paying for an autopsy?

If a hospital doctor requests the autopsy from the family, the cost of the autopsy is almost universally absorbed by the hospital and does not appear as a separate item on the patient's bill.

Why might a family want an autopsy performed?

If the cause of death is potentially genetic and treatable, or infectious, exact determination may help other family members. Also, if the cause of death may have been related to medical malpractice, autopsy findings may help to prove this. The deceased or his family may also wish to make a contribution to medical education or research.

What methods are used to obtain consent for autopsies?

The doctor who signs the death certificate usually requests the autopsy consent. While most doctors are probably straightforward in requesting autopsies, there are numerous indications in the medical literature that young interns and residents have tremendous pressure placed on them to obtain a certain high percentage of consents.

One method is to suggest "without explicit statement to that effect, that on occasion there has been delay or difficulty in the obtaining of insurance payments in the absence of specific post-mortem diagnosis." More common is to "wherever possible stress the familial tendencies of the disease . . . or the possibility of contagion."[8] While a relative's signature can often be obtained using these methods, if the inducement used was false, the consent was fraudulently obtained, and the relative may later sue the doctor and the hospital for performing an autopsy without consent.

Who has the legal authority to consent to an autopsy?

Under the statutes of most states the next of kin (the surviving spouse, if there is one, then other survivors in order of family relationship) has the right to consent to the autopsy. While it has been said by courts on numerous occasions that there can be no property interest in a dead body, the next of kin does have an interest in seeing to it that the deceased is properly buried.[9] This interest is strong enough to give the next of kin the right to possession of the body in the same condition it was in at death.[10] Only an official autopsy by a state official can override this interest, and even in this case the state official must be acting in good faith or the autopsy is illegal.[11]

A hospital can be held liable in a civil law suit for refusing to deliver a body and instead inducing a coroner to perform an autopsy.[12] It can also be held liable, of course, for performing an autopsy without permission.[13] In one case the hospital was held liable for payment of damages for mental suffering in the sum of $1,500 when an autopsy was performed without consent even though the widow did not detect the autopsy at the funeral and found out about it only when she read the death certificate 10 days later.[14] The consent form had been signed by the doctor and two nurses as witnesses before being presented to the widow. She refused to sign it, but it was placed in the record anyway, and the doctor who performed the autopsy thought that permission had been granted because of the signed form.

The general rule is that the extent of damages awarded for an unauthorized autopsy is not measured primarily by the extent of the mutilation of the body but by the effect of the procedure on the "feelings and emotions of the surviving relatives who have the duty of burial."[15]

Can a patient consent to have an autopsy performed on his body?

Laws in about half of the states specifically give the patient this right. Also, since under the provisions of the Uniform Anatomical Gift Act a person may give all or a limited part of his body for education, research, and the advancement of medical science, he may give his body to a hospital for the sole purpose of performing an autopsy. He can make this consent binding upon his survivors by executing an instrument under the provisions of the Uniform Anatomical Gift Act explained above. The probable reason doctors never ask living patients to consent in advance to autopsies is that most doctors refuse to inform patients that they are dying and thus could not very well discuss autopsy with them.[16] Moreover, few hospitals would perform the autopsy, even with this authorization, over strong family objection.

Can the hospital retain any portion of the body after autopsy?

The hospital cannot retain any tissues or organs without the permission of the person who consented to the autopsy.[17] Note, however, that standard forms for permission generally include permission to retain samples, and the general rule against retention does not cover limited small portions of organs taken for further study.[18] The person consenting to the autopsy, however, has the right to place whatever limitations on the consent he or she wishes.

A hospital is also liable if it misplaces an entire body. In a recent case in Florida a couple was awarded $150,000 in damages when a hospital lost the corpse of their premature baby. The mother testified, "I still have my doubts that Paul ever died."[19]

NOTES

1. For discussions of the Uniform Anatomical Gift Act see Sadler, Sadler & Stason, *The Uniform Anatomical Gift Act: A Model for Reform*, 206 JAMA 2501 (1968); Groll & Kerwin, *The Uniform Anatomical Gift Act: Is the Right to a Decent Burial Obsolete?*, 2 LOYOLA U.L.J. 275 (1971); Dukeminier, *Supplying Organs for Transplantation*, 68 MICH. L. REV. 811 (1970). For a discussion of the laws that the Uniform Anatomical Gift Act replaced or supplemented see Sadler & Sadler, *Transplantation and the Law: The Need for Organized Sensitivity*, 57 GEO. L. J. 5 (1968). On autopsies in general see J. Waltz & F. Inbau, MEDICAL JURISPRUDENCE, MacMillan, New York, 1971 at 203–27. The citations for the UAGAs of all 50 states appear in Note, *The Sale of Human Body Parts*, 72 MICH. L. REV. 1182, 1188–1190 (1974).

2. Copies of this form may be obtained from the National Kidney Foundation, 116 East 27th Street, New York, New York 10016.

3. These points are specifically set out in the statute. See citations in note 1, *supra.*

4. See Monger, *Functions and Limitations of an Autopsy*, 24 TENN. L. REV. 159 (1956); Gerber, *Postmortem Examinations*, 6 CLEV-MAR L. REV. 194 (1957).

5. AMA, Council on Medical Education, DIRECTORY OF APPROVED INTERNSHIPS AND RESIDENCIES: 1972-1973, AMA, Chicago, 1972 at 156. Many large teaching hospitals boast autopsy rates of 50 to 70 percent. Pediatric hospitals are often higher. *Id.*, at 61–2. The publication listed in this note gives the percentage rates for approximately 1100 large U.S. hospitals.

6. *Cremonese v. City of New York*, 267 N.Y.S. 2d 897 (Ct. App. N.Y., 1966).

7. For details concerning that autopsy, see Testimony of Comdr. James G. Hume, Comdr. J. Thornton Boswell, and Lt. Col. Pierre A. Finch before the Warren Commission, WARREN COMMISSION REPORT, Vol. VI, at 347–84; M. Lane, RUSH TO JUDGMENT, 1966, ch. 4, "The Magic Bullet"; S. White, SHOULD WE BELIEVE THE WARREN REPORT, 1968 at 40–48, 88–97; H. Wiesberg, WHITEWASH, 1965 at 178-187; J. Kirkwood, AMERICAN GROTESQUE, Simon & Schuster, New York, 1968, ch. 32, "FINCK"; and Wecht,

Pathologists' View of JFK Autopsy: An Unsolved Case, *Modern Med.*, Nov. 27, 1972 at 28.

8. Quotations are taken from a 1960 edition of the *Handbook for House Officers* of Boston City Hospital, Boston, Mass. (mimeograph); See also Joint Subcommittee, AUTOPSY MANUAL, United Hospital Fund of New York, N.Y., 1958 at 13–16, and see generally Jeffers, *The Best Way to Ask for an Autopsy*, MED. ECON., Dec., 1957 at 232.

9. See *Leno v. St. Joseph Hospital*, 302 N.E. 2d 58, 60 (Ill., 1973); Waltz, *Legal Liability for Unauthorized Autopsies and Related Procedures*, 16 J. FOR. SCI. 1 (1971); Note, *The Private Autopsy: Problems of Consent*, 41 DENVER L.J. 239 (1964); Comment, *Property Interest in a Dead Body*, 2 ARK L. REV. 124 (1947); Comment, *Property Rights in Dead Bodies*, 71 W. VA. L. REV. 377 (1969).

10. *Infield v. Cope*, 58 N.M. 308, 270 P. 2d 716 (1954).

11. *Gahn v. Leary*, 61 N.E. 2d 844 (Mass. 1945).

12. E.g., *Darcy v. Presbyterian Hospital*, 95 N.E. 695 (N.Y. 1911).

13. *Torres v. State*, 228 N.Y.S. 2d 1005 (Ct. Claims, N.Y. 1962); *Gould v. State*, 46 N.Y.S. 2d 313 (Ct. Claims, N.Y. 1944).

14. *French v. Ochsner Clinic*, 200 So. 2d 371 (La App. 1967).

15. *Id.*, and *Sworski v. Simons*, 208 Minn. 201, 293 N.W. 309 (1940).

16. See discussion in Chapter on The Terminally Ill.

17. *Hendrikson v. Roosevelt Hospital*, 297 F. Supp 1142 (D.C.N.Y. 1969); Holder, *Unauthorized Autopsies*, 214 J.A.M.A. 967 (1970).

18. *Lashbrook v. Barnes*, 437 S.W. 2d 502 (Ky. 1969).

19. Case reported in the *Boston Globe*, Nov. 28, 1973 at 2.

XVI
Payment
Of Hospital Bills

Health of mind and body is so fundamental to the
good life that if we believe that men have any personal rights as human beings, they have an absolute
. . . right to such a measure of good health that society and society alone is able to give them.

While this concept has led the United Nations to de-
clare health a basic "human right" and impelled every in-
dustrialized nation in the world except the U.S. to develop
a system of governmentally paid health services for all
their citizens, we have recognized the "right to health
care" in only a limited way in this country. This recognition has taken the form of reimbursement for rather than
provision of services.

The two major programs that reflect this recognition
are *Medicare* and *Medicaid*. This first is a *federal* program
designed mainly for those over 65 and the disabled. The
second is a cooperatively-funded, *state* program for the
needy. Discussion of the provisions of these two programs
make up the bulk of this chapter. A brief section on private health insurance is also included. It is to be hoped
that this entire chapter will soon be made obsolete by
some comprehensive system of national health insurance.

A few basic terms merit definition before beginning the
discussion:

deductible amount—the amount of medical bills the
patient must pay before the insurance program benefits
commence;

copayment—the dollar amount patient must contribute toward the bill;

coinsurance—the *percentage* (usually 20 percent) of the total bill the patient must pay;

premium—the periodic payment that must be made to continue to be covered by a program.

MEDICARE

What is Medicare?

Medicare is the name of the federal program of health insurance for the aged and disabled.[1] It was enacted in 1965 and now provides coverage for approximately 23 million Americans. The program is divided into *hospital insurance*[2] (referred to as Part A) and *medical insurance*[3] (referred to as Part B). The program is administered by the Social Security Administration (SSA), which is a part of HEW.

Who is eligible to participate in the Medicare program?

Part A (hospital insurance) and Part B (medical insurance) are distinct programs, and each involves a separate set of requirements for eligibility.

There are *five basic categories* under which a person can be eligible *for Part A*, hospital insurance. Those 65 or older and eligible for monthly social security benefits,[4] those 65 or older not eligible but who have the minimum number of quarters worked for coverage,[5] those 65 or older not otherwise eligible for Part A but who are covered by Part B,[6] those entitled to social security benefits because of disability,[7] and those with chronic renal disease.[8]

A number of the most important governmental publications available concerning disability eligibility are listed in Note 9.

The eligibility requirements *for Part B* are that *a person must be covered by Part A or be 65 or over*. Those who qualify solely on the basis of being 65 or over, or who have qualified for Part A by means of the provision for uninsured persons otherwise ineligible,[10] must meet additional requirements.[11]

While coverage under Part B is voluntary, *those persons who automatically qualify for Part A are now also automatically enrolled in Part B unless they specifically decline coverage.*[12] A requirement that a person enroll in Part B within three years of when he first became eligible was repealed in 1972. This change will allow a number of people who lost their earlier chances to enroll to now obtain coverage. However, a person is still limited to two enrollments.[13] That means if someone cancels Part B coverage (or has his coverage cancelled for reasons allowed by law, such as nonpayment of premiums) a second time, he or she permanently loses Part B coverage.

An important provision in the law allows *any person denied enrollment in either part of the program a right to judicial review of the administrative decision.*[14] This review of a decision as to entitlement is available regardless of the amount ultimately in controversy.[15] There are also various ways to have decisions denying social security benefits reviewed at local social security offices. Inquiry should be made directly to the person in charge of the local office for details.

What services does Part A (hospital insurance) cover?

Hospital insurance helps pay for three categories of expenses: inpatient hospitalization, posthospitalization extended care in a skilled nursing facility, and posthospitalization home health care administered by a home health care agency.[16]

When an insured person is an inpatient in a participating hospital, Part A pays for bed, meals, and regular nursing service in a semiprivate room. It covers operating-room charges, x-rays, laboratory tests, and medical supplies and equipment furnished by the hospital.

When an insured person has been in a hospital for at least three consecutive days and with certain exceptions enters a skilled nursing facility within 14 days after leaving the hospital, Part A will pay for services in the nursing facility. The need for skilled nursing care must arise from the same condition that originally necessitated hospitalization. Covered services include bed, meals, and regular nursing services in a semiprivate room. Drugs, medical supplies, and the use of medical appliances are also covered, as is physical, occupational, and speech therapy.

When an insured person has been hospitalized for at least three consecutive days and is subsequently confined at home, services rendered by a home health care agency under a doctor-approved *home health care* plan are covered by Part A. This coverage applies regardless of whether the person was admitted to a skilled nursing facility after hospitalization. *The plan must be established within 14 days of release from the hospital* or nursing facility, and the continuing need for treatment must result from the condition(s) that originally necessitated hospitalization. Coverage extends to part-time nursing care, physical therapy, and speech therapy. It also includes, if provided by the agency in conjunction with one of the above services, occupational therapy, medical supplies, health-aide services, and medical social services.

There are a number of *services that are not covered* by Part A, even though they may be provided by a hospital, skilled nursing facility, or a home health care agency.[17] Private-duty nurses in either facility are not covered, nor are personal comfort items such as a telephone or television (unless included in the semiprivate room charge). Private room charges are not covered unless such service is determined to be medically necessary. Home health care coverage does not include drugs, nor does it include full-time nursing care. At no time does Part A pay for a doctor's services, regardless of where they are rendered. (See Part B discussion below.) Also excluded from coverage are the first three pints of blood received during any given benefit period, although you may arrange to have blood donors make up the amount instead of paying. (See the discussion of Medicare payments for an explanation of what constitutes a benefit period).

Can a hospital require a Medicare patient to make an advance deposit as a condition of admission?

Many hospitals apparently still have this policy. The requirement is, however, against the law. Hospitals cannot require, as a condition of admission, that a patient pay any deposit.[18] Any hospital making this request should be immediately reported to your local Social Security office.

What services does Part B (medical insurance) cover?

Medical insurance covers doctors' services, outpatient hospital services, home health care services, and various other medical services.

Services of a doctor of medicine or a doctor of osteopathy are covered regardless of where they are rendered. Services of a dentist or a dental surgeon are covered only for dental surgery or services in connection with a fracture of facial or jaw bones. Any diagnostic tests performed by a doctor, as well as medical supplies provided by a doctor and drugs, that cannot be self-administered, are also covered. *Excluded from coverage* are routine physical examinations, normal dental care, and examinations for hearing aids.

Included in covered outpatient hospital services are laboratory, x-ray and diagnostic services, medical supplies, and emergency room services. Independent services are also covered, such as x-ray services, surgical dressings, diagnostic tests, durable medical equipment, and prosthetic devices. Eyeglasses, hearing aids, and false teeth are not covered.

Home health-care services are covered on a basis similar to Part A, without the prior hospitalization requirement. Ambulance service is also covered, as is outpatient physical therapy.

Part B will not pay for the first three pints of blood received in any single calender year. Coverage is extended to blood received beyond the first three pints, and Part B coverage can then be used to pay for any blood not covered by Part A (in which coverage is based on benefit periods).

How much will Medicare pay?

Part A benefits (hospitalization) are based on a concept of benefit periods. A *benefit period* begins when an insured person is hospitalized. That period continues until the person has been out of the hospital or skilled nursing facility for at least 60 consecutive days. Benefits are calculated both on the basis of a deductible charge for each benefit period (which is paid by the insured person) and a limited number of covered days or home health visits for each benefit period (beyond which the insured person must meet the full amount of his expenses).[20] *There is no lifetime limit on the number of benefit periods that an enrollee may experience.*

For each benefit period a beneficiary under Part A must pay all *hospital* charges up to a specified sum. For 1975 that figure was $92. (This is deductible.) All covered charges over the first $92 for the first 60 days of hospitalization are then paid by Medicare. For the sixty-first to ninetieth days, the patient must pay the first $23 of the costs incurred each day (this is called "copayment"). Beyond that period the patient must bear the full cost of hospitalization for that benefit period.

Each Part A beneficiary also has a *lifetime reserve* of 60 hospital days. These days can be used at a patient's option when hospitalization exceeds 90 days in a given benefit period. During each lifetime reserve day used in 1974, a patient had to pay $42 toward the costs of hospitalization (copayment). Once these days are exhausted, a benficiary must pay the full cost of any hospitalization in excess of 90 days in a given benefit period.

The first 20 days in a *skilled nursing facility* are covered fully for each benefit period. From the twenty-first to the hundredth day, for 1975, the patient had to pay $11.50 a day toward the cost of covered items and services. Any days over 100 in a given benefit period must be paid fully by the patient.

There is no coinsurance requirement applicable to Part A coverage of *home health care visits.*[21] Coverage is limited to 100 visits per year (not benefit period.) Coverage under Part B can be applied to additional visits required in a given year beyond those paid for by Part A.

There is also a lifetime limit of 190 days of inpatient care in a *psychiatric* hospital.

Part B benefits (medical care) are based on a concept of an annual deductible amount and a percentage contribution (coinsurance) by the beneficiary toward most services received.[22] For 1974 each insured person had to pay the first $60 (deductible) for services covered by Part B. This is a once-a-year charge for the first services rendered during the year. After that amount *Part B pays 80 percent* of the cost of covered services, and the *beneficiary pays the remaining 20 percent* (coinsurance). Expenses incurred in the last three months of any year are included toward the accumulation of the deductible amount for both the year in which they are incurred and the following year. *There is no absolute dollar limit on the amount payable either in any given year or during a beneficiary's lifetime.*

Two services are exempt from the deductible and coinsurance requirements and *are paid in full by Medicare.* These services are *home health care* services and *radiology and pathology services* administered by a doctor to a hospital inpatient.[23] Since these expenses are paid entirely, the cost is not included in calculating whether the deductible has been reached in a given year. Payment under Part B for home health care is limited, however, to 100 visits per year. These are in excess of any visits accumulated and paid for by Part A coverage.

It is important to note that the *deductible, coinsurance, and premium amounts can and do change every year. Thus, Medicare beneficiaries, even if fully insured, must meet increased costs for health care each year.*

How does a person receive Medicare payments to which he is entitled?

Agencies that provide individuals with services covered by *Part A* (hospitalization) automatically file claims for reimbursement. The beneficiary is billed by the agency only for those costs in excess of or not covered by Part A.

Part B (medical care) benefits are payable in two ways. An individual may be billed by the doctor or provider of services. The individual then files a Request for Medicare Payment,[24] accompanied by the bills for services and receives reimbursement to the extent of Part B coverage. Alternatively, a beneficiary may assign his or her right to reimbursement to the doctor or provider of services. The doctor or provider of services then bills the beneficiary only for the 20 percent of charges not covered by Part B. *The doctor or provider of services, not the beneficiary, has the choice of method for Part B payment.*

Payments for Medicare benefits are not made directly by the SSA. Instead, the SSA has contracted with a number of private insurance companies—variously called carriers or intermediaries—to handle the paperwork and make payments on behalf of the SSA.

In many situations the intermediaries also have some discretion in the administration of Medicare. For example, within the confines of the Social Security Act and the relevant regulations, the intermediaries may establish what amounts are proper charges for various services. It is possible for a beneficiary to have payment denied on the basis that the charge was too high or that the service was not covered or not necessary.

In any case in which the payment is denied, a beneficiary has the *right to a reconsidered determination*[25] (Part A benefits) or to an *informal review of determination*[26] (Part B benefits). If the beneficiary loses at that level, he or she has *a right to a fair hearing.*[27] Details about how to obtain these hearings can be obtained from your local Social Security office where the hearing will usually be conducted. You should demand this review as soon after receiving a negative determination as possible. Requests for such hearings must almost always be made in writing on a form provided by your local SSA office. The Part B fair hearing is conducted by the organization administering Medicare in the state, usually Blue Cross, and is available only if the amount in controversy is at least $100. In the case of Part A benefits, the beneficiary may skip the reconsidered determination and request a fair hearing at the outset. If the amount in controversy is over $1,000, in regard to Part A benefits, *judicial review* of the administrative decision is available.[28] No judicial review of fair-hearing decisions on the amount of Part B benefits is available.

What does Medicare coverage cost?

With one exception, coverage under *Part A is provided at no cost to the beneficiary.* For persons obtaining coverage by the provision for persons otherwise ineligible, a monthly premium is assessed.[29] For the twelve-month period beginning July 1, 1974, that premium was $36 per month, up from $33 per month during the prior twelve months.

A monthly premium charge is assessed for every person

186 THE RIGHTS OF HOSPITAL PATIENTS

enrolled in Part B. Until at least July 1, 1976 that charge will be $6.70 per month.

There are provisions in the Social Security Act for states to establish plans whereby these premiums are paid for those persons who cannot afford the payments but meet other criteria.[30] Most states have such plans.

Can an individual purchase insurance to cover those items not covered by Medicare?

In most areas of the country there are a number of so-called "Medicare policy" plans available from private insurance companies. While using the term "Medicare," these programs are in no way endorsed, approved, or issued by the federal government. There are some excellent plans, however, that are designed to pay all *deductibles* under Medicare and extended benefits for inpatient, outpatient, and nursing home care. It may be important to purchase such a policy since Medicare itself pays only an average of 50 percent of an individual's total health care bill.

On the other hand, caution must be exercised in selecting a supplementary plan. One policy, for example, provides no benefits until a patient has been hospitalized for more than 60 days. The odds against this happening to someone over 65 have been computed to be 100 to 1.[31] Make sure you understand the coverages, deductibles, and co-insurance features of this type of policy before you purchase it.

Where can an individual get more information about Medicare?

Your local SSA office can answer your questions about Medicare, as can personnel from the Teleservice Centers that the SSA has established in major metropolitan areas around the country.

The primary publication of the SSA for beneficiaries of Medicare is *Your Medicare Handbook*. This booklet is printed in English and Spanish editions and is available from any SSA office. Every new Medicare enrollee should automatically receive a copy of the handbook from the SSA. While the handbook is helpful, it does not explain many of the intricacies of Medicare coverage. If you are unsure of a question, you should pursue it with someone from the SSA.

If you are not satisfied with the treatment you receive from the SSA, most U.S. Congressmen have at least one member of their staff who is an expert on Social Security matters. If your own efforts fail, do not hesitate to seek advice and assistance from the office of your Congressman or Senator.

MEDICAID

What is Medicaid?

Medicaid is the name given to a system of medical assistance plans for low-income people.[32] It is cooperatively financed by the federal and state governments, with the federal government paying at least 50 percent of the cost of each plan. Unlike Medicare, however, *each state designs and administers its own plan,* within the requirements of the Social Security Act. While a state is not required to have a Medicaid program, since 1970 participation has been the only way a state can obtain federal reimbursement for providing medical assistance to poor people.[33] Currently 49 states, Puerto Rico, the Virgin Islands, and the District of Columbia have Medicaid plans.[34]

Since each state plan differs to some extent, answers to specific questions concerning Medicaid must be directed to the state agency (usually the Health or Welfare Department), which administers the program in the patient's state. What follows is an outline of rules all states must observe.

Who is eligible for Medicaid?

Although each state may design its Medicaid program to cover a variety of persons, there are certain groups for whom coverage is mandatory, for example, for all considered to *be categorically needy.* This means essentially people receiving assistance under the Aid to Families with Dependent Children (AFDC) program,[35] the Supplemental Security Income for the Aged, Blind and Disabled (SSI) program[36] or a state supplementary SSI program.[37] However, not everyone receiving benefits under SSI is necessarily covered by a given state's Medicaid plan.[38]

In addition to those receiving payments under one of the above plans, there are also certain people who are excluded from the above programs by the rules of the state in which they live but who must nonetheless be covered by the state's Medicaid program.[39] An example is someone under 21 who is excluded from AFDC because he is not attending school. He must, however, be covered by Medicaid since the school attendance stipulation is not permitted by the minimum federal Medicaid standards.

A state has the option of extending coverage to any categorically needy persons not mandatorily covered, as well as to medically needy persons. An example of a categorically needy person who could be covered if the state chose is someone who meets all the requirements for AFDC but has not applied. Another example would be a person under 21 who met the financial requirements for AFDC eligibility but was nonetheless ineligible because of some other provision in that state's AFDC plan.

A *medically needy person* is an individual whose income and resources equal or exceed his or her state's standards for financial assistance but whose resources are insufficient to meet his or her medical insurance premiums and medical expenses. A state may decide which persons it will cover out of the potentially large number who could fit the description of medically needy. The state may not, however, include anyone whose income exceeds 133⅓ percent of the state's highest corresponding AFDC payment for an equivalent family.[40]

There may be provisions for even broader coverage, but a state whose plan covers such persons will receive no federal reimbursement for its costs.

What services does Medicaid cover?

There are two categories of medical services covered by Medicaid. The first category consists of those services that must be included in a plan and must be available to persons for whom Medicaid coverage is *federally mandated*.[41] The second category includes those *additional services* that may be made available to mandatory enrollees. Taken together, these categories make up the range of services a state may provide for optional enrollees.[42]

The first category consists of five services,[48] for which a state plan must cover at least some of the expenses. These are *inpatient hospital services,* (in other than a tuberculosis or, except for persons under 21,[44] a psychiatric institution), *outpatient hospital services,* other *laboratory and x-ray services, skilled nursing facility services* for those over 21 and *comprehensive diagnostic services* for those under 21, and *physicians services.*

The second category consists of eleven other specified types of services as well as a blanket provision for any other medical care.[45] Such services as dental care, physical therapy, prescription drugs, dentures, and prosthetic devices are among the specified services.

In determining the scope of coverage for those persons to whom a state has chosen to extend optional coverage, a state has the choice of two minimum plans. It may include the basic five listed above, or it may choose any seven from the total of seventeen categories.

All care in each category must be "medically necessary," or Medicaid will not reimburse the provider for it. Medicaid must provide all enrollees with transportation to and from the providers of such necessary medical services, which may be by ambulance, taxi, or other means of transportation.

One particularly important aspect of Medicaid coverage is the provision for comprehensive services for persons under 21, referred to as Early and Periodic Screening, Diagnosis and Treatment (EPSDT).[46] These services must be extended to every person under 21 who is eligible for Medicaid. Although to date implementation has been sketchy, this provision could mean a significant improvement in the health care provided to poor children throughout the country. States that have not yet met the regulatory requirements for implementation are subject to a penalty, which can be subtracted from their federal Medicaid funds.

All states that participate in Medicaid are also required to set up a program to meet the cost of "family planning services and supplies furnished to individuals of childbearing age (including sexually active minors) who are eligible" for Medicaid and desire such services.[47] Very few states have met their legal obligation to develop such comprehensive services to date.[48]

What does Medicaid coverage cost?

Categorically needy recipients of Medicaid are not charged any premiums or enrollment fees.[49] Medically needy persons must be charged either an enrollment fee or a premium, which is graduated according to income.[50] The premiums must be at least $1 per month, and may be graduated upward within a ceiling established by HEW regulations.

Both categorically needy and medically needy persons may be required to pay deductibles, co-insurance amounts, and co-payments.[51] However, categorically needy persons may not be subjected to such charges for those services that are mandatory for state plans. The co-payment amounts have a variable ceiling of between 5 and 10 percent of the cost of service. Deductible amounts are limited to a maximum of $2 per month. The co-insurance amount is limited to a maximum of 5 percent of the state's payment to a recipient.[52]

Must a hospital make special efforts to ascertain a patient's eligibility for Medicaid?

At least one court has found that a hospital has a duty to determine the patient's eligibility for Medicaid, give the patient adequate directions and instructions concerning the Medicaid program, and take some steps to be sure that the required application forms are filed by the patient and that appropriate action is taken regarding payment of hospital bills by Medicaid.

The case involved a premature baby who was transferred to the special-care unit of another hospital. A hospital employee there learned that the child's mother was eligible for Medicaid and referred her to a Medicaid representative who had an office in the hospital. The forms were given, but for some reason were returned to the appropriate hospital employee incomplete. No bill was sent to the patient for some years. Finally one was sent, and the hospital sued to collect. The court, noting that the fundamental purpose of the Medicaid program was to help needy persons pay for their medical care, said that achievement of that purpose required the cooperative effort of the hospital, the patient, and the state Medicaid program. The court found that the hospital personnel were almost certain to know more about the Medicaid program than a patient and that the hospital also had an ongoing relationship with the state's Medicaid program that would permit ready correction of any misunderstandings. Because of this the court determined that the hospital had a legal responsibility toward the patient to ensure that the proper forms were filed and appropriate action on them was taken. The suit against the child's mother was dismissed.[53]

Where can an individual get more information about Medicaid?

Each state with a Medicaid plan is required to designate a single state agency to administer the program. In most states it is the Department of Public Welfare, but in some states it is the Department of Public Health. That agency can provide you with information about Medicaid and process applications for assistance. If you are unable to determine what agency administers Medicaid in your state, your local Social Security office can give you that information.

PRIVATE HEALTH INSURANCE

What should consumers know about private health insurance plans?

Both the Medicare and Medicaid programs outlined above can be described as "basic health insurance" programs, which means simply that they pay a *major* portion of hospital-related expenses. If you are not covered by one of these programs or by a group program through your place of employment, you should have some form of hospital insurance.

Basic policies will typically cover 80 percent of your total hospital bills *after* you have paid an annual deductible amount (which may range from $50 to over $500).

To get an idea of the amount of coverage you should have, you can estimate that doctor and hospital charges average about $200 per day in the hospital. Persons aged 15 to 44 average about a 6-day stay per hospitilization.

This would cost about $1,200. Add to this your loss of income for 6 days in the hospital and 6 days recuperation, if your policy does not cover (and most don't) disability income after your sick leave is used up.

In deciding which policy to purchase, you should be aware of optional coverages, waiting periods (usually 15 to 30 days for diseases, 9 months for pregnancy, etc.) during which time you are *not* covered, pre-existing conditions which you have that are *not* covered by many policies, exclusion provisions, and cancellation provisions. The most important terms of the insurance contract will normally be the premium, the coverages, the deductible, and the coinsurance amounts. More detailed information on purchasing private health insurance is set out in *A Shopper's Guide to Health Insurance*, published by the Insurance Dept. of Pennsylvania, and is available for $1 from Consumer Information, 813 National Press Building, Washington, D.C., 20004.

Not only does this guide set forth some of the basics of private health insurance, it also ranks the 25 largest commercial insurance companies by "loss ratios" of individual (nongroup) policies (the percentage of premiums that are returned to policy holders in terms of benefits), financial strength, and total premiums collected in 1972. The Blue Cross and Blue Shield plans, with average loss ratios of over 90 percent come out better than any of the private plans. The top six insurance companies by this study on the basis of loss ratio were American National, Equitable, Physicians Mutual, Metropolitan Life, American Republic, and National Liberty.[54]

How much will private health insurance pay?

Private health insurance pays about 30 percent of the average American's health bills. The problem of payment is one faced by almost every American. Nonetheless, the U.S. remains the only major industrial nation in the world that has not adopted a system of government-funded health insurance for all its citizens. With increasing costs, however, some form of national health insurance is likely within the next 2 to 3 years. As with private health insurance, the most important aspect will be the *coverage* provided in terms of health care services. A system of reimbursement for the cost of care does not, however, ensure that patients will have access to medical services. This fact is well documented by the Medicare and Medicaid experience and means that much work remains to be done to develop a health-care system that can deliver quality services to all citizens.

NOTES

1. Title XVIII of the Social Security Act, Pub. Law 89-97, 42 U.S.C. 1385-1395 (1973). The regulations governing the program appear at 20 C.F.R. §§404 and 405. Also see C.C.H., *Medicare and Medicaid Guide* (loose leaf) and J. K. Lasser's, YOUR GUIDE TO SOCIAL SECURITY AND MEDICARE BENEFITS, 1973. The story of how this legislation finally made it through Congress is related by Richard Harris in A SACRED TRUST, Penguin Books, Baltimore, 1969. Much legal material about Medicare is collected in a volume put out by the Health Law Project of U. Penn. Law School entitled *MEDICARE*, (1972 revised ed.) (mimeograph).

2. 42 U.S.C. §§1395c-1395i-2 (1973).

3. 42 U.S.C. §§1395j-1395w (1973).

4. This is the primary category and consists of those persons 65 or older who are eligible for monthly social-security retirement or survivor benefits or who are qualified railroad-retirement beneficiaries. Railroad Retirement Act of 1937, 45 U.S.C. §228a et seq (1973). A person may obtain Medicare coverage even if he or she declines social security or railroad-retirement benefits. Likewise, if the benefits payable are reduced to zero, as in the situation in which annual earned income exceeds permissible limits, Medicare coverage is still available. *Anyone over 65 who applies for and establishes entitlement to social-security or railroad-retirement benefits is automatically covered by Part A.*

5. This category is referred to as *transitional* and consists of those persons who turned 65 before 1968 or earned three quarters of Social Security coverage for each full year after 1966 and before reaching the age of 65. 42 U.S.C. §427 (1973). The number of quarters of coverage required to qualify on this basis increases for each year after 1967 that a person reaches the age of 65. By 1974 for women and by 1975 for men, the number of quarters re-

quired will equal the number required for retirement-ben-
efit coverage, thus phasing this category out of existence.

6. This category consists of those persons 65 or over who
   are not otherwise eligible for coverage under Part A but
   who are covered (or apply simultaneously for coverage)
   under Part B. 42 U.S.C. §1395i-2 (1973). As of July 1,
   1973, persons in this category were eligible for Medicare
   upon application, but are under different financial obliga-
   tions than those persons qualifying under other eligibility
   categories.

7. This category covers those persons entitled to cash benefits under either the social security or railroad retirement
   program because they are disabled.

   42 U.S.C. §426 (b) (1973). This coverage has no
   minimum-age limitation of its own. Thus, within the limitations imposed by the various disability programs persons of any age may become eligible for Medicare. To
   obtain coverage, a person must have been disabled and
   eligible for disability payments for 24 months, but need
   not have been actually receiving disability payments for
   that period. Included in this category *in addition to those
   meeting the 24-month requirement* are disabled widows
   and disabled dependent widowers if 50 years old or older,
   and those 18 or over who are both disabled and are receiving social-security benefits. More than 3 million
   Americans will apply for disability or supplementary payments under social security in fiscal 1975. One study in
   late 1973 found 65 percent of 100,000 welfare recipients
   had "severe disabilities". *New York Times,* Sept. 24,
   1973, p. 1.

8. This category consists of those persons, regardless of age,
   who are fully or currently insured or entitled to monthly
   benefits from either social security or railroad retirement
   and who have chronic renal disease. 42 U.S.C. §§426 (e),
   1395c (1973). The spouse or dependent child of a person
   covered by the retirement programs is eligible for Part A
   if the child or spouse has chronic renal disease, regardless
   of whether the person eligible for retirement benefits has
   such a disease. Payment begins under the program only
   after the third complete month of dialysis treatment.

9. The following publications may be obtained through the
   Social Security Administration, Bureau of Disability Insurance, Room 7140, Dickerson Tower, Baltimore, Md.
   21241. When ordering, cite title and publication number.
   If You Become Disabled (The basic facts about all
   phases of the social-security disability program ... how

they affect the average worker and dependents) 31 pages, July 1972, DHEW (SSA) 72-10029. *Your Social Security* (The basic facts in simple language about all phases of social security coverage. Certain sections concentrate on disability payments for insured workers) 46 pages, July 1972, DHEW (SSA) 72-10035. *Social Security Information For Young Families* (Special emphasis is placed on how social-security benefits may be paid to young workers and their dependents if the worker becomes disabled) 19 pages, February 1972, DHEW (SSA) 72-10033. *Your Right to Question the Decision On Your Claim* (Explains what a person may do if he thinks the decision on his claim is not correct. Lists the steps for re-examination of claims.) 5 pages, October 1970, SSI-58. *Disability Evaluation Under Social Security: A Handbook For Physicians* (Presents the medical evaluation criteria used by the Bureau of Disability Insurance to determine impairment.) 71 pages, July 1970, SSI-89. *Psychological Reports in Social Security Disability Cases* (Simple guidelines for the physician showing areas of psychological evaluation that are helpful in determining disability.) 5 pages, August 1970, SSI-689. *Social Security: What It Means To You* (Illustrated booklet written in conversational style, telling what makes social-security work and how it pays benefits to almost all workers: retirement, disability, medical, survivors.) 40 pages, July 1972, DHEW (SSA) 72-1003. *Social Security Checks for Students 18 to 22* (Focuses on social security benefits available to students whose parent or parents are receiving social security payments due to death, disability or retirement.) 7 pages, March 1972, DHEW (SSA) 72-10048.

See also in the medical literature:

The Social Security Disability Program (a 3-part series) by Bernard Popick, Director, Bureau of Disability Insurance; *Journal of Occupational Medicine.* (Part 1 "Characteristics of the Program", May 1971; Part II "Medical Evaluation of Claims", June 1971; Part III "Black Lung Benefits—An Administrative Case Study" July 1971). *Psychiatric Evidence Needed in Social Security Disability Evaluation,* by Nussbaum, et al., *Journal of the Indiana State Medical Association* (March 1968).

10. 42 U.S.C. §1395i-2 (1973).
11. They must be residents of the United States, and either be citizens or aliens lawfully admitted for permanent residence, and have resided in the United States continuously for the five years prior to seeking Medicare cov-

erage. 42 U.S.C. §§1395i-2,1395o (1973). A federal district court has recently declared the five-year requirement and the permanent-resident-status requirement unconstitutional as to Part B. *Diaz v. Weinberger,* 361 F.
Supp. 1 (D.S.D. Fla. 1973), appeal filed 42 U.S.L.W.
3439 (Jan. 29, 1974). If the case is upheld, the application of the same requirements to Part A will probably
be subject to a constitutional challenge.

12. The individual must, of course, pay for this additional
coverage. See *infra.* section on costs.

13. 42 U.S.C. §1395p(b) (1973).

14. 42 U.S.C. §1395ff(b) (1973).

15. Ridgely v. Sec. of H.E.W., 345 F. Supp. 983 (D.Md.
1972); Cardno v. Finch, 311 F. Supp. 251 (D.La. 1970).

16. 42 U.S.C. §1395d (1973).

17. 42 U.S.C. §1395y (1973).

18. 20 C.F.R. 405.10.

19. 42 U.S.C. §1395k (1973).

20. 42 U.S.C. §1395e (1973).

21. 42 U.S.C. §1395e (1973).

22. 42 U.S.C. §13951 (1973).

23. 42 U.S.C. §13951(a) (1973).

24. SSA Form 1490.

25. 20 C.F.R. §405.710.

26. 20 C.F.R. §405.807(a).

27. 42 U.S.C. §1395ff (b) (2) (1973), 20 C.F.R. §405.720
(Part A benefits); 42 U.S.C. §1395u(c) (1973), 20 C.F.R.
§405.820 (Part B benefits).

28. 42 U.S.C. §1395ff(b) (2) (1973).

29. 42 U.S.C. §1395i-2(a) (1973).

30. 42 U.S.C. §1395v (1973).

31. See generally, *Consumer's Guide to Health Insurance*
(1974) at 10. Issued and distributed by Executive Office
of Human Services, Commonwealth of Massachusetts,
100 Cambridge Street, Boston, Massachusetts 02202.

32. Title XIX of the Social Security Act, 42 U.S.C. §1396 et
seq (1973). The regulations governing Medicaid appear
at 45 C.F.R. §200 et seq. See also C.C.H., *Medicare and
Medicaid Guide* (loose leaf). The Health Law Project of
the University of Pennsylvania put out a volume of legal
materials on *Medicaid,* 1972 (rev. ed.) (not published).

33. P.L. 89-97, §121b.

34. See 2 C.C.H., *Medicare and Medicaid Guide* §15,501
et seq. Arizona is the only state without a program.

35. Title IV-A of the Social Security Act, 42 U.S.C. §601 et seq (1973).

36. Title XVI of the Social Security Act, 42 U.S.C. §1381 et seq (1973).

37. 42 U.S.C. §1396d(j) (1973).

38. 42 U.S.C. §1396a(f) (1973).

39. 42 U.S.C. §1396a(b) 1-4 (1973).

40. 42 U.S.C. §1396b(f) (1) (B) (i) (1973). *See* 2 C.C.H. Medicare and Medicaid Guide §14,311.

41. 42 U.S.C. §139a (a) (13) (B) (1973).

42. 42 U.S.C. §1396a(a) (13) (C) (1973).

43. 42 U.S.C. §1396d(a) (1973).

44. 42 U.S.C. §1396d(h) (1973).

45. 42 U.S.C. §1396d(a) (17) (1973).

46. 42 U.S.C. §1396d(a) (4) (B) (1973).

47. 42 U.S.C. §602 (a) (14) (15) and §606 (d).

48. A booklet describing the types of services required by the law, *Family Planning Services for Poor Women* is available from Health Law Project, 133 South 36th Street, Philadelphia, Pa. 19174.

49. 42 U.S.C. §1396a (14) (A) (i) (1973).

50. 42 U.S.C. §1396a (14) (B) (i) (1973).

51. 42 U.S.C. §§1396a (14) (A) (ii); 1396a (14) (B) (ii) (1973).

52. Regulations concerning payments by recipients appear at 45 C.F.R. §249.40, as amended by 39 *Fed. Reg.* 5552 (Feb. 13, 1974).

53. *Mount Sinai Hospital v. Kornegay*, 347 N.Y.S. 2d 807 (N.Y., Civ. Ct. of City of N.Y.) (1973).

54. The complete company ranking is reprinted in *Medical World News*, Feb. 8, 1974 at 78. For a critical look at Blue Cross see S. Law, BLUE CROSS: WHAT WENT WRONG? Yale U. Press, New Haven, Conn., 1974.

XVII

Legal Actions Patients Can Take Against Doctors and Hospitals

Physicians have described themselves as being "truly alarmed at the increase of malpractice claims" for over 125 years. In 1847, thirteen years before the Civil War, one surgeon wrote: "Legal prosecutions for malpractice in surgery occur so often that even a respectable surgeon may well fear for the results of his surgical practice."[1]

More recently the cry has escalated. In 1973, for example, an AMA spokesman wrote, "The habit of litigation has been increasing to virtually orgy proportions ... New rules of procedure make it easier for any injured person to recover substantial damages from someone for virtually any injury he suffers."[2]

Although most are likely to be so viewed by the physician-defendant, there is no evidence that the rising number of lawsuits is composed of "nuisance" actions. On the contrary, the evidence that does exist suggests that consumers in all areas are becoming more aware of their rights and are increasingly seeking compensation for injuries caused by others. The medical profession's real objections appear to be the time and energy it takes to defend malpractice action no matter how meritorious, the public cross-examination a defendant must undergo should the case go to trial, and the fear that a malpractice charge may damage a defendant's reputation, and high insurance rates.

In this chapter both the present malpractice system and the alternatives that are proposed to supplement or replace it will be examined.

What must an injured patient prove to win a lawsuit against a doctor or a hospital?

In asserting that "the bringing of a malpractice action does not even suggest that the claim has merit," the medical profession is correct. A suit in malpractice, like any other civil action, is an assertion that a wrong has been done that the defendant should answer for, and nothing more. To prevail in the lawsuit, the patient must demonstrate four things: (1) that the doctor or hospital had a *duty of care* (e.g., to perform surgery up to the standards of the average surgeon); (2) that the duty was *breached* (the surgery performed was below *standards*); (3) that *damages* to the patient resulted; and (4) that the damages to the patient were *caused* directly by the breach of duty. Only by proving all of these in court can the plaintiff prevail. In the unusual case in which a physician guarantees a particular result and the treatment is less successful than promised (e.g., plastic surgery guaranteed to make one look more beautiful), a patient may also sue for breach of contract. This legal action usually has a longer statute of limitations, also. A malpractice suit remains an infrequent occurrence, however. Statistically, only about one out of every 226,000 patient visits to doctors results in a malpractice action, and the majority of hospitals, no matter how large, go through an entire year without having a single claim filed against them.[8]

Since complicated medical issues of standard of care and causation are involved, a medical malpractice suit can be an expensive venture. In order to permit the low- and middle-income client to sue, most lawyers will take malpractice cases on a contingency basis.

What is a contingency-fee agreement?

Under a contingency-fee agreement, the client pays only for the *expenses* directly involved in bringing the lawsuit. The attorney is compensated for his time only if the suit is won. His fee is said to be "contingent" on winning and is a percentage of the verdict, usually 30 to 35 percent. A common argument is that nuisance suits are encouraged by this system. The simple fact that 30 percent of nothing is nothing, however, usually means that the contingency fee actually reduces the number of claims that might otherwise be brought against doctors and hospitals. HEW's *Report on Medical Malpractice*, for example, found that lawyers accept only about one of every eight claims that they are asked to handle. A strong argument can thus be made that lawyers, far from encouraging such suits, are actually discouraging them. Experienced malpractice lawyers hire experts to evaluate claims and go ahead only with those that such an expert finds have merit.

The problems with this system are that even under it a patient may have to come up with over $1,000 for expenses before an attorney will take a case, and cases that promise final verdicts of under $10 to 20,000 may never be taken. Thus the poor and those with small claims may be discriminated against by this system.

What is defensive medicine?

Defensive medicine is generally defined as the alteration of modes of medical practice for the sole purpose of avoiding legal liability.

A Duke Law School study attempted to assess the problem by distributing questionnaires to physicians in North Carolina and California. The response indicated that the threat of malpractice does induce many physicians to practice with an eye toward their legal status. There was, however, little evidence to support the claim that the practice of negative defensive medicine, the conscious avoidance of certain inherently dangerous tests or procedures, has increased. The conclusion was that a lack of cost constraints, not malpractice actions, was responsible for unnecessary tests either overtly or covertly performed in the interests of defensive medicine.[5] On the other hand, in an AMA survey, over 70 percent of doctors reported that they practiced defensive medicine.[6] The problem with both of these studies, however, is that any questionnaire declaration by a physician who dislikes the present system (as most do) will be an unreliable indicator of the way he really practices medicine. Hard data, thus, are difficult to find.

The only study I have been able to locate that lends any support to the "defensive medicine" position is one from the University of Washington, which indicated that in the course of one year 34 percent of skull films taken in a Seattle emergency room were taken for "medicolegal" reasons. This amounted to 509 x-rays, 2 of which revealed a fracture, a much lower incidence than patients x-rayed because of clinically significant findings. At $30 per series, it cost $7,650 to find each fracture, and in neither case was the mode of treatment altered.[7]

On the other hand, another emergency-room study, done about the same time but without the focus on medical malpractice, concluded that on the sample group (non-emergency patients with gastrointestinal symptoms seen at the Baltimore City Hospital emergency room) "the staff performed incomplete physical examinations and too few routine laboratory tests."[8] The only conclusion that one can draw is that the state of practice of defensive medicine is conjectural at best, and that there is no solid evidence to support the claim that the practice exists.

Moreover, the doctor who complains about positive defensive medicine, such as excessive testing, is defaming himself. The legal standard is "good medical practice" judged by what the average practitioner does. Thus, the doctor is saying either that he is wasting his patient's and society's money by performing unnecessary tests or that his own standard for diagnostic testing is so far below that of the "average practitioner" that he meets the legal requirement only when he performs more tests than he would have performed without the threat of a malpractice suit. In short, the law should not affect the practice of a competent physician, but only serve to encourage a less than average practitioner to raise his standards. The argument of the American College of Surgeons, for example, that some of their members "feel compelled to treat patients under a concept which stresses avoidance of litigation rather than application of their best clinical judgment"[9] is a non sequitur if their best clinical judgment conforms with the standards of good medical practice. If it does not, the surgeons are simply confirming the powerful policing role of medical malpractice litigation. In blaming the legal profession for the manner in which

they practice medicine, they join the ranks of those who
blame the police for crime.

What are the real problems with the current malpractice system?

Costs of malpractice insurance premiums have risen
from 50 to 1000 percent during the past five years. At
times, some physicians have found it difficult to purchase
insurance, even at higher rates. Much of this can be
directly traced to the increased exposure to liability faced
by today's physician who has an increasing array of
drugs and devices at his disposal and is therefore far more
able to treat and cure disease than his counterpart of 50
or even 20 years ago. Nor do the high insurance premiums
paid by physicians ensure that injured patients will be
compensated. Many injured patients never sue and so are
not compensated at all by the system. Of those that do
sue, only about half ever receive any money, and of monies
awarded to plaintiffs by juries (plaintiffs win only
about 20 percent of all jury cases), they themselves receive
only 17 to 38 cents of each dollar. The rest is absorbed
in costs for legal fees, court costs, and witnesses.
Also, the suit may take two to six years, and in the meantime
the plaintiff may have no money to pay his bills and
may be unable to continue his preinjury occupation.

On an interprofessional level, malpractice suits exacerbate
already strained relationships between doctors and
lawyers. There will always be a significant minority of
claims that have little or no merit. Doctors involved may
justifiably feel persecuted. Likewise, many doctors whose
colleagues would judge their performance well below average
may never be sued.

It can be argued, nonetheless, that the tort system is an
adequate, albeit erratic, method of quality control. Compared
with county medical societies, hospital utilization
review committees, or proposed professional standards
review organizations, it is more effective. The system,
however, is not cost efficient, nor does it provide universal
coverage for injury. The conclusion is that while most
of the major complaints with the system voiced by the

medical profession are trivial, there are other real major problems with litigation as the sole method of injury compensation. Total cost might also be considered high, but at a population per capita rate of less than $2.00 per year, it is unlikely that any other system would be significantly less expensive.

What are screening panels and defense committees?

A screening panel is a group, usually of doctors and other professionals, that evaluates the merits of a malpractice action before it goes to court. A defense committee is usually an arm of the local medical society and evaluates claims only from the standpoint of helping member physicians defend against them.

The idea of having preliminary boards or panels review malpractice claims with an eye toward settlement or dismissal is not novel. In 1869 the AMA proposed that lawsuits requiring expert testimony be decided by a committee of physicians appointed by a judge. This "blue ribbon jury" approach remains the medical profession favorite solution to the problem of potentially conflicting expert testimony. In 1886, the formation of cooperative unions for the defense of physicians was urged, and in the following year the Michigan State Medical Society declared it unethical for one physician to testify against another. By 1910, 13 medical societies had developed defense committees for members.[10]

The screening panel is a more sophisticated tool for settling disputes. It draws part (usually half) of its membership from the legal profession. While with a defense committee the plaintiff does not get an opportunity to present his side of the case, under the screening panel system both sides are represented by counsel. If the panel finds the complaint has merit, they advise the doctor and his insurance company to settle. They also make their services available to the plaintiff in preparing for court, usually helping to locate expert witnesses. If they find the case without merit, they will not assist the plaintiff, who must usually either settle for a small sum or drop the suit.

That the decisions of the screening panels are not binding and do not set damages are problems. Therefore, review by these committees is no guarantee that a long

court battle will be avoided. Moreover, insurance companies have been strongly opposed to such panels both because they must disclose their defense with no guarantee
of a final decision and because if they find the doctor at
fault, the plaintiff can hold out for a larger settlement.[11]

**How does binding arbitration of a malpractice claim
work?**

An arbitration agreement is signed between the doctor
and the patient, or the hospital and the patient, *before* any
treatment is administered. It provides that in the event of
a medical injury, the amount of damages that the doctor
or hospital will have to pay the patient will be set by an
arbitration panel.

An arbitration case is initiated when the plaintiff notifies
the defendant that there is a case or claim against him.
Each side then has a period of time, usually thirty days, to
select an arbitrator. The two arbitrators in turn have another thirty days to select a third arbitrator. The court se-
lects this "neutral" arbitrator if the two cannot agree. After another brief period for preparation, this three-man
panel hears the arguments of each side in a private, unre-
corded hearing, renders an unpublished decision that is
binding, and sets the amount of the award, if any. Appeals
ar available only on very limited due process grounds.[12]

The advantages to the doctor are the privacy of the entire proceeding, the elimination of public cross-examination, and cheaper malpractice insurance premiums. The
mechanics of signing a binding arbitration agreement, with
all of the legal requirements that void contracts made under stress, duress, or necessity, can present real problems.
They can probably only be solved by prepaid group plans,
and then only by giving the patient at least an annual opportunity to rescind the contract.

It is hard to see how consumers will benefit, except for
speed. Indeed, it currently seems the advantages are all
stacked in favor of the providers. If providers really believe arbitration would be advantageous to the patients,
they should allow the patient to have the right of binding
arbitration at his option after the medical injury complained of occurs. While there is little doubt that many
would opt for this method in small claims cases, it seems

equally clear that in cases of serious injury most patients would prefer to use the current legal structure.

How would no-fault malpractice insurance work?

When an injury is insured against by its victim, regardless of the negligence of the person who caused it, the victim has "no-fault insurance." The result is to eliminate the lawsuit (and usually any compensation for "pain and suffering") and compensate the injured party directly for his out-of-pocket expenses. If this were done in all cases of bodily injury, the result would be a system of National Health Insurance. If the plan were limited to medical injuries caused by medical personnel involved in treating the patient for another separate injury, illness, or disability, the result would be "no fault malpractice insurance."

Such a system works in the automobile field because once the issue of "fault" is eliminated, the only issue remaining is how much money should be awarded. By eliminating awards for "pain and suffering" we are left with the readily ascertainable out-of-pocket expenses. The situation is not so simple in the malpractice area. Even eliminating fault, one still must decide what portion of the plaintiff's injury is attributable to medical treatment and what portion to injury, illness, or disability that the patient had when he initially sought treatment. Not only this, but medical "mishaps" are not as discrete as automobile accidents, and determining what is and what is not a "compensable event" or a "less than average" outcome may be so uncertain as to create more arbitrariness and waste than anything the present system might breed. Besides this major objection, such a system could cost up to eight times as much as the current one and would not only eliminate all "quality control" mechanisms but could even tend to encourage sloppiness.[18]

What is the future likely to bring in terms of consumer remedies?

The three major goals of a medical-injury compensation scheme should be: effective quality control, complete coverage, and cost effectiveness. None of the proposed alternatives to the present system addresses all of these goals adequately. None of them alone, therefore, offers a final solution to the malpractice problem.

Instead of adopting any of these alternatives wholesale, we are likely to see increased experimentation with combinations of the proposed alternatives. Screening panels, for example, will probably be made a formal part of the pretrial conference under the direct supervision of the trial judge in some states. This should help decrease the number of suits going to trial. Compulsory binding arbitration is unlikely to win widespread consumer support. But binding arbitration at the option of the injured party may prove beneficial to both the medical profession and patients, and arbitration may be widely used in the Health Maintenance Organization context. The introduction of catastrophic health insurance should also decrease the number of actions brought for bad results since it will eliminate one of the main incentives to sue: high medical bills in the face of a less than optimal result. An effective patient's rights advocate should decrease the number of suits by resolving some conflicts at the hospital level.

None of these modifications will drastically affect either cost or quality control. Unless an effective alternative to litigation can be found, malpractice suits will have to be retained as an imperfect, but viable method of quality control.

How can a patient take legal action against a doctor or hospital for the violation of any of the specific rights outlined in this book if the violation did not directly result in any personal or bodily injury?

Various legal actions can be brought for the denial of essential services such as emergency care or constitutionally protected services like abortion. Actions can also be brought to challenge the denial of payment against Medicare and Medicaid or against a private health insurer. Invasion of one's right to informational or bodily privacy, breach of confidentiality, denial of access to medical records, etc., can also be challenged in court. Patients who have problems related to the denial of access to abortion services, refusal of payment by a public or private insurance company for abortion, or insistence on the husband's consent before an abortion will be performed, should contact their local office of the American Civil Liberties Union (ACLU).

Patients who are denied any of the other rights outlined in this book, and who qualify financially, should contact their local legal services office for help. Others should contact an attorney, any of the organizations listed in Appendix E, or both. All patient-consumers must realize that unless they complain about conditions that they don't like and take strong legal action when their rights are violated, hospitals will have no incentive or rationale, other than general principles, to change their policies to reflect consumer wishes.

NOTES

1. Burns, *Malpractice Suits in American Medicine Before the Civil War*, 43 BULL. HIST. MED. 41, 52 (1969); See also *Malpractice and the Physician*, A Report of the Committee on Medicolegal Problems, AMA, 1951 (prepared by Louis J. Regan). For a somewhat more complete discussion of the issues dealt with in this chapter see G. Annas, *Medical Malpractice: Are the Doctors Right?* 10 *Trial* 59-63 (July, 1974).
2. Dissenting Statement of Charles A. Hoffman, former president, AMA, to *MEDICAL MALPRACTICE: REPORT OF THE SECRETARY'S COMMISSION ON MEDICAL MALPRACTICE*, Dept. HEW, DHEW Pub. No. (OS) 73-88 (U.S. Gov. Print. Office, Stock #1700 00114) 1973, at 114. And see Bird, Malpractice Insurance: A Crisis in Health Care, *New York Times*, Jan. 19, 1975 at 1, col. 1.
3. *MEDICAL MALPRACTICE: supra.* note 2, at 12.
4. Dietz, Baird & Berul, The Medical Malpractice Legal System, *APPENDIX, MEDICAL MALPRACTICE, Id.* at 97.
5. Note, *Medical Malpractice Threat: A Study of Defensive Medicine*, 39 DUKE L. J. 957 (1971).
6. *1972 Opinion Survey of the AMA Membership*, Center for Health Services, Research and Development, AMA, Chicago, Ill., 1973. And see *Trial*, March/April, 1973, at 59.
7. Bell & Loop, *The Utility and Futility of Radiographic*

Skull Examination for Trauma, 284 NEW ENG. J. MED. 236, 239 (1971).

8. Brook & Stevenson, *Effectiveness of Patient Care in an Emergency Room,* 283 NEW ENG. J. MED. 904 (1970). A 1973 study found that 98% of a sample population of patients received fewer tests and procedures than a group of medical experts thought they should have received. Brook & Appel, *Quality-of-Care Assessment: Choosing a Method for Peer Review,* 288 NEW ENG. J. MED. 1323, 1327 (1973). The situation regarding defensive medicine may, however, shift if other courts take the lead of the Supreme Court of Washington in *Helling v. Carey,* 519 P.2d 981 (1974) (Ophthalmologists found negligent for not administering routinely a diagnostic test for glaucoma even though the other ophthalmologists in the state did not think that the routine administration of such tests to persons under 40 was good medical practice).

9. *Boston Globe,* Nov. 14, 1970 at 3.

10. Konold, A HISTORY OF MEDICAL ETHICS: 1847-1912, Madison: U. Wisc. Press, 1962 at 49.

11. *Doctor-Lawyer Panels: The Verdict Is Mixed,* MED. ECON., March 1, 1971, p. 128; Lee, *The Medical Malpractice Mediation Program,* 9 TRIAL LAW. Q. 85 (1973); and Note, *Medical Legal Screening Panels as an Alternative Approach to Malpractice Claims,* 13 WM. & MARY L. REV. 695 (1972).

12. See Baker, *Proposal for a Medical Malpractice Arbitration Plan Using Cleveland, Ohio as a Model,* ILL. INS. L. J. 625 (1972); Henderson, *Contractual Problems in the Enforcement of Agreements to Arbitrate Medical Malpractice,* 58 VA. L. REV. 947 (1972); Henderson, *Arbitration and Medical Services,* 28 ARB. J. 15 (1973).

13. See generally, Keeton, *Compensation for Medical Accidents,* 121 U. PA. L. REV. 590 (1973); Dornette, *Medical Injury Insurance—A Possible Remedy for the Malpractice Problems,* 78 CASE & COMMENT 25 (1973).

XVIII
The Patient's Rights Advocate

Because patients are, by definition, sick when in the hospital, they are unlikely to be able to assert the rights discussed in this book without some assistance. Hopefully, after a period of education, doctors and nurses will begin to afford patients their rights as a matter of course. Until this goal is attained, however, it will be necessary to set up some mechanism that can help ensure that patient's rights are protected. The mechanism I favor is the patient's rights advocate.[1]

Who should the patient's rights advocate represent?
Don't let a hospital representative tell you he's *your* representative! The most important thing about a patient advocate, regardless of title, is that he or she *must actually represent the patient* since the goal is to enhance the patient's position in making decisions concerning his health care. This contrasts with almost all current programs, which are offshoots of hospital administrations and whose goal is to help smooth over patient complaints, make the hospital function more smoothly, and help improve the hospital's image in the community. These public relations programs are *not* patient advocate programs.

To illustrate, in a recent survey of 2,000 hospitals with more then 200 beds, 462 of the 1,000 responding to a survey questionnaire said they had at least one employee who worked as a patient representative. The primary function of this person, however, was "to serve as management's direct representative to patients." The job descriptions generally confined the activities of these people to nonmedical housekeeping matters such as quality of food, décor of room, and telephone and television service.[2] As is clear from their own descriptions, these people are *management* representatives, not patient representatives. They represent the hospital administration and act on it's behalf, not on behalf of the patients.

Dr. Mitchell T. Rabkin, Director of Boston's Beth Israel Hospital has defined this distinction. He writes of his hospital's "patient representative" program as follows: Representatives deal only with "non-medical and non-nursing matters that have to do with patient comfort and convenience, such as a room improperly cleaned or a misplaced dietary tray." The representative is "introduced to the patient as the representative of the administration."[3] Ms. Anne Alexis Coté, the patient services coordinator at the New York Hospital, has described the role as "someone who will greet him [the patient] with a smile, listen to him, get to know him as a person and be his voice."[4] While her description holds out some possibility for aiding patients in making health care decisions, the system she describes does not come to grips with the major problems patients face in exercising their rights in the hospital context.

What powers should the patient's rights advocate have?

A patient's rights advocate should be defined as an individual whose primary responsibility is to assist the patient in learning about, protecting, and asserting his or her rights within the health care context. It is essential that the specific rights of patients be *spelled out in a bill of rights that the hospital adopts as policy and which the advocate has the power to enforce.* A model bill of rights is set forth in this book as Appendix D. The word advocate is used in its classical sense, *advocare,* "to summon to one's assistance, to defend, to call to one's aid." Connotations of adversariness, contentiousness, and deliberate antagonism are both unfortunate and unnecessary.

The goals of a patient's rights advocate system should be:

1. To protect patients, especially those at a disadvantage within the health care context (e.g., the young, the illiterate, the uncommunicative, those without relatives, those unable to speak English);

2. To make available to those who seek it the opportu-

nity to participate actively with their doctor as a partner in a personal health care program;

3. To restore medical technology and pharmaceutical advances to proper perspective by confronting the exaggerated expectations of the modern American medical consumer; and

4. To reflect in the doctor-patient relationship the reality of the health-sickness continuum and assert the humanness of death as a natural and inevitable reality.

The advocate should exercise, at the direction of the patient, powers that belong to the patient. They include:

1. *Complete access to medical records* and the ability to call in, at the direction of the patient, a consultant to aid or advise the patient;

2. *Active participation in those hospital committees* responsible for monitoring quality care within the health-care context, especially utilization review and patient care;

3. *Access to support services* for all patients who request them;

4. *Participation at the patient's request and direction in discussion of the patient's case.*

5. *Ability to delay discharges;*

6. *Ability to lodge complaints directly to hospital director and Executive Committee.*

Most of the criticism directed against the patient's rights advocate has involved the alleged "introduction of conflict into the hospital setting." This seems less a reaction to the concept itself than to one way of carrying out the responsibilities. The advocate as adversary would confront the hospital with a number of problems. The relegation of all serious decision-making to adversary proceedings, for example, would raise a number of questions. How can an independent decision be reached? Should the doctor retain final authority to do what he judges to be in the best interests of the patient? How could such a program be supervised? Would a state of paralysis engulf the health care facility? The advocate would probably improve the doctor-patient relationship by promoting openness and honesty.

What is usually meant by the term ombudsman in the hospital setting?

The ombudsman is an alternative approach, although both an advocate and an ombudsman could function in the same facility. The *ombudsman's* role is to seek out broad problem areas, to research facts, to publicize grievances to appropriate audiences, and to make suggestions about resolving those problems. He has no participation in the actual resolution. What results is active representation without direct personal influence on the outcome of the decision. While such an approach would eliminate the problems created by an adversary system, the danger is that such a person would have no influence on important decisions. Another suggestion is to combine the best aspects of both approaches while discarding those aspects that would have a detrimental effect on its proper functioning.

Part of the patient's rights advocate's function could, however, be as an ombudsman with respect to protecting patient's rights. While available to respond to all patients who desired his services, he could compile lists of recurring situations in which the rights of the patient are affected, and classify them according to seriousness, taking action via publication when warranted.

What qualifications should an advocate have?

As is inherent in his task, the advocate must have both a basic knowledge of medicine—know the language and how to read medical charts—and law. He or she must also be able to communicate with patients, nurses, doctors, and the hospital administration. How and by whom this person should be trained is a question that will take experience to answer. In the beginning, however, it is essential that persons chosen for this role be over- rather than under-qualified in terms of both knowledge and community acceptance so that the usefulness of the advocate in improving patient care and enhancing patient rights gets a fair trial. There must, of course, be a sufficient number of advocates to ensure patient access to their services.

Who should have the power to hire and fire the advocate?

Financing and supervising an advocate system is a complex problem. In order to ensure, however, that advocates are not transformed from patient to management representatives, it would seem essential that they be hired by someone outside the hospital (or possibly by the board of trustees) and be accountable only to the patients they serve. In the future an advocate program might be built into H.M.O. contracts (in which case the advocate could work for the consumer-dominated board of directors), be required as a condition of accreditation or participation in Medicare (or any forthcoming program of National Health Insurance), or be funded by a statewide consumer agency.

How would a patient's rights advocate improve health care while safeguarding human rights?

Examples of how such a system would improve patient care and enhance human rights are legion. In presenting his patient's rights advocate proposal to the trustees of Boston City Hospital, Dr. David F. Allen, former chief resident in psychiatry and president of the House Officers Association, told of the time he was called to the emergency ward to talk with a woman whose stomach had just been pumped out. He was the first person on the scene able to speak Spanish to the Puerto Rican woman and was told by her that she had had some very distressing news at home, had taken two Alka Seltzers, and had come to the hospital to talk with someone. The staff at the emergency room had assumed she was an overdose case "because most Puerto Ricans who demonstrate symptoms like those shown by the woman have overdosed."[5] Only an advocate on duty constantly with the capability of speaking Spanish could have prevented this "routine treatment."

Senator Edward Kennedy's book on health care recounts the following true story.[6]

Paul, a ten year old boy, had a seizure at his home and passed out. His father picked him up and rushed him to a police station. The nearest hospital was a private institution. Paul had been receiving treatment at the County Hospital which was some distance away. The police said they could not take him there because it was out of their district. When they arrived at the hospital, Paul's father was subjected to an interview about his finances and insurance. No one would look at Paul until his father had answered such questions as: "Do you own your own home?" "Who do you work for?" "How long have you worked there?" The interviewer also refused to call the County Hospital. In frustration, Paul's father left the emergency room at the hospital and drove the long distance to the County Hospital. In the course of his trip, he passed several hospitals but was afraid to stop because of the possibility that they would treat him as the first hospital had. He arrived at the County Hospital where his son died within an hour.

The case illustrates the tragic results that occur when a hospital places housekeeping chores above medical duty in an emergency situation. An advocate could have asserted the right of the patient to receive emergency care promptly without reference to ability to pay. Failure to provide an opportunity for the right to be asserted was a significant factor in the loss of a life. An advocate could have played a key role in saving it.

A college professor wrote of his own experiences.[7]

He was admitted to the hospital for a series of tests to determine the identity of the condition he was suffering from. A neurologist and three medical students ran him through a neurological examination. In his words: "I got a reinforcement of the sense of not only am I a patient who is supposed to behave in a certain way, but I'm almost an object to demonstrate to people that I'm not really people any more, I'm something else. I'm a body that has some very interesting characteristics about it.... I began to feel not only the fear of this unknown, dread thing that I have, that nobody knows anything about—and if they know, they're not going to tell me—but an anger and a resentment of 'Goddamn it, I'm a human being and I want to be treated like one!' And feeling that if I expressed anger, I could be retaliated against, because I'm in a very vulnerable position."

Some of his frustrations would find an outlet in the person of the patient's rights advocate. The advocate would be a person that the patient could talk to without fear of retaliation; a person who could pull his medical records and tell him whether or not a diagnosis had been made; a person who, on behalf of a busy medical staff, could take the time to explain the reason for the tests, why medical students were present, that he could have them excluded if he wished, that no matter what his attitudes toward the medical staff or his expressions of fear and resentment, no retaliatory action would be taken against him in any manner. Tension and conflict would be reduced and the quality of medical care improved.

On a more routine matter, John Haggerty recounts her experiences with childbirth:[8]

> She and her husband had attended classes on natural child birth. They had discussed the matter with the doctor in the out-patient clinic of the hospital where the child would be delivered. The hospital had a policy of allowing the husband in the delivery room "at the doctor's discretion." They entered the hospital and spent three hours together in the labor room. As she was being transferred to the delivery room the doctor (a resident) said to the husband, "Sorry, you can't come in, you make me nervous."
> In the delivery room Ms. Haggerty, who had previously given birth by the natural method in England, demanded that the stirrups be removed. The attendants laughed at her and held her down as her wrists were strapped to the table by leather thongs.

Under the current system a couple has little, if any, recourse. Under a patient advocate system, with an advocate assigned to the maternity ward, the advocate would be in charge of advising the medical personnel about the couple's desires concerning natural childbirth, would make whatever preparations were deemed necessary, and be present at the parents' request to be sure that the father was not denied access to the delivery room during birth (e.g., by assuring an alternative obstetrician is available). The advocate would also see to it that the mother was not subjected to coercion or ridicule during birth. (This latter function would probably not be necessary if the husband were allowed to be present in the delivery room as a matter of course.) The advocate would function similarly in the emergency room when delays could be cut or when an interpreter was needed. Again, doctor-patient relationships would be improved by the advocate.

Responses to the patient advocate proposal tend to fall into three general categories: (1) there should be no interference with the current doctor-patient relationship; (2) patients' rights are already being protected by all members of the hospital staff; (3) the entire health care delivery system is fundamentally defective, and this "band-aid" approach will only serve to delay inevitable and radical system restructuring. The first two responses have been shown to be without merit.

Before one resorts to the third position, experimentation with the patient's rights advocate as herein outlined is called for. While certainly no miracle cure-all, the advocate could help not only the individual patient but society and the medical profession as well in working toward what must be a common goal: ensuring that human rights are not sacrificed to medical progress.

NOTES

1. Parts of this chapter are adapted from Annas & Healey, *The Patient Rights Advocate: Redefining the Doctor-Patient Relationship in the Hospital Context,* 27 VAND. L. REV. 243 (1974), which examines the patient rights advocate proposal in considerably more detail.

2. Thompson, Lupton, Rench & Feldesman, *Patient Review Mechanisms in Health Care Institutions,* APPENDIX, SECRETARY'S REPORT ON MEDICAL MALPRACTICE, HEW, U.S. Gov. Printing Office, 1973 at 758.

3. Rabkin, *The Needs of Patients,* 288 NEW ENG. J. MED. 1019 (1973). See also: M. Rabkin, *The Personal Dimension of Patient Care,* (monograph), Massachusetts Hospital Research and Education Association, Inc., 1974. TWA was responding to this view when it developed a "be nice to patients" course taught by ex-airline stewardesses from its stewardess training school and designed to help improve the attitudes of hospital personnel. *Medical World News,* Aug. 2, 1974 at 44.

4. Cote, *The Patient's Link,* 9 TRIAL 30 (March 1973).

Other nurses have expressed a somewhat more positive view of their role as patient representative, e.g., Kosik, *Patient Advocacy or Fighting the System*, 72 AM. J. NURSING 694 (1972); Nations, *Nurse-Lawyer is Patient Advocate*, 73 AM. J. NURSING 1039 (1973).

5. Oral presentation of a personal experience by Dr. Allen to the Trustees of Boston City Hospital during discussion of a patient advocate system for the hospital, Boston, Mass., Sept. 26, 1973.

6. Kennedy, IN CRITICAL CONDITION: THE CRISIS IN AMERICA'S HEALTH CARE (Pocket Books, N.Y., 1973) at 49–51.

7. Hanlan (originally published anonymously), *Notes of a Dying Professor, Penn Gazette*, Feb. 1972 at 23 (his disease was eventually diagnosed as A.L.S., amatrophic lateral sclerosis).

8. Haggerty, *Ms.*, Jan., 1973 at 16-17.

Appendix
A
Common Medical Terms

(including some common prefixes and suffixes)

anaphylactic—extreme allergic reaction

anatomy—study of body and body parts

angiography—radiographic technique for studying vessels of the body; contrast media is injected into an artery or vein and photographed as it travels through the body

anterior—front, forward

AP/PA—referring to positioning in x-rays; full front or rear (anterior-posterior; posterior-anterior)

arteriography—angiography that studies arteries

arth—joint

biopsy—removal of tissue for microscopic examination

bronchoscopy—tube passed through the trachea for direct visualization of airway

cardiac—relating to the heart

cardiac arrest—heart stopped; heart attack

catheterization—insertion of a small tube into a vein or artery to measure pressure or place angiography equipment

cephal—relating to the head

cyanotic—blue

cystoscopy—tube with light inserted into urethra to examine bladder and lower urinary tract

-dema—swelling

derma—referring to skin

dys—ill, difficult, or abnormal

-ectomy—removal by cutting

electrocardiogram—(EKG or ECK) contacts to chest used to measure pattern of the heart *electroencephalogram*—(EEG) contacts attached to skull and measurements taken to measure electrical impulses of brain

endocrinology—dealing with glands and their secretions

epidemiology—study of incidence and distribution of disease

epi—upon, beside, over

epidural—under the skin

exo—out, outside

gastro—referring to the stomach

gyn—female, woman (e.g., gynecology: dealing with female reproductive system)

hem—blood (e.g., hematology: study of blood)

hematocrit—measures ratio of red cells to whole blood

hematoma—local collection of blood

hemi—half

hemoglobin—measure of oxygen-carrying substance in red cells

hemorrhage—bleeding

hepa—liver

hetero—other, different

hyper—above, excessive

hysterectomy—removal of the uterus

inferior—below

intermittent positive pressure breathing (IPPB)—apparatus used to assist breathing and aid in clearing lung congestion

intravenous pyelogram (IVP)—use of contrast media to study kidneys

-itis—inflammation

laminectomy—excision of part of vertebra for removal of intervertebral disc or other operation on the spinal column

laparotomy—abdominal surgery

lateral—side

lytes—electrolyte studies of the blood

-mania—madness

mastectomy—removal of breast tissue

mening—membranes surrounding spinal cord (meninges)

myelogram—introduction of dye into cerebrospinal fluid space for diagnostic purposes

nasogastric tube (NG tube)—introduced via nose and

swallowed into stomach for direct access to stomach contents

necro—dead

nephr—kidney

oculo—eye

-ology—study of

-oma—growth, tumor, swelling

oncology—study of tumors

ophthalmology—dealing with the eye

orthopedics—dealing with repair of bone and joint injuries

os-; osteo—bone

otolaryngology—dealing with ear, nose, throat, larynx, and trachea

pan—all, entire

PAP test—Papanicolaou; technique for studying state of cervical cells

patch test—skin test to determine sensitivity

pathology—study of disease

pathology services—study of tissue removed from body; also, autopsy procedures

ped—child or foot (e.g., pediatrics: childrens' medicine)

peri—around, about

phlebo—vein

pharmacology—study of drugs

pneumoencephalogram—introduction of air into the ventricles of brain

posterior—back, behind

proctology—dealing with lower intestinal tract

proctoscopy—introduction of a tube with light to view interior of rectum

protime—measure of extrinsic blood-clotting mechanism

psychiatry—dealing with mental disease

pulmo—lungs

radiology—use of x-rays for diagnosis and treatment

ren—kidney

retro—backward

scler—hard

sigmoidoscopy—introduction of viewing apparatus into sigmoid colon

sub—underneath or beneath

super; supra—above, excess

thermo—heat

thoracic—referring to chest
thrombo—clot
-tony—cutting
toxi—poison
urology—dealing with kidney and urinary tract
vaso—vessel
vessel—artery or vein

Appendix
B

Common Medical
Abbreviations

a.—artery
Ab—antibody
Abd.—abdomen
A.C.—before meals
Ag.—antigen
AHA—American Hospital Association
AMA—American Medical Association
APHA—American Public Health Association
ARD—acute respiratory disease or distress
ASA—acetylsalicylic acid (aspirin)
ASHD—arteriosclerotic heart disease
ASD—arterial septal defect
BBT—basal body temperature
BHI—Bureau of Health Insurance
b.i.d.—twice a day
BMR—basal metabolic rate
BNDD—Bureau of Narcotics and Dangerous Drugs
BP—blood pressure
Bx—biopsy
CA—cancer
cath—catheter
CBC—complete blood count for red and white cells and platelets
CC—chief complaint
CCU—coronary care unit
CDC—Center for Disease Control
CHAMP—Certified Hospital Admission Monitoring Program

CHAMPUS—Civilian Health and Medical Program of the Uniformed Services

CHD—coronary (artery) heart disease

CHF—congestive heart failure

chol.—cholesterol

CHP—Comprehensive Health Planning

CNS—Central Nervous System

C.O.—cardiac output

CPC—clinicopathological conference

CSF—cerebrospinal fluid

CVA—cerebrovascular accident

CVS—clean voided specimen

D&C—dilation (of cervix) and curettage (scraping of uterus)

DI—diabetes insipidus

diff—differential

dig—digitalis

Disch—discharge

DL—danger list

DM—diabetes mellitus

D/NSS—dextrose with normal saline solution

DOA—dead on arrival

DTs—delirium tremors

D/W—dextrose with water

Dx—diagnosis

EEG—electroencephalogram

EKG or ECG—electrocardiogram

EMS—emergency medical services

ENT—ear, nose, and throat

ER or EW—emergency room or emergency ward

f—frequency

FBS—fasting blood sugar (taken after 12 hours fast)

FDA—Food and Drug Administration

FH—family history

fract—fracture

GI—gastrointestinal (stomach and intestines)

gm%—grams per 100 ml. of blood or serum

gr—grain

gtt—drop

GTT—glucose tolerance test (follows FBS)

GU—genitourinary (genitals and urinary tract)

GYN—gynecologist
HCT—hematocrit
HEW—U.S. Department of Health, Education and Welfare
Hgb—hemoglobin
H.M.O.—Health Maintenance Organization
HPI—history of present illness
H.R.—heart rate
h.s.—hours of sleep
H.T.—hypertension
Hx—history
ICU—intensive care unit
I.D.—infectious disease
I&D—incision and drainage
IM—intramuscular
incr—increased or increasing
I/O—intake-output
IPPB—intermittent positive pressure breathing
IV—intravenous
IVP—intravenous pyelogram
JCAH—Joint Commission on Accreditation of Hospitals
KJ—knee jerk
L—left
lab—laboratory
LCA—left coronary artery
LLQ—lower left quadrant of abdomen
LMP—last menstrual period
LP—lumbar puncture
LUQ—left upper quadrant of abdomen
m—meter
MCH—mean corpuscular hemoglobin
MCHC—mean corpuscular hemoglobin concentration
MCV—mean corpuscular volume of red blood cells
Mg—milligram
MI—myocardial infarction (heart attack)
MICU—medical intensive care unit
mm—millimeter
MS—multiple sclerosis
n.—nerve
N-G tube—nasogastric tube
NIH—National Institutes of Health

NLM—National Library of Medicine
NMA—National Medical Association
NPO—nothing by mouth (non per os)
O.D.—right eye (also denotes overdose)
Op—operation
OPD—outpatient department
OR—operating room
O.S.—left eye
OT—occupational therapy
PAT—Preadmission test
P.C.—after meals (post cibum)
pcn—penicillin
PDUR—predischarge Utilization Review
P.E.—physical examination, or pulmonary embolism
PERLA—pupils equal, responding to light & accommoda-
    tion
PFP—Prevailing Fee Plan (Blue Shield)
PHS—Public Health Service
PI—present illness
PICU—pediatric intensive care unit
PNHSA—Physicians National House Staff Association
P.O.—by mouth
p.r.—administer through the rectum
prep.—prepare for
PRN—as often as necessary (pro re nata)
PSRO—Professional Standards Review Organization
pt.—patient
PTA—prior to admission
PTT—partial thromboplastin time (blood clotting test)
Px—prognosis
Q—flow
q—every
QAP—Quality Assurance Program
q.d.—every day.
q2h—every two hours
q3h—every three hours, etc.
qid—four times a day
qn—every night
qns—quantity not sufficient
R—right
RBC—red blood count

RDS—respiratory distress syndrome

ref. doc.—referring doctor

RHD—rheumatic heart disease

RMP—Regional Medical Program

RN—registered nurse

RQ—respiratory quotient

RR—respiratory rate

RRE—round, regular, and equal

RUQ—right upper quadrant of abdomen

RV—right ventricle

Rx—therapy or treatment

s—without

SH—social history

SICU—surgical intensive care unit

SNS—sympathetic nervous

s.o.b.—shortness of breath

S.O.S.—may be repeated once if urgently required

spec.—specimen

S.R.—systems review

S & S—signs and symptoms

ss—half

SSA—Social Security Administration

ss enema—soapsuds enema

staph.—staphylococcus

strep.—streptococcus

surg—surgery

Sx—symptoms

T&A—tonsillectomy and adenoidectomy

TB—tuberculosis (also abbreviated Tbc)

TID—three times daily

TPR—temperature, pulse and respiration (vital signs)

Tx—treatment

u—unit

UCG—urinary chorionic gonadotropic test

UR—utilization review

URI—upper respiratory infection

UTI—urinary tract infection

v.—vein

VD—venereal disease

vol.—volume

Wass.—Wasserman
WBC—white blood count
WDWN—well-developed, well-nourished
wt.—weight

Appendix C

Introduction to the Medical and Legal Literature

It is probably true that very few practicing lawyers know how to properly use the law library, and very few practicing doctors know how to fully utilize the medical library. The purpose of this brief appendix is not to teach potential patients and clients something few professionals have taken the time to understand but to give potential patients enough information so that if they want to go out of their way to find something out about a particular legal issue or medical condition, they will be able to do so. The first rule of research in any unfamiliar library is to *ask the reference librarian for assistance*. Do not, however, request such assistance until you have narrowed down your topic to the precise question that interests you.

THE LEGAL LITERATURE

All law schools have substantial libraries, as do many bar associations. To obtain admission to the law library of your local law school, you may need special permission from the school or the assistance of a law student. Once inside, you will discover the principal problem with writing about "the law" in the United States. Specifically, there are 50 states, each with its own court system and state legislature. Superimposed on this structure is a system of federal district courts and federal appeals courts. Over them all is the United States Supreme Court. There are not only the laws of the U.S. (which are set out in a set of books called *U.S. Code Annotated*), but also all of the regulations adopted under federal statutes by the executive branch of government such as the FDA, HEW, and the

Department of Agriculture. (These are set forth in another set of books called the *Code of Federal Regulations*.)

The legal literature you are most likely to be interested in locating is *statutes, court decisions* (case law), *regulations, legal periodicals,* and *legal encyclopedias*. Each of these will be discussed briefly. Statutes are arranged by state, each having its own set of books (usually 50 to 100 volumes). These statutes are usually arranged by subject matter, and each provision of the statute has a number. If you know the number, the task of locating the law is not difficult. If you do not, look up the subject matter in the index to the set. Note that since new statutes are passed each year, these volumes have "pocket parts" at the back in which current material is kept.

If you are looking for a particular case, you probably have the case name and citation. For example, the famous *Darling* case referred to in a number of places in this volume is properly cited as *Darling v. Charleston Community Memorial Hospital*, 33 Ill. 2d 326, 211 N.E. 2d 253 (1965), cert. denied, 383 U.S. 946 (1966). To locate this case in the library, either find the set of books for the state of Illinois or the set labeled "Northeastern Reports" (abbreviated "N.E."). In the Illinois set, locate the second series (2d) (most states begin renumbering their reports after volume 200 or 300, but some do not), and within that set, find volume 33. The *Darling* case begins in volume 33 at page 326 (or in the N.E. 2d series in volume 211, page 253). The final part of the citation refers to the fact that the United States Supreme Court refused to hear an appeal. This refusal can be found in the U.S. Supreme Court reports, volume 383, at page 946. The year in parenthesis following the case is the year in which it was decided.

Regulations are promulgated under statutory authority. Federal regulations are collected in the Code of Federal Regulations, parts of which are changed daily. These changes are reported in the *Federal Register*. State regulations are found in various, non-uniform state publications.

Legal encyclopedias, Corpus Juris Secundum (the one Perry Mason used), and *American Jurisprudence* are usually located side by side in a conspicuous part of the library. They are, as the name implies, general works on various aspects of the law arranged alphabetically by subject matter.

The other type of legal material cited in many of the footnotes in this volume is *legal periodicals*. These are usually published at individual law schools and are named after these law schools. For example, 54 *B.U.L. Rev.* is the fifty-fourth volume of the set of Boston University's Law Reviews. There is a rather unsophisticated and spotty index to these periodicals called the *Guide to Legal Periodicals* that is arranged by subject matter and author's last name.

For those desiring detailed information on legal research, reference should be made to one or both of the following excellent volumes: M. Price & H. Bitner, *Effective Legal Research* (3rd ed.), Little, Brown, Boston, 1969; or E. Pollock, *Fundamentals of Legal Research* (3rd ed.), Foundation Press, Brooklyn, N. Y. 1967.

THE MEDICAL LITERATURE

In many ways the medical library is a much easier library to deal with since the "laws" of anatomy and pharmacology do not vary from state to state. Medical libraries are generally divided into three sections relevant to the consumer-patient: the *reference* section, *books*, and *periodicals*. The reference section will contain such materials as the list of medical specialists. The book section will contain such things as textbooks on various parts of the body or various medical specialities. (About 2,000 new medical books are published annually.) The heart of the medical library, however, is in its periodical collection because it is here that new discoveries and reports on currently used procedures show up first. A good medical library will receive from 2,000 to 6,000 periodicals. The largest collection of medical literature in this country is located at the National Library of Medicine in Bethesda, Maryland. It consists of over 1,500,000 volumes. Under the Medical Library Assistance Act of 1965 (79 Stat. 1059, 42 U.S.C. 28b) the Congress attempted to make this knowledge available to all "qualified persons" regardless of their geographical location. To date, nine regional medical libraries have been funded to further this purpose. They are: (1) The New England Regional Medical Library Service at the Countway Library of Medicine at Harvard Medical School, 10 Shattuck St., Boston; (2) the New York and New Jersey Regional Medical Library Service at the New York Academy of Medicine, 2 East 103rd St., New York City; (3) the Mid-Eastern Regional Medical Library at the Library of the College of Physicians, 19 South 22 St., Philadelphia; (4) the Mid-Atlantic Regional Medical Library Service of the National Library of Medicine, P.O. Box 30260, Bethesda, Md.; (5) the Kentucky, Ohio, Michigan Regional Library at the Health Sciences Library at Wayne State University, 645 Mullett St., Detroit; (6) the Southwestern Regional Medical Library, A. M. Calhoun Medical Library, Woodrust Research Building, Emory University, Atlanta, Ga.; (7) the Midwest Regional Medical Library at the John Crerar Library, Chicago; (8) the Pacific Northwest Health Sciences Library at the University of Washington, Seattle; (9) the Pacific Southwest Regional Medical Library Service at the Biomedical Library of the University of California, Los Angeles.

The statute provides that "qualified persons and organizations shall be entitled to free loan services." While some of these regional libraries have attempted to restrict the meaning of qualified to other medical libraries, this definition is not consistent with the wording of the statute or its purpose. An excellent argument can be made for the proposition that any individual who can read and who has a desire to research a particular medical question is a "qualified" user under the act and should not only be given access to the library, but free loan privileges as well. This proposition has not yet been argued in court. See 42 C.F.R. 59a.31 et seq.

Once you obtain access to the medical library, your main source of information will be the card catalog for books and medical indices for periodicals. The major index is *Index Medicus*, which is put out by NIH and indexes about 3,000 world wide medical periodicals under approximately 8,000 subject headings. These subject headings are constantly being updated and appear each year as Part II of the January issue designated "Medical Subject

Headings." Listings are also grouped by author's last name. In addition to the yearly indices, there is also a *Cumulative* edition and an *Abridged* edition of *Index Medicus*. There are also approximately 15 other more specialized indices to the medical and biological literature.

Finally, a service unique to the medical and scientific literature is computer searches of the literature. These searches can locate a complete listing of all articles published over a given period of time on a particular subject matter. Further information on ordering these done and their cost can be obtained through the reference librarian of your local medical library.

Those wanting more specific information on searching the medical literature are directed to: W. Beatty, *Searching the Literature Comes before Writing the Literature*, 79 ANN. OF INTERNAL MED. 917-924 (1973) and E. Sagall, "Lawyer's Guide to Medical Writings," *Trial* Oct/ Nov, 1970.

Appendix D

A Model Patient's Bill of Rights

PREAMBLE

As you enter this health care facility, it is our duty to remind you that your health care is a cooperative effort between you as a patient and the doctors and hospital staff. During your stay you will have a patient's rights advocate available. The duty of the advocate is to assist you in all the decisions you must make and in all situations in which your health and welfare are at stake. The advocate's first responsibility is to help you understand who each of the people are who will be working with you and to help you understand what your rights as a patient are. Your advocate can be reached at any time of the day by dialing ———. The following is a list of your rights as a patient. Your advocate's duty is to see to it that you are afforded these rights. You should call your advocate whenever you have any questions or concerns about any of these rights.

1. The patient has a legal right to informed participation in all decisions involving his health care program.
2. We recognize the right of all potential patients to know what research and experimental protocols are being used in our facility and what alternatives are available in the community.
3. The patient has a legal right to privacy respecting the source of payment for treatment and care. This right includes access to the highest degree of care without regard to the source of payment for that treatment and care.
4. We recognize the right of a potential patient to complete

and accurate information concerning medical care and procedures.

5. The patient has a legal right to prompt attention especially in an emergency situation.

6. The patient has a legal right to a clear, concise explanation of all proposed procedures in layman's terms, including the possibilities of any risk of mortality or serious side effects, problems related to recuperation, and probability of success, and will not be subjected to any procedure without his voluntary, competent, and understanding consent. The specifics of such consent shall be set out in a written consent form, signed by the patient.

7. The patient has a legal right to a clear, complete, and accurate evaluation of his condition and prognosis without treatment before he is asked to consent to any test or procedure.

8. We recognize the right of the patient to know the identity and professional status of all those providing service. All personnel have been instructed to introduce themselves, state their status, and explain their role in the health care of the patient. Part of this right is the right of the patient to know the physician responsible for his care.

9. We recognize the right of any patient who does not speak English to have access to an interpreter.

10. The patient has a legal right to all the information contained in his medical record while in the health-care facility and to examine the record upon request.

11. We recognize the right of a patient to discuss his condition with a consultant specialist at his own request and his own expense.

12. The patient has a legal right not to have any test or procedure, designed for educational purposes rather than his direct personal benefit, performed on him.

13. The patient has a legal right to refuse any particular drug, test, procedure, or treatment.

14. The patient has a legal right to both personal and informational privacy with respect to: the hospital staff, other doctors, residents, interns and medical students, researchers, nurses, other hospital personnel, and other patients.

15. We recognize the patient's right of access to people outside the health care facility by means of visitors and the telephone. Parents may stay with their children and relatives with terminally ill patients 24 hours a day.

16. The patient has a legal right to leave the health care fa-

cility regardless of physical condition or financial status, although he may be requested to sign a release stating that he is leaving against the medical judgment of his doctor or the hospital.

17. No patient may be transferred to another facility unless he has received a complete explanation of the desirability and need for the transfer, the other facility has accepted the patient for transfer, and the patient has agreed to transfer. If the patient does not agree to transfer, the patient has the right to a consultant's opinion on the desirability of transfer.

18. A patient has a right to be notified of discharge at least one day before it is accomplished, to demand a consultation by an expert on the desirability of discharge, and to have a person of the patient's choice so notified.

19. The patient has a right, regardless of source of payment, to examine and receive an itemized and detailed explanation of his total bill for services rendered in the facility.

20. The patient has a right to competent counseling from the facility to help him obtain financial assistance from public or private sources to meet the expense of services received in the institution.

21. The patient has a right to timely prior notice of the termination of his eligibility for reimbursement for the expense of his care by any third-party payer.

22. At the termination of his stay at the health care facility we recognize the right of a patient to a complete copy of the information contained in his medical record.

23. We recognize the right of all patients to have 24 hour a day access to a patient's rights advocate who may act on behalf of the patient to assert or protect the rights set out in this document.

Appendix E

Organizations Involved in Legal Rights of Patients

Center for Law and Health Sciences
Boston University School of Law
209 Bay State Road
Boston, Massachusetts   02215

National Urban Coalition
2100 M Street, N.W.
Washington, D.C.   20036

National Health Law Program
10995 LeConte Avenue
Los Angeles, California   90024

Joint Center for the Study of Law, Medicine & the Life
Sciences
Boston College Law School—Tufts Medical School
Brighton, Massachusetts   02135

American Society of Law & Medicine
454 Brookline Avenue
Boston, Massachusetts   02215

Health Policy Advisory Center
558 Capp Street
San Francisco, California   94110
            and
17 Murray Street
New York, New York   10007

Children's Defense Fund
1520 New Hampshire Avenue
Washington, D.C. 20056

Charles Drew Health Rights Center
1621 East 120 St.
Los Angeles, California 90059

Health Research Group
2000 P Street, N.W.
Washington, D.C. 20036
(and local Public Interest Research
Group affiliates—PIRGs)

Medical Committee for Human Rights
New York, Boston, St. Louis,
San Francisco, and other cities

On the state level contact:
Attorney General's Office
Insurance Commissioner
State Comprehensive Health Planning Agency
Department of Public Health

Center for Law & Social Policy
1751 "N" Street, N.W.
Washington, D.C. 20036

Committee in Health Law, Am. Public Health Assoc.
1015 18th St., N.W.
Washington, D.C. 20036

Health Law Project Library, U. Pa.
133 S. 36th Street, Rm. 410
Philadelphia, Pa. 19104

INDEX